THE QUEEN'S CLASSICS

CERTIFICATE BOOKS

*

JOHN EVELYN & SAMUEL PEPYS

Selections from the Diaries

THE QUEEN'S CLASSICS

CERTIFICATE BOOKS

General Editor: DENYS THOMPSON, M.A.

JOHN KEATS
Selected Letters and Poems
Edited by J. H. Walsh, B.A.

GEORGE CRABBE
Selections from his poetry
Edited by Frank Whitehead, M.A.

JOHN MILTON
Paradise Lost: Books I & II
Edited by R. R. Pedley, M.A.

THE ELIZABETHAN VOYAGES
Edited by James Winny, M.A.

LORD TENNYSON
Selected Poems
Edited by B. C. Southam, M.A.

QUEEN VICTORIA
Lytton Strachey

RHYME AND REASON
An Anthology of Poetry
Edited by Denys Thompson, M.A. and Raymond O'Malley, M.A.

THREE ELIZABETHAN PLAYS
Edited by James Winny, M.A.

ALDOUS HUXLEY
Selected Essays
Edited by Harold Raymond, O.B.E. and Frank Whitehead M.A.

ALEXANDER POPE
Selected Poems and Letters
Edited by R. P. C. Mutter, M.A., and M. Kinkead-Weekes, M.A.

LORD BYRON
Selections from his Poetry and Prose
Edited by Ian C. S. Gregor, M.A., and Andrew Rutherfold, M.A.

SIX MODERN POETS
An Anthology
Edited by J. R. Osgerby, M.A.

WILFRED OWEN
Poems
Edited with a Memoir by Edmund Blunden

VIRGINIA WOOLF
Selection from her Essays
Edited with an Introduction by Walter James, B.A.

SELECTIONS FROM THE DIARIES OF JOHN EVELYN AND SAMUEL PEPYS

Edited
with an Introduction and Notes by
JAMES GIBSON, M.A.
CANTERBURY TEACHERS' TRAINING COLLEGE

QC

Chatto and Windus
Educational

Granada Publishing Limited
Published by Chatto and Windus Educational
Frogmore St Albans Hertfordshire AL2 2NF
and
3 Upper James Street London W1R 4BP

Clarke, Irwin & Co Ltd
Toronto

First published in 1957, and reprinted in 1967 and 1973

ISBN 0 7010 0250 6
Printed in Great Britain by
Fletcher & Son Ltd, Norwich

PREFACE

My aim in compiling this selection has been to arouse the interest of readers in Evelyn and Pepys so that they will try to find out more about these two important writers for themselves. I have therefore chosen what seemed to me to be the entries which would most stimulate their attention while at the same time conveying to them a true picture of the nature of the two diaries. It would have been easy to make a superficially more attractive selection by cutting snippets from the entries, but I have resisted this temptation. With few exceptions the entries contained in this book are complete, and the reader will be able to read all the items which the diarist chose to mention on the days I have selected.

The difficulty of reproducing as accurately as possible in two hundred pages the atmosphere which is built up in six thousand pages of the original diaries has been great. I have, however, chosen my entries carefully in order to portray as truthfully as any summary can the picture of Evelyn and Pepys which emerges from the complete diaries. It has been possible for me to give in their entirety all Evelyn's entries for the second half of 1666, but for obvious reasons this cannot be done with Pepys. I have kept my own notes to a minimum in the belief that the text is the most important part of a book of this kind.

I should like to acknowledge my gratitude to Dr Esmond de Beer who has most generously given me advice in the preparation of this book, and to Mr John Evelyn and the Delegates of the Clarendon Press for permission to make use of the Evelyn text. I should also like to pay tribute to my publishers whose idea this book was, and who have been most courteous and helpful throughout its growth.

J. C. G.

CONTENTS

INTRODUCTION

I

JOHN EVELYN was born in 1620 at Wotton, near Dorking, in Surrey, and was a member of a family which had risen to fortune in the sixteenth century through the manufacture of gunpowder. His early education was at the free school at Southover, near Lewes, in Sussex, and in 1637 he went to Balliol College, Oxford. Subsequently he spent some time in travelling. He visited the Netherlands in 1641, and was in France and Italy from 1643 to 1646.

In Paris in 1646 he married Mary Browne, the daughter of the English Ambassador, and he returned to England in 1647, leaving his wife in France. In July 1649 he made another visit to Paris and remained there until 1652 when he came back to England. His wife, who had been only twelve when he married her, joined him in England shortly afterwards, and in the same year he obtained possession of his father-in-law's estate of Sayes Court at Deptford, then in the country south-east of London, which was to be his home for more than forty years. His wife bore him eight children, of whom only one survived the parents. Of his five sons only one lived to be grown-up. In 1654 Evelyn and his wife made a tour of England, and visited Bath, Oxford, Salisbury, York, Lincoln and Cambridge.

Evelyn was a supporter of the Royalists and he welcomed the Restoration of Charles II in 1660. In 1662 he was appointed a member of the Commission for "reforming the buildings, ways, streets, and encumbrances, and regulating the hackney coaches in the City of London". His most arduous public work came when he was made Commissioner for Sick and Wounded Seamen and for Prisoners of War. Evelyn's district for this work was Kent and Sussex, and he was kept busy raising money and attending to his many duties which were particularly onerous during the two Dutch wars of 1665-7 and 1672-4. It was through these duties that he first met Pepys. He was appointed a member of the Council for Foreign Plantations—an early ancestor of the Colonial Office—in 1671. and a Commissioner of the Privy Seal by James II in 1685. Nevertheless his relations with James II were not so close as they had been with Charles II, and, on the accession of William and Mary, he tended to take a diminishing part in public life. He was by now a man of sixty-nine and was naturally less active, but one notable post which he filled at this time was the Treasurership for Greenwich Hospital. In 1696 he left his house at Deptford and spent most of the remaining part of his life either in London or at Wotton which he inherited in 1699. He died on the 27th February 1706.

II

Evelyn was essentially a gentleman of education, culture and taste. Among his many friends were such distinguished figures as Jeremy Taylor, Robert Boyle, Richard Bentley, Christopher Wren, Abraham Cowley, and Archbishop Tenison. Evelyn's motto was *Omnia explorate*, *meliora retinete* (Prove all things, retain the best), and in a famous age of mental exploration Evelyn was a keen explorer. His travels on the Continent were designed to satisfy his thirst for knowledge and to develop his taste, and throughout his life he showed an active interest in the world around him. During his lifetime human knowledge was advancing with exciting speed, and we learn from his writings of his versatility and energy. The desire for knowledge was widespread at the time of the Restoration, and the founding of the Royal Society which began its formal meetings at Gresham College in 1660 was one of the most significant events of the time. Evelyn was one of its first and most distinguished members, and was appointed its Secretary in 1673. His library was carefully catalogued under six headings and one hundred and twenty sub-headings and well demonstrated his widespread interests. In fact it has been suggested that he ranged too widely and seldom thought deeply enough with the result that some of his written work gives the impression that he is weighed down by his knowledge rather than illuminated by it. This is so, but nevertheless he has left us in his work the impression of a keen and studious man conscientiously trying to "prove all things" at a time when it was believed that a man might know all there was to know.

His writings are many and varied and consist for the main part of discourses, tracts, occasional papers, essays, translations and his diary. His first published work, which appeared when he was twenty-nine, was a translation from the French of a short treatise entitled *Of Liberty and Servitude.* In 1656 he wrote a translation into verse of Book I of Lucretius's *De Rerum Natura.* In 1659 there was a translation from the Greek of *The Golden Book of St. John Chrysostom,* and about the same time he wrote an entertaining satire called *A Character of England.* Among the criticisms of his countrymen are to be found such remarks as "All Englishmen ride so fast upon the road that you would swear there were some enemy in the ariere." In 1661 he translated Gabriel Naudé's *Avis pour dresser une Bibliothèque,* and in the same year there appeared one of the most interesting and often quoted of all his works, *Fumifugium.* In this he discusses a subject still much in the news today, the fog and smoke in London:—

> "For where in all other places the Air is most serene and pure, it is here eclipsed with such a cloud of sulphur, as the sun itself, which gives day to all the world besides, is hardly able to penetrate and impart it here; and the weary traveller, at many miles distance sooner smells than sees the City to which he repairs. This is that pernicious smoke which sullies all her glory, super-inducing a sooty crust or fur upon all that it lights, spoiling the moveables, tarnishing the plate, gildings and furniture and corroding the very iron bars and hardest stones with those piercing and acrimonious spirits which accompany its sulphur; and executing more in one year, than exposed to the pure Air of the country it could affect in some hundreds."

Evelyn suggested that factories and works should be removed from the City, and that sweet-smelling flowers and shrubs should be planted to the south-west of London so that the prevailing wind would bring sweet odours. Modern campaigners against the smoke nuisance in our big towns often quote from *Fumifugium*, and it has been several times republished, the last edition appearing as recently as 1933.

Another publication of 1661 was *Tyrannus or the Mode*, in which he attacked the prevailing custom of following the French fashions in clothes. In 1662 came *Sculptura, or the History and Art of Chalcography and Engraving on Copper.* It is dedicated to Robert Boyle, and from this dedication we can get an insight into Evelyn's public spirit and devotion to learning:

> "I professe to have nothing so much in my desires, and which I more avowe the pursuite of, than to employ the whole remainder of the life, which God shall assigne me, and that I can redeem from its impertinences, in contributing to that great and august designe, which your illustrious, and happy Genius does prompt you to, of cultivating the Sciences, and advancing of useful knowledge."

In 1664 there appeared a translation from the French of R. Freart's *Parallel of Antient Architecture with Modern.* As an example of the taste of the time it is interesting to find that Evelyn in a dedication of the work written in 1697 refers to Gothic architecture as "congestions of heavy, dark, melancholy and monkish piles, without any just proportion, use or beauty". The main English and Continental cathedrals are dismissed as "mountains of stone . . . not worthy the name of architecture". Freart's work was important as it was a repository of the Five Orders, that is a sort of pattern book for architects. Its importance can be estimated by the new editions of Evelyn's translation which appeared in 1707, 1727 and 1737.

In 1664 he also published *Kalendarium Hortense or the Gardener's Almanack*, and the work by which he was best known during the seventeenth and eighteenth centuries, *Sylva or a Discourse of Forest Trees*. Evelyn was keenly interested in forestry and gardening, and he was more of an authority on these subjects than on some of the others he wrote about. The great landowners of the Restoration were proud of their gardens, and Evelyn, a recognised expert, was sometimes consulted by them when they were designing and laying out their estates. He has been described as "bridging the transition from the formal to the landscape garden". Certainly his knowledge and love of trees proved important in making English landowners realise the need for growing and using their own timber. It is difficult to estimate exactly the influence of *Sylva*. It has passed through many editions, the last one being as late as 1908, and the *Quarterly* in 1813 described it as a work of national importance. In 1821 Scott mentioned it as still being the manual of British planters. Even within the last few years Mr W. G. Hiscock has claimed that because of the effect that *Sylva* had on the planting of trees "the battle of Trafalgar was won in Evelyn's study". This claim may be regarded as too big, but nevertheless there is no doubt that *Sylva* was very important because of its use by landowners as a text-book on the planting of trees which often were to be used eventually as timber for the Navy.

One of Evelyn's lists shows that at one time he had treatises, papers and books in preparation on "The Dignity of Man", "Of Stones", "Of Reason in Brute Animals", "Animadversions on Spinoza", "Education" and "Mathematics". It is not surprising that among his manuscripts at the time of his death was found one entitled "Rules for Spending my Pretious Tyme well". Few men can have wasted less time and yet, of his written work, little survived after his death except *Sylva*, *Fumifugium* and his diary.

III

His diary, with which we shall be concerned in this book, is not strictly a diary but a series of memoirs. Early in his life

Evelyn developed the habit of writing notes on the events of the day. "In imitation of what I had seene my Father do, I began to observe matters more punctualy, which I did use to set down in a blanke Almanac." Between 1660 and 1664 he seems to have written up his original notes to the middle of 1645. He resumed this task some time after 1680 and probably brought his notes up to date in 1684. This gave them a more permanent form, and the main manuscript is in a bound volume entitled *Kalendarium*. From 1684 he probably made entries once or twice a week and it becomes a record of contemporary events. There is ample evidence in such phrases as "about this time" of alterations made to the original entries, and the whole diary is very much of a patchwork. The result of this revision is that the diary loses a good deal of the freshness, spontaneity and vigour which is to be found in a diary such as that of Pepys. There is evidence too that in writing up his notes Evelyn added greatly to what he had originally written, and sometimes his memory failed him and the additions are incorrect. Thus about one-sixth of the diary is concerned with his travels on the Continent, and long sections of this have been taken years later from the travel books of the time. But even in these sections we come across such comments as "indeed very extra-ordinary, but of far greater expense than use or beauty", and we are immediately brought face to face with Evelyn himself.

Even after 1684, when the diary becomes a diary in the true sense, items of news are taken straight from the newspapers of the time. There was no intention to deceive in borrowing from guide-books and newspapers, rewriting and adding comments. He wished merely to remind himself as the years slipped away of the places he had seen, the people he had met and the things that had happened. But it is probable that Evelyn did consider that his descendants might read this story of his life, and this means that to some extent it was written with an eye to the impression being made. This may account in part for a feeling of self-consciousness and of self-righteousness which is communicated to us by some of the entries. It will also account in part for the objective nature of most of the entries, although it should be said that Evelyn as a man of "breeding and good manners" could never have written with the candour and complete self-revelation of a Pepys.

About 1700 Evelyn started yet another recension of his diary and this is found in a volume entitled *De Vita Propria*, but in this work he did not get further than the middle of his Italian travels. For over a hundred years after his death the volumes of his diary, and his other manuscripts, lay almost undisturbed at Wotton. Then in 1814 a London antiquary, William Upcott, while staying with Lady Evelyn, mentioned that his hobby was collecting the handwriting of famous men. "Oh, if that is your taste," said Lady Evelyn, "we can easily satisfy you. There is a whole washing-basket full of letters of old 'Sylva' Evelyn in the garret which I was so tired of seeing that I ordered the House-maid the other day to light the fires with them." Fortunately the manuscripts had not been destroyed, and an edited selection of the diary was published by William Bray, assisted by Upcott, in 1818. It was a success, and further editions followed throughout the last century, but it was not until 1955 that the first complete edition appeared, edited by Dr E. S. de Beer. His edition is the authoritative one to which the student of Evelyn should go. Dr de Beer has shown how the first editors have erred by misreading what Evelyn wrote—this is to a certain extent excusable as Evelyn often crammed 1,000 words on to a comparatively small page—by changing words, making interpolations, and frequently by indiscreet cutting. But even more damaging was the attempt of the early editors to 'improve' Evelyn's style. Dr de Beer tells us that "in making what Evelyn wrote suit the taste of his own time, Bray deprived it of much of its life, of the changing accents of the voice". Evelyn was not a great prose writer, but his diary, as it was written, does bear the imprint of his character, and there is a personality about Evelyn's own words which is lacking from what has been well called Bray's "Victorian secretaryese".

It is, however, for the light it throws on the seventeenth century that Evelyn's diary is of special value to us, for it is a major authority on the social, cultural and religious life of the time. He does not tell us as much about himself as we should like to know, but he does provide us with a fine contemporary view of the great figures and great events of this period. The diary has been described as a running commentary on his life and times. Charles II, James II, William and Mary, Clarendon and Shaftesbury, Monk and Sandwich, Boyle and Wren, all these and many others pass through his pages. In a short selection it is difficult to do justice to the great sweep of time and history covered in the diary, but the reader will at least be able to make the acquaintance of one of the most interesting books on the seventeenth century.

We must not go to Evelyn's diary for bursts of self-revelation. He was not a Pepys, a Boswell or a Rousseau. We shall learn how a cultivated, intelligent gentleman of the seventeenth century lived, we shall learn about his interests and his attitude to the world around him, but we shall learn little about his emotions. Perhaps because of this when Evelyn does reveal his feelings the effect is all the greater.

> "After evening prayer was my child buried neere the rest of his brothers, my deare children."

There are occasions such as this which are worth far more than any number of carefully constructed 'purple' passages.

What is to be our final estimate of Evelyn? To many people in the nineteenth century he was a pious, almost saintly, man whose diary was to be read for moral edification. Some in this century regard him as a pompous, conceited bore. Neither of these judgements can be accepted by itself. Each is an attempt to simplify what cannot be simplified. Evelyn's character is complex, and its very complexity lends it interest. There can be no doubt of his religious sincerity, and occasional notes of priggishness cannot mar the air of genuine piety which is apparent throughout the diary. Nor is it possible to doubt his devotion to learning and his public spirit. His was an inquiring rather than a creative mind, and he has produced no great masterpiece of English Literature, but some of his works were regarded during his lifetime and for many years afterwards as authorities on the subjects he discussed, and his diary is still read today because of its great historical interest, and because it tells us something about a man of whom the shrewd Pepys could write:

"... a very ingenious man, and the more I know him the more I love him."

IV

SAMUEL PEPYS was born in London in 1633, and was therefore thirteen years younger than Evelyn. Although his own branch of the family was humble, he was related to more important households, and one of the most important was that of the Montagues. His great-aunt had married Sir Sidney Montague, and their son, Edward, played an important part in the life of Pepys. Edward Montague was a neighbour of Oliver Cromwell and supported him in the Civil War, to be rewarded in 1656 with the appointment of Joint Commander of the English Fleet. Meanwhile Pepys had been to St. Paul's School and won an Exhibition to Magdalene College, Cambridge. Shortly after coming down, probably about 1656, he went into the service of Montague, and acted as the head of his London household and his secretary.

In 1655 he married Elizabeth St. Michel, the beautiful, but often trying, fifteen-year-old daughter of a French Huguenot, and although their married life was not quarrel-free they appear to have been generally happy enough. They did not have any children. At this period of his life Pepys was poor, but his income was slightly increased in 1658 when he secured a post as clerk to the Exchequer. Montague obviously had great trust in his young kinsman for, when he decided that the time had come to go over openly to the side of the exiled Charles, Pepys was on board his flagship as his secretary as they sailed to the Hague in May 1660 in order to bring the King back to England.

In the distribution of rewards at the Restoration Montague became the Earl of Sandwich, and through his support Pepys secured in June 1660 the position of Clerk of the Acts to the Navy. This was an important step forward for it meant that Pepys became one of the principal officers responsible for the administration of the Navy. At that time he knew little about ships and the sea, but he was an industrious man and he soon became an expert. On taking up this position Pepys went to live in the Navy Office, a large building near the Tower of London, and this was his home throughout most of the period when the diary was being written.

Further honours and successes soon came to Pepys. In 1662 he was elected a Younger Brother of the Trinity House, and later in the same year he was made one of the Commissioners for the affairs of Tangiers, an appointment which helped to increase his influence and his fortune. Other members of the Commission were the Duke of York, Prince Rupert, the Duke of Albemarle and Lord Sandwich. In October 1665 he was given the additional appointment of Surveyor-General of Victualling for His Majesty's Navy. That Pepys was well suited to this particular task can be assumed from one of his best-known Naval Minutes:

> "Englishmen, and more especially seamen, love their bellies above anything else, and therefore it must always be remembered in the management of the victualling of the Navy that to make any abatement from them in the quantity or agreeableness of the victuals is to discourage and provoke them in the tenderest point, and will sooner render them disgusted with the King's service than any one other hardship that can be put upon them."

In the middle of 1669 he obtained leave of absence and went with his wife on a tour of France and Holland. Some months after his return, in November 1669, his wife died. In 1673 he was elected Member of Parliament for Castle Rising in Norfolk, and in the same year he took up a new appointment as Secretary of the Admiralty, a position of even greater responsibility than that which he had previously held as Clerk of the Acts. This new position brought him closely into touch with Charles II. In 1676 came his election as Master of the Trinity House, and further honours which were conferred on him about this time were his appointments as a Governor of Christ's Hospital and Master of the Clothworkers' Company. A set-back occurred in 1679 when he was committed to the Tower on a charge of complicity in the "Popish Plot". The attempt to implicate Pepys by spreading false accusations against him, the way in which he was finally cleared of these charges, and the part played in this by the remarkable villain, John Scott, is an exciting story. Pepys was deprived of his office at this time and was out of public employment until July 1683 when he accompanied Lord Dartmouth, as his secretary, on an expedition to Tangier. This had been part of Catharine of Braganza's dowry when she married Charles II in 1661, but it had brought him little but expense, and it had now been decided to destroy and evacuate the place.

While on this expedition he kept a journal which is often referred to as his "Second Diary". This is an interesting document, but it lacks many of the qualities which are to be found in his earlier and more famous diary. Shortly after his return to England in March 1684 he was again appointed Secretary of the Admiralty, and there begins the second of his two periods of rule over the administrative affairs of the Navy. This period was to last four years. In December 1684 the Royal Society elected him their president, and in 1685 he became Member of Parliament for Harwich. With the accession of James II, who had long known and respected Pepys, there seemed to be opening out for him a long vista of prosperity and official power, but the Revolution of 1688 brought this to an abrupt end. Pepys as a right-hand man of the exiled king was removed from his position and went into retirement. This was spent in developing his many interests, in cultivating his many friends, and in adding to his collection of books, prints and curiosities. On the 26th May 1703 he died.

V

One of Pepys's most valued possessions was his library. At his death he bequeathed it first to his nephew, and, on his death, to his old College. Among the many books which eventually went to Cambridge in 1724 were six bound volumes of the diary which he had kept from the 1st January 1660 until the 31st May 1669. These were written in shorthand and consisted of about 1,300,000 words covering over 3,000 quarto pages. For over a hundred years these volumes were to lie untouched, and if the eighteenth century remembered Pepys at all it was as an able administrator of the Navy. But just as Evelyn and Pepys were associated in life, they were associated in death, for it was the publication of Evelyn's diary in 1818 with its references to Pepys which led the Master of Magdalene College to remember the dusty volumes lying in the library and to ask John Smith, an undergraduate, to decipher them. The system of shorthand used was that of Thomas Shelton, and a key to this was also to be found among Pepys's books, but Smith did not know this. If he had, he would have been saved some of his very hard work. It is interesting to read his description of his task:

"In the spring of 1819 I engaged with the late Master of Magdalene College, Cambridge, to decipher the whole of the diary from the six closely written volumes of the original shorthand MS., little thinking how difficult, how laborious, and how unprofitable a task I had undertaken. The distinguished stenographer the late William Brodie Gurney to whom I showed the MS. at the outset, positively assured me that neither I nor any other man would ever be able to decipher it; and two eminent professors of the art confirmed his opinion. I persevered nevertheless; and worked for nearly three years at it usually twelve and fourteen hours a day with frequent wakeful nights. The MS. extended to 3,012 pages of shorthand which furnished 9,325 pages in longhand and embraced 314 different shorthand characters, comprising 391 words and letters, which all had to be kept continually in mind, whilst the head, the eye and the hand of the decipherer were all engaged on the MS. Much of it was in minute characters, greatly faded, and inscribed on almost transparent paper, very trying and injurious indeed to the visual organs."

It was soon realised that here was a literary find of great value, and in 1825 Lord Braybrooke issued the first edition, which was followed by others in 1828, 1848 and 1854. In 1875 the whole manuscript was again deciphered by the Rev. Mynors Bright, and he produced a new edition. The best and most complete edition to be obtained at present is that of H. B. Wheatley which appeared in 1899, but an important new edition of the diary is at present in preparation by Mr R. C. Latham of London University. For the purposes of this text-book I have made use of the Wheatley edition. Everyone should read eventually one of the fuller editions for no selection can do full justice to the flavour and humanity of the diary. Really to know and understand this most interesting of all diarists one must read consecutive entries and follow him through his life day by day. Many of the entries are written on the days they cover, and it is seldom that Pepys allows himself to fall more than two or three days behind with his entries. In the whole nine and a half years during which he kept this record of his life hardly a day was missed. Sometimes the entries are long and cover two or three pages, sometimes they consist of two or three lines.

VI

What are the special merits of the diary which have led our finest critics to describe it as "a work of genius", "a remarkable achievement", and "the work of the only writer of his kind known to history"? Most outstanding perhaps is his gift of selecting the incidents and bringing to life the happenings of the day. It requires an artist to select from the countless incidents of the day the vital moment and the vital experience. But it is not enough to choose the right incidents; they must be clothed in the personality of the writer and expressed in language which vividly sums up the scene or person for the reader. Pepys had the ability to bring a person before us with a few deft words:

> "With Colonel Slingsby and a friend of his, Major Waters (a deaf and most amorous melancholy gentleman, who is under a despair in love, as the Colonel told me, which makes him bad company, though a most good-natured man)."

Pepys is brilliantly successful in doing this again and again, and he secures his effect in terse, lucid, precise language. There is no striving for effect, no feeling of self-consciousness in the style, because it is certain that Pepys never envisaged his beloved diary's being read by other eyes than his own. Nothing essential is left out even if it tells against himself, and there is a candour and honesty about the writing which comes through to the reader in every entry. This is at once the most subjective and objective of all writing. We learn almost everything there is to know about Pepys, his strength and his weakness, his virtues and vices, his likes and dislikes, his interests and hobbies, the big and little things in his life. We get to know him better than we shall ever know our closest friends. To be interesting we must be interested and one of Pepys's outstanding characteristics is his interest in himself and the world around him. We learn too a great deal about the history of those years because Pepys was not only a keen observer of the social scene and "a greate Cherisher of Learned men", but in his official duties he came into contact with some of the great historical figures of the seventeenth century. Finally, for us ordinary mortals who have tried to keep a diary for a year and given it up after a few weeks what will stand out is the industry and enthusiasm which could drive this man after a hard day's work to write his diary by candlelight whilst outside the bell-man was calling out "Past one of the clock, and a cold, frosty, windy morning".

To the nineteenth century Pepys was famous as a diarist, and his work as a naval administrator was almost forgotten. Yet the diary covered less than ten years of a very busy life, and Pepys was to live for thirty-four years after he had written the last word of it. It is to two scholars of our own century, Dr J. R. Tanner and Sir Arthur Bryant, that we are indebted for the more balanced view of Pepys's achievement which now prevails. Sir Arthur Bryant has described Pepys as the creator of three remarkable, and still surviving things—the diary, the civil administration of the Royal Navy, and the administrative principles which still govern the Civil Service. Just as it has been claimed that the Battle of Trafalgar was won in Evelyn's study, so it has been claimed that Pepys in his work for the Navy made "the scabbard for the sword that Nelson, and the heirs of Nelson, used". This book will be concerned with Pepys the diarist, but everyone who wants to know more about Pepys the administrator of the Navy should read Sir Arthur Bryant's trilogy—*Samuel Pepys, the Man in the Making*; *The Years of Peril*; and *The Saviour of the Navy*.

VII

The diaries of Evelyn and Pepys can tell us about the history of the periods during which they were written. In both we shall find descriptions of great events and great people. From Pepys's diary we can learn a great deal about Pepys himself, and, perhaps, if we look closely at Evelyn's diary, we shall learn more about him than appears at first sight. But in addition to this the diaries are important in telling us much about the immense intellectual development and progress in experimental science which marked the seventeenth century. At the beginning of the period science had still been mainly medieval in conception and method. Mr R. G. Cox in his essay "From Donne to Marvell" (in the admirable Penguin Guide to Literature) well sums up the change which is taking place when he says, "There is a conscious modernity in the air". Three great names are associated with this movement away from a superstitious and towards an empiric science—Galileo, Descartes and Francis Bacon. The latter in *The Advancement of Learning* (1605) had advocated a transfer of interest away from abstract speculation and towards direct observation and experiment. This change can be seen clearly in the interest which both Evelyn and Pepys frequently reveal in observation and experiment. We see it again in their interest in the activities of the Royal Society. As we read their diaries we can feel the excitement which they felt as the "spirit of enquiry began to probe into the secrets of nature". In the very midst of all his troubles over the Dutch attack in 1667 we find Pepys writing as his boat brings him back up the Thames at the end of a weary day, "So I homeward as long as it was light reading Mr. Boyle's book of Hydrostatics, which is a most excellent book as ever I read, and I will take much pains to understand him through if I can, the doctrine being very useful".

As great a change can be seen in the prose style of the period. Although at the beginning of the century such pieces of writing as we find in James Winny's selection *The Elizabethan Voyages* and in the introduction to the 1611 Bible are already straightforward prose, it was still regarded as fashionable to write in a style which was ornate and ostentatiously literary. After the Restoration a fashionable prose style was one that was plain, simple and lucid, as was that of Pepys, and as Evelyn's could be in such passages as the description of his robbery by the footpads. Pepys's style is particularly interesting because in spite of its spontaneity which gives it the ring of conversation there is an order in its association of ideas and a clarity about the description of events that show the analytical mind at work. There is an easy intelligibility and modernity about his writing which is in contrast with the archaism of much of the writing of the earlier part of the century. On the other hand Evelyn's style still retains at times those qualities which had been fashionable earlier in the century, even if his intellectual attitude was as modern as that of Pepys.

1660 is important not only as the date of the Restoration of Charles II, and to us as the year in which Pepys started to write his diary, but because, if it is possible to say a literary movement begins anywhere, one begins there. The seeds planted by Bacon now burst into flower, and a spirit of disciplined enquiry makes itself increasingly felt in every mental activity. This spirit of enquiry can be felt in both Evelyn and Pepys. Even the growing habit of writing diaries was in a sense a reflection of the spirit of the time. It showed the enquiring mind looking in at itself. In Donne and other great writers of the seventeenth century there can be seen an increasing interest in introspection and self-analysis. Part of Shakespeare's greatness lay in his interest in human character and in the motives which governed human action, and this interest which he developed in the drama became general as the century advanced. Men became more interested in themselves, in their actions and the reasons for them, and in what we should call nowadays psychology. The proper study of mankind was rapidly becoming man. In reading Evelyn and Pepys we become acquainted with two of the most active minds of their time, and our own experience of life and understanding of human nature is enlarged. It would be a dull person who could come away from a reading of these two diaries without having learnt something about life, and, perhaps more important, about himself.

EXTRACTS FROM THE DIARY OF JOHN EVELYN

[1644] The Summer now drawing neere, and determining to spend the rest of it in some more remote Towne upon the river of Loyer; On the 19 of Aprill I tooke leave of Paris, and by the way of the Messenger agreed for my Passage to Orleans:

The Way from Paris to this City (as indeede most of the roades of France) is paved with a small square free-stone; so that the Country dos not much molest the Travelor with dirt and ill way as ours in England dos; onely 'tis somewhat hard to the poore horses feete which causes them to ride more temperately, seldome going out of the trot, or *grand pas*, as they call it:

We passed by divers Wall'd Townes or Villages as the manner is frequently to secure them: Amongst others of note Chartres & Estampes where we lay the first night: This has a faire Church: The next day we had excellent Way; but had like to come short home; for no sooner were we entred two or three leagues into the Forest of Orleans (which extends it selfe for many miles) after dinner; but the Company behind us, were set on by Rogues who shooting from the hedges and frequent Covert, slew fowre upon the spot, the rest flying: Amongst the slayne was a Captaine of Swisses of the Regiment of Picardy, a person much lamented: This disaster made such an Alarme in Orleans at our arival; that the Prevost-Martial with his assistants going in pursuite, brought in two whom they had shot, and exposed them in the greate Market-place, to see if any would take cognizance of them. I have greate Cause to give God thankes for this Escape; this happend on

Apr: 20 when comming to Orleans, and lying at the White-Crosse (where I found Mr. John Nicholas, eldest sonne to Mr. Secretary) there kitten'd a Cat on my bed, which left on it a Young one having 6 Eares, eight leggs, two bodys from the navil downewards, & two tayles: which strange Monster, I found dead; but warme by me in the Morning when I awaked.

Octob: 7 we had a most delicious journey to Marselles through a Country, sweetely declining to the South & Mediterranean Coasts, full of Vine-yards, & Olive-yards, Orange trees, Myrtils, Pomegranads & the like sweete Plantations, to which belong innumerable pleasantly situated Villas, to the number of above 15 hundred; built all of Free-stone, and most of them in prospect shewing as if they were so many heapes of snow dropp'd out of the clowds amongst those perennial greenes: It was almost at the shutting in of the Gates that we got in at

Marcelles: This Towne stands on the Sea-Coast upon a sweete rising; tis well wall'd, & has an excellent Port for Ships, & Gallys, securd by an huge Chayne of Yron which draw crosse the harbour at pleasure; & there is a well fortified tower: besides this, there are also three other Forts or small Castles, especialy that cald the If built on a rock: Ratonneau, & that of St. John strongly garnison'd. But the Castle commanding the Citty, is that of Nostre dame de la Guard: In the Chapel hang up divers Crocodiles Skinns: We went then to Visite the Gallys being about 25 in number. The Captaine of the Gally royal gave us most courteous entertainement in his Cabine, the Slaves in the interim playing both on loud & soft musique very rarely: Then he shew'd us how he commanded their motions with a nod, & his Wistle, making them row out; which was to me the newest spectacle I could imagine, beholding so many hundreds of miserably naked Persons, having their heads shaven cloose, & onely red high bonnets, a payre of Course canvas drawers, their whole backs, & leggs starke naked, doubly chayned about their middle, & leggs, in Cupples, & made fast to their seates: and all Commanded in a trise, by an Imperious & cruell sea-man: One Turke amongst them he much favourd, who waited on him in his Cabine, but naked as he was, & in a Chayne lock'd about his leg; but not coupled.

Then this Gally, I never saw any thing more richly carv'd & Guilded (the Sovraigne excepted) and most of the rest were exceeding beautiful: Here, after we had bestow'd something amongst the Slaves, the Cap: sent a band of them to give us musique at dinner where we lodged. I was amaz'd to contemplate how these miserable Catyfs lye in their Gally, considering how they were crowded together; Yet was there hardly one but had some occupation or other: by which as leasure, in Calmes, & other times, permitts, they get some little monye; in so much as some have after many Yeares of cruel Servitude been able to purchase their liberty: Their rising forwards, & falling back at their Oare, is a miserable spectacle, and the noyse of their Chaines with the roaring of the beaten Waters has something of strange & fearfull in it, to one unaccostom'd. They are ruld, & chastiz'd upon their backs, & soles of their feete upon the least dissorder, & without the least humanity: Yet for all this they are Cherefull, & full of vile knavery:

On the 11th we lay at Canes, which is a small port on the Mediterranean; here we agree'd with a Sea-man to transport us to Genöa, so having procurd a bill of Health (without which there is no admission at any Towne in Italy) we embarq'd on the 12 of Octob: . . . on the 15 . . . we encounterd a little foule Weather, which made us creepe *Terra*, *Terra* as they call it; and so a Vessell that encounter'd us advis'd us to do: But our Patron, striving to double the point of Savona, making out into the Wind, put us all into an incredible hazard; for blowing very hard from Land 'twixt those horrid gapps of the Mountaines, it set so violently, as rais'd on the sudaine an over growne Sea, so as we could not then by any meanes recover the Weather shore for many houres, inso much that what with the Water already enterd, & the confusion of fearfull Passengers (of which one was an Irish Bishop & his Bro: a Priest, confessing some as at the Article of Death) we were almost uterly abandon'd to despaire; Our Pilot himselfe giving us for gon: But so it pleas'd God on the suddaine (and as now we were almost sinking downe right, wearied with pumping, & laving out the Water) to appease the Wind, that with much adoe & greate perill we recover'd the Shore, which we now kept within lesse then halfe a league, in view & sent of those pleasant Villas, & fragrant Orchards which are situated on this Coast, full of Princly retirements for the Sumptuousnesse of their buildings & noblenesse of the plantations; especially those at St. Pietro d'Arena, from whence (the wind spiring as now it did) might perfectly be smelt the peculiar joys of Italy, in the natural perfumes of Orange, Citron, & Jassmine flowres, for divers leagues to seaward.

Octo: 16 we got to Anker under the Pharos or Watch-towre erected on an high rock, at the mouth of the Mole of Genoa; the weather being yet so fowle, that for two houres at least we dast not stand in to the haven: Towards the evening adventur'd and came on shore by the Prattique-house, where after strict examination of the Syndics, we were had to the Ducal Palace, and there our names beeing taken, we were conducted to our Inne, which was at one Zacharias an Englishmans, where we were almost amazd at the consideration of the danger we had escaped, never thinking to have seene that evening alive: I shall never forget a story of our host Zacharye, who upon the relation of our perill, quitted us with another of his owne, being shipwrack'd as he affirm'd solemnly, in the middle of a greate sea some where in the West-Indies: That he swam no lesse then 22 leagues to another Iland, with a tinder-box wraped up in his hayre, which was not so much as wett all that way: That picking up the Carpenters tooles with other provisions in a Chest, he & the Carpenter, that accompany'd him (good swimmers it seemes both) floated the Chest before them, and arriving at last in a place full of Wood, they built another Vessell, and so escaped; the rest being all cast away: After this story we no more talk'd of our danger, for Zachary put us quite downe, though we were all Travellors.

[1645] So soone as we came on shore we were conducted to the Dogana, where our Portmanteaus were visited, & so got to our lodging, which was at honest Signor Paulo Rhodomants at the Aquila Nera neere the Rialto, & one of the best quarters of the Towne. This journey from Rome to Venice, cost me 7: Pistoles & 13 Julios.

June. The next morning finding my-selfe extreamly weary, & beaten with my Journey, I went to one of their Bagnias, which are made, & treate after the Eastern manner, washing one with hot & cold water, with oyles, rubbing with a kind of Strigil, which a naked youth puts on his hand like a glove of seales Skin, or what ever it be, fetching off a world of dirt, & stretching out ones limbs, then claps on a depilatorie made of a drug or earth they call Resina, that comes out of Turky, which takes off all the haire of the body, as resin dos a piggs. I think there is orpiment & lime in it, for if it lie on to long it burns the flesh: The curiosity of this Bath, did so open my pores that it cost me one of the greatest Colds & rheumes that ever I had in my whole life, by reason of my comming out without that caution necessary of keeping my selfe Warme for some time after: For I immediately began to visite the famous Places of the Citty And Travellers, do nothing else but run up & downe to see sights, that come into Italy: And this Citty, for being one of the most miraculously plac'd of any in the whole World, built on so many hundred Ilands, in the very sea, and at good distance from the Continent, deserv'd our admiration: It has neither fresh, nor any other but salt Water, save what is reserved in Cistrens, of the raine, & such as is daily brought them from *Terra firma* in boates: Yet it wants nor fresh water, nor aboundance of all sorts of excellent Provisions, very cheape. 'Tis reported that when the Hunns overran all Italy, some meane fishermen & others left the Maine land, & fled to these despicable & muddy Ilands for Shelter, where in processe of time, & by Industry, it is growne to the greatnesse of one of the most considerable states in the World, consider'd as a Republique & having now subsisted longer, than any of the foure antient Monarchies, & flourishing in greate State, welth & glory by their Conquests of greate Territories in Italy, Dacia, Greece,

Candy, Rhodes, Slavonia, & at present challenging the Empire of all the Adriatique Sea, which they yearly espouse, by casting a gold ring into it, with greate pomp & ceremony upon Ascention day: the desire of seing this, being one of the reasons, that hastned us from Rome: First the Dodge or Duke (having heard Masse) in his robes of State (which are very particular & after the Eastern) together with the Senat in their gownes, Imbarkd in their gloriously painted, carved & gilded Bucentoro, invirond & follow'd by innumerable Gallys, Gundolas, & boates filled with Spectators, some dressed in Masquerade, Trumpets, musique, & Canons, filling the whole aire with din: Thus having rowed out about a league into the Gulph, the Duke at the prow casts into the Sea a Gold ring, & Cup, at which a loud acclamation is Echod by the greate Guns of the Arsenale, and at the Liddo: & so we returned: Two days after taking a Gundola which are their Water Coaches, (for land ones many old men in this Citty never saw any, or rarely a horse) we rowed up & downe the Channells, which are as our Streetes; These Vessells are built very long & narrow, having necks and tailes of steele, somewhat spreading at the beake like a fishes taile, & kept so exceedingly polish'd as gives a wonderfull lustre: some are adornd with carving, others lined with Velvet, commonly black, with Curtains & tassals, & the seates like Couches to lie stretch'd on, while he who rowes, stands on the very edge of the boate, upright, and with one Oare (bending forward as if they would precipitate into the Sea) rows, & turnes, with incredible dexterity, thus passing from Channell to Chanell, & landing his fare or patron, at what house he pleases: The beakes of these vessells are not unlike the Roman antient Rostrums: The first thing I went to see of publique building was the Rialto, celebrated for passing over the grand Canale with one onely Arch, so large as to admitt a Gally to row through it, built of good Marble, & having on it, besides many pretty shops, three stately & ample passages for people, without any incumbrance, the 2 outmost nobly balustr'd with the same stone, a piece of Architecture to be admir'd. It was Evening & the Canale (which is their Hide-park, where the Noblesse go to take the aire) was full of Ladys & Gent; & there are many times very dangerous stops by reason of the multitude of Gudalos, ready to sink one another, & indeede they affect to leane them so on one side, that one who is not accostom'd to it, would be afraid of over setting: Here they were singing, playing on harpsicords, & other musick & serenading their Mistriss's: In another place, racing, & other *passe tempi* on the Water, it being now exceeding hot: I went next day to their Exchange, a place like ours, frequented by Merchants, but nothing so magnificent; from thence by Guide had me to the Fondigo di Todeschi which is their magazine, & here the Merchants (as in a Coledge) having their lodging and diet many of them, especially Germons; the outside of this stately fabric is painted by Geo: Castel Franco, & Titian himselfe; hence I pass'd through the Merceria, which I take to be the most delicious streete in the World for the sweetenesse of it, being all the way on both sides, continualy tapissry'd as it were, with Cloth of Gold, rich Damasks & other silks, which the shops expose & hang before their houses from the first floore, & with that variety, that for neere halfe the yeare, which I spent chiefly in this citty, I hardly remember to have seene the same piece twice exposd, to this add the perfumers & Apothecaries shops, and the innumerable cages of Nightingals, which they keepe, that entertaines you with their melody from shop to shop, so as shutting your Eyes, you would imagine your selfe in the Country, when indeede you are in the middle of the Sea; besides there being neither rattling of Coaches nor trampling of horses, tis almost as silent as the field: This streete, pav'd with brick, and exceedingly cleane, brought us through an arch into famous Piazzo St. Marco, over this Porch, stands that admirable Clock, celebrated next to that of Strasburg, for its many movements, amongst which, about 12 & 6, which is their houre of Ave Maria, when all the towne are on their knees, comes forth the 3 Kings led by a Starr, & passing by the Imoge of Christ in his Mothers armes, do their reverence, & enter into the Clock by another doore: at the top of this turret another Automat strikes the quarters; & this I mention for a storie affirmd to me by an honest merchant, That walking one day in the Piazza he saw the fellow who kept the Clock, struck with this hammer so forcably, as he was stooping his head neere the bell to mend something amisse, at the instant of striking, that being stunn'd, he reel'd over the battlements, & brake his neck. The buildings about this Piazza are all Arched, on Pillars, within pav'd with white & black polish'd Marble, even to the Shops, the rest of the fabric as stately as any in Europ, being not onely marble, but the architecture of the famous Sansovini, who lies buried in St. Jacomo at the End of the Piazzo: The battlements of this noble range of building is raild with stone, & thick set with excellent statues, which add a wonderfull ornament; yet is one of the sides, much more Roman like than the other, I meane that which reguards the Sea, & where the church is placd: The other range is plainly Gotic, & so we entred into St. Marks Church, before which stand two brasse piedestals exquisitely cast, & figur'd, which beare as many tall masts, painted red, on which upon greate festivals, they hang flags & streamers: This famous Church is also Gotic, yet for the preciousnesse of the Materials, being of severall rich marbles, aboundanc of Porphyrie, serpentine &c: far exceeding any of Rome, St. Peters hardly excepted; & first I much admired the splendid historie of our B: Saviour, composd all of Mosaic over the faciata, below which, & over the chiefe Gate, are 4 horses cast in Coper, as big as the life, the same that formerly were transported from Rome by Constantine to Byzantium, & thence by the Venetians hither: Being come into the Church, you see nothing, & tread on nothing but is precious, The floore all inlayed with Achats, Lazulis, Calcedons, Jaspers, Porphyrie and other rich marbles, in admirable sort for the work, the walls sumptuously incrusted, & presenting to the Imagination the Shapes of Men, birds, trees, houses, flowers & a thousand varieties: . . . But when all is said, as to this Church, tis in my opinion much too dark, & dismal, & of heavy work: The fabric, as is much of Venice, both for buildings & other fashions & circumstances much after the Greekes, their next neighbours: . . .

Twas now Ascention Weeke, & the greate Mart or faire of the whole yeare now kept, every body at liberty, & jollie; the Noblemen stalking with their Ladys on Choppines about 10 foote high from the ground. These are high heeld shoos particularly affected by these proude dames, or as some say, invented to keepe them at home, it being so difficult to walke with them, whence one being asked how he liked the Venetian Dames, replyd, they were Mezzo Carne, Mezzo Legno; & he would have none of them: The truth is their Garb is very odd, as seeming allwayes in Masquerade, their other habite also totaly different from all Nations: They weare very long crisped haire of several strakes and Colours, which they artificially make so, by washing their heads, & dischevelling them on the brims of a broade hat that has no head, but an hole to put out their head by, drie them in the Sunn, as one may see them above, out of their windos: In their tire they set silk flowers & sparkling stones: Their Sleeves are made exceeding wide, under which their smock sleeves as wide & commonly tucked up to the shoulder, & shewing their naked arme, through false Sleeves of Tiffany girt with a bracelet or two: besides this they go very bare of their breasts and back, with knots of poynts richly tagg'd, about their shoulders & other places, of their body, which they usualy cover with a kind of yellow Vaile of Lawn very transparent. Thus attir'd they set their hands on the heads of two Matron-like servants or old women to support them, who are mumbling their beades: Tis very ridiculous to see how these ladys crawle in & out of their Gundolas by reason of their Choppines, & what dwarfes they appeare when taken down from their Wooden scafolds: Of these I saw neere 30 together stalking, halfe as high more, as the rest of the World; for Curtezans or the Citizens may not weare Chopines, but cover their bodies & faces with a vaile of a certaine glistring Taffata or Lustrèe, out of which they now & then dart a glaunce of their Eye, the whole face being otherwise intirely hid with it: Nor may the

Common Misses or Whores, take this habite, but go about beare fac'd: To the corners of these Virgin Vailes hang broad but flat tassels of curious Point de Venize: The Married Women go in black Vailes: In the same Colour, but of fine Cloth, do all the Nobility weare, lind with taffata in Summer, with furre of the bellys of Squirills in the Winter, which all put on at a certaine day, girt with a girdle emboss'd with silver: The Vest, not much different from what our Batchelors of Art weare in Oxford, & an hood of Cloth made like a sack, cast over their left shoulder, & a round cloth black Cap, frieng'd with wooll: which is not so comely: They also weare their Collar open, to shew the diamond button of the Stock of their Shirt: But never have I seene pearle for oriency & bignesse comparable to what the Ladys weare, most noble families being very rich in jewells, especialy Pearle, which allways is left to the son or brother who is destin'd to Marry, which the eldest seldome do: The Dodges vest is of Crimson Velvet, the Procurator's &c. of Damasc very stately: Nor was I lesse surpriz'd with the strange variety of the severall Nations which we every day met with in the Streetes & Piazza of Jewes, Turks, Armenians, Persians, Moores, Greekes, Sclavonians, some with their Targets & boucklers, & all in their native fashions, negotiating in this famous Emporium, which is allways crouded with strangers. This night, having with my Lord Bruce taken our places before, we went to the Opera, which are Comedies (& other plays) represented in Recitative Music by the most excellent Musitians vocal & Instrumental, together with variety of Seeanes painted & contrived with no lesse art of Perspective, and Machines, for flying in the aire, & other wonderfull motions. So taken together it is doubtlesse one of the most magnificent & expensfull diversions the Wit of Men can invent: The historie was Hercules in Lydia, the Seanes chang'd 13 times, The famous Voices Anna Rencia a Roman, & reputed the best treble of Women; but there was an Eunuch, that in my opinion surpass'd her, and a Genoveze that sung an incomparable Base; This held us by the Eyes and Eares til two in the Morning when we went to the Chetto de San: Felice, to see the Noblemen & their Ladies at Basset, a Game at Cards which much use, but play not in publique & with all that have inclination to it, in Masquerad, without speaking so much as one word, & so come in, play, loose, or gaine, & go away as they please: This time of Licence is not all the yeare long, but onely in Carnoval, & this Ascention Weeke, neither are their Theaters open for that other Magnificenc, or for ordinary Comedians, save on these solemnities; they being a frugal & wise people and exact observer of all sumptuarie Laws.

There being at the time a ship bound for the Holy Land, I had now resolved to imbarke myselfe, intending to see Jerusalem, & other parts of Syria, Egypt, & Turky: but after I was provided of all necessaries, laied in Snow to coole our drink, bought some Sheepe, Poultry, Bisquit, Spirits & a little Cabinet of Drouggs &c. in case of sicknesse; our Vessell (whereof Cap: Powell was Master) happnd to be press'd for the service of the State, to Carry Provisions to Candia, which was now nuly attacqu'd by the Turkes; which altogether frustrated my designe, to my greate sorrow, it being but two or 3 daies before we hoped to set saile.

August. The next morning Cap: Powell (Master of the Vessell which had been stop'd by the State, to go to Candy, & in which I was to Embark towards Turky) invited me on board, lying about 10 miles from Venice, where we had a good dinner, of English pouderd beefe, & other good meate, with store of Wine, & greate Gunns, as the manner is: After dinner the Captaine presented me with a stone he lately brought from Grand Cairo, which he tooke from the Mumy-pitts, full of Hieroglypics, which I designd on paper, with the true dimensions & sent in a letter to Mr. Henshaw, to communicate to Father Kircher, who was then setting forth his greate work *Obeliscus Pamphilius*, where it is described, though without mentioning my Name at all: The stone was afterward brought for me into England, landed at Wapping, where before I could heare of it, it was broken into severall fragments, & utterly defaced to my no small affliction: The Boateswaine of the ship also gave me an hand &

foote of rare Mummy, the nailes wheroff had been overlaid with thin plates of Gold, & the whole body perfect, when he brought it out of Egypt, but the avarice of the Sailers & Ships Crue, brake it in pieces & divided the body among them, which was greate pitty: he presented me also with 2 Egyptian Idols, & some loaves of the Bread which the Coptics use in the H: Sacrament, with other curiosities:

[1646] In January Signor Molino was chosen Dodge, but the extreame snow that fell, & the cold hindred my going to see the solemnity, so as I stirred not from Padoa til Shrovetide, when all the world repaire to Venice to see the folly & madnesse of the Carnevall; The Women, Men & persons of all Conditions disguising themselves in antique dresses, & extravagant Musique & a thousand gambols, & traversing the streetes from house to house, all places being then accessible, & free to enter: There is abroad nothing but flinging of Eggs fill'd with sweete Waters, & sometimes not over sweete; they also have a barbarous costome of hunting bulls about the Streetes & Piazzas, which is very dangerous, the passages being generally so narrow in that Citty: Likewise do the youth of the severall Wards & parrishes contend in other Masteries or pastimes, so as tis altogether impossible to recount the universal madnesse of this place during this time of licence: Now are the greate banks set up for those who will play at Basset, the Comedians have also liberty & the Operas to Exercise: Witty pasquils are likewise thrown about, & the Mountebanks have their stages in every Corner: The diversion which chiefely tooke me up, was three noble Operas which I saw, where was incomparable Voices, & Musique: The most celebrated of which was the famous Anna Rencha, whom we invited to a Fishdinner, after 4 daies in Lent, that they had given over at the Theater; when accompanied with an Eunuch (whom she brought with her) she entertaind us with rare Musique, both of them singing to an Harpsichord: It growing late a Gentleman of Venice came for her, to shew her the Gallys now ready to set sayle for Candia:

This Entertainement produc'd a second, which was given us by the English Consul of the Merchants, inviting us to his house, where he had the Genoèze, the most celebrated base in Italy, who was of the late Opera: this diversion held us so late at night, that conveying a Gentlewoman (that supped with us) to her Gundola at the usual place of landing; we were shot at by two Carbines from out another Gundola, in which was a Noble Venetian & his Curtezana, unwilling it seemes to be disturb'd, which made us run in, and fetch other weapons, not knowing what the matter was, 'till we were informed of the danger we might incurr, by pursuing it farther.

Three daies after this, I tooke my leave of Venice, and went to Padoa to be present at the famous Anatomie Lecture, which is here celebrated with extraordinary apparatus, & lasting almost the whole Moneth, during which I saw three, a Woman, a Child, & a Man dissected, with all the manual operations of the Chirurgion upon the humane body: The one performed by Cavaliere Vestlingius, & Dr. Jo. Athelsteinus Leoncenas, of whom I purchased those rare Tables of Veines & Nerves, & causd him to prepare a third of the Lungs, liver, & Nervi sexti par: with the Gastric vaines, which I transported into England, the first of that kind had ben ever seene in our Country, & for ought I know, in the World, though afterwards there were others: (Given after to the R: Society:) . . .

March: 20 I return'd to Venice where I tooke leave of my Friends: The 22d was invited to excellent English potted Venison, at Mr. Hobbsons a worthy Merchant: The 23d, I toke my leave of the Patriarcke, & the Prince of Wertenburg, & Monsieur Grotius (sonn to the learned Hugo,) now going a Commander to Candia, & in the afternoone receiv'd my Bills of Exchange of 300 ducati for my Journey of Vandervoort my Merchant, who shewed me his rare Collection of Italian Books, esteem'd very curious & of good value: The next day I was conducted to the Ghetta where the Jewes dwell (as in a Tribe & Ward) together, where I was present at a Mariage: The Bride was clad in White, sitting in a lofty chaire, & coverd also with a white vaile; Then two old Rabbies joynd them together, one of them holding a glasse of Wine in his hand, which in the midst of the ceremony, pretending to deliver to the Woman, he let fall, the breaking wherof, was to signifie the frailty of our nature, & that we must expect dissasters & crosses amidst all enjoyments: This don, we had a fine banquet, & were brought into the Bride chamber, where the bed was dress'd up with flowers, & the Counterpan, strewed in workes: At this ceremony we saw divers very beautiful Portuguez-Jewesses, with whom we had some conversation, & so went to dinner at our Lodging. . . .

Having pack'd up my purchases, of Books, Pictures, Glasses, Treacle, &c (the making and extraordinary ceremonie whereof, I had been curious to observe, for tis extremely pompous & worth seeing) I departed from Venice, accompanied with Mr. Waller (the celebrated Poet) now newly gotten out of England, after the Parliament had extreamely worried him, for attempting to put in execution the Commission of Aray, & for which the rest of his Collegues were hanged by the Rebells:

(May) In a Word Milan is a sweete place, & though the streetes are somewhat narrow, they abound in rich Coaches, are full of Noblesse, who every night frequent the Course.

Passing towards our Lodging, & Walking a turne in the Portico before the Dome a Cavaliero who pass'd by, hearing some of our Companie speaking English, looked a good while earnestly on us, and by & by sending his servant towards us, desired that we would honour him the next day at Dinner; This we looked on as an odd kind of Invitation, he not speaking at all to us himselfe: We returnd his Civilitie, with thanks, not full resolv'd what to do, or what might be the meaning of it, in this jealous place: But on inquirie, 'twas told us he was a Scots Colonel, that had an honorable Command in the Citty, so we agreed to go: This Afternoone we were wholy taken up in seeing an Opera, represented by some Neapolitans, & performed all in excellent Musick, & rare Sceanes: in which there acted a celebrated Beauty:

Next morning we went to the Colonels, who had sent his servant againe to conduct us to his house; which in truth we found a noble Palace, richly furnish'd. There were also other Guests, all Souldiers, and one of them a Scotch man, but not one of all their names could we learn: At dinner he excusd his rudenesse, that he had not himselfe spoken to us, telling us it was his costome, when he heard of any English Travlors (who but rarely would be knowne to passe through that Citty, for feare of the Inquisition) to invite them to his house, where they might be free: And indeede we had a most sumptuous dinner, with plenty of Excellent provision, & the wine so tempting, that after some healths had gon about, & we rissen from Table, the Colonel leade us into his hall, where there hung up divers Colours, Saddle, bridles, pistols & other Armes, being Trophies which he had with his owne hands taken from the Enemy: & amongst them would needes bestow a paire of Pistols on Cap: Wray, one of our fellow Travelors, & a good drinking Gent: & on me, a Turkish bridle woven with silk & very Curiously embossd, with other silk Trappings, to which hung an halfe moone finely wrought, which he had taken from a Basshaw that he had slaine: With this glorious spoile, I rid the rest of my Journey as far as Paris & brought it afterwards into England. Then he shew'd us a stable of brave horses, with his Menage & Cavalerizzo. Some of the horses he causd to be brought forth, which he mounted, and perform'd all the motions of an Excellent horse-man: When this was don, & he alighted, contrary to the advice of his Groome & Pages, (who it seemes knew the nature of the beast, & that their Master was a little spirited with Wine) needes he would have out a fiery horse, that had not yet ben Menag'd, & was very ungovernable; but was else a very beautifull Creature: This he mounting, the horse getting the raines, in a full carriere, rose so desperately, as he fell quite back, crushing the Colonell so forceably against the Wall of the Manege, that though he sat on him like a Centaure, yet recovering the Jade on all foure againe, he desir'd to be taken down, & so led in, where he cast himselfe upon a Pallet, where with infinite lamentation, after some time, we tooke our leaves of him, being now speechlesse; and the next morning coming to visite him, we found before the doore, the Canopie, which they usualy carry over the Host, and some with lighted tapers, which made us suspect he was in very sad condition, & so indeede we found him, an Irish frier standing by his bed side, as Confessing him, or at least disguising a Confession & other Ceremonies, used *in extremis*; for we afterwards learn'd, that the Gent: was a Protestant, and had this Frier his confident; which doubtlesse was a dangerous thing at Milan, had it ben but suspected: At our enterance he sighed grievously and held up his hands, but was not able to speake: After vomiting some bloud, he kindly tooke us all by the hand, & made signes, that he should see us no more, which made us take our leave of him with extreame reluctancy, & affliction for the Accident: This sad disaster made us Consult that very Evening about our departure from this Towne as soone as we could, not knowing how we might be enquird after, or engag'd, The Inquisition heare being so cruelly formidable, & inevitable on the least suspicion: The very next morning therefore discharging our Lodgings we agreed for a Coach to Carry us to the foote of the Alpes, not a little concernd for the death of the Colonell, which we now heard of, & that had so courteously entertain'd us:

We ariv'd at night to Marguzzo an obscure village at the end of the Lake, & very foote of the Alpes, which now rise as it were suddainly, after some hundred of miles of the most even Country in the World, & where there is hardly a stone to be found, as if nature had here swept up the rubbish of the Earth in the Alpes, to forme & cleare the Plaines of Lumbardy, which hitherto he had pass'd since our coming from Venice:

In this wretched place, I lay on a bed stuff'd with leaves, which made such a Crackling, & did so prick my skin through the tick, that I could not sleepe: The next morning I was furnish'd with an Asse (for we could not get horses) but without stirrops, but we had ropes tied with a loope to put our feete in, that supplied other trappings, & thus with my gallant steede, bridld with my Turkish present, we pass'd thro a reasonable pleasant, but very narrow Vally, 'til we came to Duomo, where we rested, & having shew'd the Spanish passe, we brought from the Ambassador; The Governor would presse another on us: though onely that his Secretary might get a Croune: Here we exchang'd our Asses for Mules sure footed on the hills & precipices, as accustom'd to passe them, & with a Guide, which now we hired, we were brought that night, through very steepe, craggy, & dangerous passages, to a Village cal'd Vedra, being the last of the King of Spaines Dominion in the Dutchy of Milan, a very infamous wretched lodging:

Next morning we mount againe through strange, horrid & firefull Craggs & tracts abounding in Pine trees, & onely inhabited with Beares, Wolves, & Wild Goates, nor could we any where see above a pistol shoote before us, the horizon being terminated with rocks, & mountaines, whose tops cover'd with Snow, seem'd to touch the Skies, & in many places pierced the Clowdes. Some of these vast mountaines were but one intire stone, 'twixt whose clefts now & then precipitated greate Cataracts of Mealted Snow, and other Waters, which made a tirrible roaring, Echoing from the rocks & Cavities, & these Waters in some places, breaking in the fall, wett us as if we had pas'd through a mist, so as we could neither see, nor heare one another, but trusting to our honest Mules, jog on our Way: The narrow bridges in some places, made onely by felling huge Fir-trees & laying them athwart from mountaine to mountaine, over Cataracts of stupendious depth, are very dangerous, & so are the passages & edges made by cutting away the maine rock: others in steps, & in some places we passe betweene mountaines that have been broken & falln upon one another, which is very tirrible, & one had neede of a sure foote, & a steady head to climb some of these precipices, harbours for the Beares, & Woulves, who sometimes have assaulted Travellers: In these straits we frequently alighted, freezing in the Snow, & anon frying by the reverberation of the Sun against the Cliffs as we descend lower, where we meete now & then a few miserable

Cottages, built so upon the declining of the rocks, as one would expect their sliding down: Amongst these inhabite a goodly sort of People having monstrous Gullets or Wenns of flesse growing to their throats, some of which I have seene as big as an hundred pound bag of silver hanking under their Chinns; among the Women especialy, & that so ponderous, as that to Ease them, they many of them were a linnen cloth, bound about their head & coming under the chin to support it, but *quis tumidum guttur miratur in Alpibus?* Their drinking so much snow water is thought to be the Cause of it, the men using more wine, are not so strumous as the Women: but the very truth is, they are a race of people, & many greate Water-drinkers here have not those prodigious tumors: It runs as we say in the bloud, & is a vice in the race, & renders them so ougly, shrivel'd & deform'd, by its drawing the skin of the face downe, that nothing can be more fritefull; to which add a strange puffing habit, furrs, & barbarous Language, being a mixture of corrupt high German, French, & Italian: The people are of gigantic Stature, extreamely fierce & rude, yet very honest & trustie: This night, through unaccessible heights, we came in prospect of Mons Sempronius, now Mount Sampion, which has on its summit a few hutts, & a Chapell: Approaching this, Captaine Wrays Water Spaniel, (a hugh filthy Curr, that had follow'd him out of England), hunted an heard of Goates downe the rocks, into a river made by the dissolutions of the Snow: Ariv'd at our cold harbour (though the house had in every roome a Stove), supping with Cheeze & Milke & wretched wine to bed we go in Cupbords, & so high from the floore, that we climb'd them by a Ladder, & as we lay on feathers, so are Coverd with them, that is, betweene two tickes stuff'd with feathers, & all little enough to keepe one warme: The Ceilings of the roomes are strangely low for those tall people. The house was now in September, halfe cover'd with Snow, nor is there ever a tree or bush growing in many miles: from this unhospitable place then we hasted away early next morning.

(July) The next day we ariv'd at Orleans, taking our turn to row through all the former passages, & reckoning that my share amounted to little lesse than 20 legues; sometimes footing it through pleasant fields & medows, sometimes we shot at fouls & other birds, nothing came amisse, sometimes we play'd at Cards, whilst other sung, or were composing Verses; for we had the greate Poet Mr. Waller in our Companie, & some other ingenious Persons: At Orleans we abode but one day, the next (leaving our mad Captain behind us) I arrived at Paris, strangely rejoyc'd, after so many dissasters, & accidents, of a tedious Peregrination, that I was gotten so neere home, & therefore resolved to rest myselfe before I set on any farther Motion.

It was now October, & the onely time that in my whole life I spent most idly, tempted from my more profitable recesses; but I soone recovered my better resolutions, & fell to my study, & learning of the high-dutch & Spanish tongues, & now & then refreshing my Dauncing, & such exercises as I had long omitted, & which are not in such reputation among the sober Italians.

[1647] January 28, I chang'd my Lodging in the Place de Monsieur de Metz neere the Abby of St. Germains, & thence on the 12 feb: to another in Rue Collumbiers, where I had a very faire Appartment, which cost me 4 pistols per Moneth: The 18 I frequented a Course of Chymistrie, the famous Monsieur Le Febure operating upon most of the Nobler processes: 3 March, Monsieur Mercure began to teach me on the Lute, though to small perfection.

Octob: 4: I seald & declard my Will: & that morning went from Paris taking my journey thro Rouen, Dieppe, Ville Dieu, St. Vallerie, where I staied one day, with Mr. Waller, with whom I had some affaires, & for which cause I tooke this Circle to Calice, where I ariv'd on the 11th and that night Imbarking in the Paquet-boate, was by one aclock gott safe to Dover; for which I heartily put up my Thankes to God, who had conducted me safe to my owne Country, & ben mercifull to me through so many aberrations: Hence taking Post, I ariv'd at London the next day at Evening, being the 2d of October New-style.

[1649] On the 19 (January) I return'd home, passing an extraordinary danger of being drown'd, by our Whirries falling fowle in the night, on another vessell there at Anker, shooting the Bridge at 3 quarter Ebb, for which his mercy, God Almighty be prais'd.

21. was published my Translation of *Liberty & Servitude*, for the Preface of which I was severely threatn'd: 22d I went through a Course of Chymistrie at S. Court & now was the Thames frozen over, & horrid Tempest of Winds, so different was this part of the Winter from the former:

The Villanie of the Rebells proceeding now so far as to Trie, Condemne, & Murder our excellent King, the 30 of this Moneth, struck me with such horror that I kept the day of his Martyrdom a fast, & would not be present, at that execrable wickednesse; receiving that sad account of it from my Bro: Geo: & also by Mr. Owen, who came to Visite this afternoone, recounting to me all Circumstances.

[1652] 4 June I set out for Rie to meete my Wife, now upon her journey from Paris, after she had obtain'd leave to come out that Citty, which had now ben besieged some time, by the Pr: of Condys armie, in the Time of Rebellion: & after she had now ben neere 12 Yeares from her owne Country, that is since 5 yeares of age, at which time she went over: 5 I lay this night at Sennock, ariv'd the next at Rie, where was an Embargo, upon occasion of the late Conflict with the Holland Fleete, the two Nations being now in Warr; & which made sailing very unsafe: 6: Whitsonday, I went to Church (which is a very faire one) heard one of their Canters, who dismiss'd the Assembly rudely, & without any blessing: I was displeasd when I came home, that I was present at it, having hitherto kept my Eares incontaminate from their new fangled service: Here I stayed til the

10th with no small impatience, when I walked over to survey the ruines of Winchelsea, that antient Cinq-port, which by the remaines & ruines of ample Streetes, & publique structures, discovers it to have formerly ben a considerable & large Citty, There are to be seene vast Caves & Vaults, Walls, & Towers, ruines of Monasteries, & of a sumptuous Church in which some handsom monuments, especialy of the Templars buried just in the manner of those in the Temp: at Lond: This place being now all in rubbish, & a few despicable hovells & cottages onely standing, hath yet a Major: The sea which formerly renderd it a rich & commodious port, having now forsaken it: so we walked back to Rie:

11 About 4 in the after-noone, being at bowles on the Greene, we discoverd a Vessel, which proved to be that in which my Wife was, & got into harbour about 8 a clock that Evening to my no small joy: They had ben 3 days at Sea, & hardly Escaped the whole Dutch Fleete, through which they pass'd taken for Fishers; which was a greate good fortune; there being 17 bailes of furniture, & other rich plunder, which I blesse God came all safe to land, together with my Wife, & my Lady Browne her mother, accompanying her Daughter: But my Wife discompos'd with being so long at sea, we set not forth towards hom 'til the 14th, when hearing the Small-pox was very rife in and about Lond: and that my Lady had a greate desire to drink Tunbridge Waters; I carried them thither, where I staied in a very sweete place, private & refreshing, and also tooke the Waters my selfe a few daies, 'til the 23d when buisinesse calling me homewards, & to prepare for the reception of my little family (leaving them for the present in their Cottage by the Wells) The morning growing excessivly hot, I sent my footman some hours before, and so rod negligently, under favour of the shade, 'til being now come to within three miles of Bromely, at a place calld the procession Oake, started out two Cutt-throates, & striking with their long staves at the horse, taking hold of the reignes, threw me downe, & immediately tooke my sword, & haled me into a deepe Thickett, some

quarter of a mile from the high-way, where they might securely rob me, as they soone did; what they got of mony was not considerable, but they tooke two rings, the one an Emrald with diamonds, an Onyx, & a pair of boucles set with rubies & diamonds which were of value, and after all, barbarously bound my hands behind me, & my feete, having before pull'd off my bootes: & then set me up against an Oake, with most bloudy threatnings to cutt my throat, if I offerd to crie out, or make any noise, for that they should be within hearing, I not being the person they looked for: I told them, if they had not basely surpriz'd me, they should not have made so easy a prize, & that it should teach me hereafter never to ride neere an hedge; since had I ben in the mid way, they durst not have adventur'd on me, at which they cock'd their pistols, & told me they had long guns too, & were 14 companions, which all were lies: I begg'd for my Onyx & told them it being engraven with my armes, would betray them, but nothing prevaild: My horses bridle they slipt, & search'd the saddle which they likewise pull'd off, but let the horse alone to grace, & then turning againe bridld him, & tied him to a Tree, yet so as he might graze, & so left me bound: The reason they tooke not my horse, was I suppose, because he was mark'd, and cropt on both Eares, & well known on that roade, & these rogues were lusty foote padders, as they are cald: Well, being left in this manner, grievously was I tormented with the flies, the ants, & the sunn, so as I sweate intollerably, nor little was my anxiety how I should get loose in that solitary place, where I could neither heare or see any creature but my poore horse & a few sheepe stragling in the Coppse; til after neere two houres attempting I got my hands to turne paulme to paulme, whereas before they were tied back to back, and then I stuck a greate while ere' I could slip the cord over my wrist to my thumb, which at last I did, & then being quite loose soone unbound my feete, & so sadling my horse, and roaming a while about, I at last perceiv'd a dust to rise, & soone after heard the rattling of a Cart, towards which I made, and by the help of two Country fellows that were driving it, got downe a steepe bank, into the highway againe; but could heare nothing of the Villains: So I rod to Colonel Blounts a greate justiciarie of the times, who sent out hugh & Crie immediately: and 25, The next morning weary & sore as I was at my wrists & armes, I went from Deptford to Lond, got 500 ticketts printed & dispers'd, by an officer of Gould Smiths-hall, describing what I had lost, and within two daies after had tidings of all I lost, except my Sword which was a silver hilt, & some other trifles: These rogues had paund my Rings &c for a trifle to a Goldsmiths Servant, before the tickets came to the shop, by which meanes they scap'd, the other ring was bought by a Victualer, who brought it to a Goldsmith, that having seene the ticket, seiz'd upon him; but whom I afterwards discharg'd upon the mediation of friends, & protestation of his innocency: Thus did God deliver me from these villains, & not onely so, but restor'd to me what they tooke, as twise before he had graciously don, both at sea & land, I meane, when I had ben rob'd by Pyrates and was in danger of a considerable losse at Amsterdam, for which & many, many signal preservations I am eternaly obligd to give thanks to God my Saviour.

[1654] 27 June We all went to see Bathe, where I bathed in the Crosse bathe; amongst the rest of the idle diversions of the Towne, one Musitian was famous for acting a Changling; which indeede he personated strangely: The Faciate of this Cathedrall is remarkable for the Historical Carving: The Kings Bath is esteemed the fairest in Europe; The Towne is intirely built of stone, but the streetes narrow, uneven & unpleasant: Here we trifled & bath'd, & intervisited with the company who frequent the place, for health &c: till 30th & then went to Bristoll a Citty emulating London, not for its large extent, but manner of building, shops, bridge: Traffique: Exchange, Marketplace &c. The Governor shew'd us the Castle, of no greate concernment: The City wholy Mercantile, as standing neere the famous Severne, commodiously for

Ireland & the Western world: Here I first saw the manner of refining Suggar, & casting it into loaves, where we had collation of Eggs fried in the suggar furnace, together with excellent Spanish Wine; but what was most stupendious to me, was the rock of St. Vincent, a little distance from the Towne, the precipice whereoff is equal to any thing of that nature I have seene in the most confragose cataracts of the Alpes: The river gliding between them after an extraordinary depth: Here we went searching for Diamonds, & to the hot Well of Water at its foote: There is also on the side of this horrid Alp, a very romantic seate: & so we returned that Evening to Bathe, & on 1 of July to Cadenam, where on the Sonday, preachd Dr. Hayward Chaplaine to the late A: Bish: Lawde, on 15: Luke 7 describing the Joyes of Heaven at the conversion of a sinner:

On the 20th (July) We proceede to Salisbury; We went to see the Cathedral, which I take to be the compleatest piece of Gotic-Worke in Europe, taken in all its uniformitie; a neate fabric, but the pillars (reputed to be cast) are of stone manifestly cut out of the cuarry: Most observable are those in the Chapter-house: There are some remarkable Monuments, particularly the antient Bishops founders of the church; Knights Templars, the Marques of Hartfords: Also the Cloysters of the Palace & Garden to it, & greate Mural dial.

In the afternoone we went to Wilton, a fine house of the E. of Penbrochs, in which the most observable are the Dining-roome in the modern built part towards the Garden, richly gilded, & painted with story by De Creete, also some other apartments, as that of Hunting Landskips by Pierce: some magnificent chimny-pieces, after the French best manner: Also a paire of artificial winding-stayres of stone, & divers rare Pictures: The Garden (heretofore esteem'd the noblest in all England) is a large handsom plaine, with a Grotto & Water-works, which might be made much more pleasant were the River that passes through, clensed & rais'd, for all is effected by a meere force: It has a flower Garden not inelegant: But after all, that which to me renders the Seate delightfull, is its being so neere the downes & noble plaines about the Country & contiguous to it. The stables are well order'd, & yeild a gracefull front, by reason of the Walks of limetrees, with the Court & fountaine of the stable adorn'd with the Caesars heads:

We return'd this evening by the Plaine, & 14 mile-race, where out of my Lords Hare-Waren we were entertain'd with a long course of an hare for neere 2 miles in sight: Neere this a Pergola or stand, built to view the Sports; so we came to Salisbury, and view'd the most considerable parts of that Citty, the Merket place, which together with most of the streetes are Watred by a quick current & pure streame, running through the middle of them, but are negligently kept, when with small charge they might be purged, & rendred infinitely agreable, & that one of the sweetest Townes in Europe; but as 'tis now, the common buildings are despicable, & the streetes dirty.

22 We departed & dined at a ferme of my U. Hungerfords cald Darneford magna, situate in a Vally under the Plaine, most sweetly water'd, abounding in Trowts and all things else requisite, provisions exceeding cheape: They catch the Trouts by Speare in the night, whilst they come wondring at a light set in the sterne: There were Pigeons, Conys, & foule in aboundance, & so we had an excellent dinner at an houres warning: After dinner continuing our returne we passd over that goodly plaine or rather Sea of Carpet, which I think for evennesse, extent, Verdure, innumerable flocks, to be one of the most delightfull prospects in nature and put me in mind of the pleasant lives of the Shepherds we reade of in Romances & truer stories: Now we were ariv'd at Stone-henge, Indeede a stupendious Monument, how so many, & huge pillars of stone should have ben brought together, erected some, other Transverse on the tops of them, in a Circular area as rudly representing a Cloyster, or heathen & more natural Temple: & so exceeding hard, that all my strength with an hammer, could not breake a fragment: which duritie I impute to their so long exposure: To

number them exactly, is very difficult, in such variety of postures they lie & confusion, though they seeme'd not to exceede 100; we counted onely 95: As to their bringing thither, there being no navigable river neere, is by some admir'd; but for the stone, there seemes to be of the same kind about 20 miles distant, some of which appeares above ground: About the same hills are divers mounts raisd, conceiv'd to be antient intrenchments, or places of burial after bloudy fights: We now went by the Devizes a reasonable large Towne, so passing over Tan-hill (esteemed one of the highest in England) we came late to Cadenam:

7 (August) I went to Upingham the Shire-towne of Rutland, pretty & well built of stone, which is a rarity in that part of England, where most of the rural parishes are but of mud, and the people living as wretchedly as in the most impoverish'd parts of France, which they much resemble being idle & sluttish: The Country (especialy Licester shire) much in Commune, the Gentry greate drinkers:

1 September. Cambridg, & went first to see St. Johns Colledge & Librarie, which I think is the fairest of that Universitie: one Mr. Benlous has given it all the ornaments of Pietra Commessa, whereof a Table, and one piece of Perspective is very fine, other trifles there also be of no greate value, besides a vast old song book or Service, & some faire Manuscripts: This Coll: is well built of brick: There hangs in the Library the Picture of Williams ABishop of York, & sometime Ld: Keeper, my Kindsman, and their greate benefactor. Next we saw Trinity Coll, esteemed the fairest Quadrangle of any University in Europ, but in truth far inferior to that of Christ-Church Oxford: the Hall is ample, & of stone, the fountaine in the Quadrangle is gracefull, The Chapell & Library faire, there they shew'd us the prophetic MS. of the famous Grebner; but the passage & Emblem which they would apply to our late King, is manifestly relating to the Swedish; in truth it seemes to be a

meere fantastic rhapsody, however the Title bespeake strange revelations: There is an Office finely miniatur'd MS, with some other antiquities given by the Countesse of Richmond mother of Hen: 7: and the formentioned Bishop Williams when Bishop of Lincoln: The Library is pretty well stor'd: Here the Greeke Professor had me into another halfe Quadrangle, cloistred & well built, and gave us an handsome Collation in his owne Chamber: Then we went to Caius, then to Kings Coll, where I found the Chapel altogether answerable to expectation, especialy the roofe all of stone, which for the flatnesse of its laying & carving may I conceive vie with any in Christendome; The contignation of the roofe (which I went upon), weight, and artificial joyning of the stones is admirable: The lights are also very faire: The library is too narrow: here in one Ile, lies the famous Dr. Collins so celebrated for his fluency in the Latine Tongue: from this roofe we could discry Elie, and the Incampment of Sturbridge faire now beginning to set up their Tents & boothes: also Royston, New-Market &c: houses belonging to the King. Thence we walked to Clare-hall of a new and noble designe, but not finish'd: hence to Peterhouse formerly under the charge & government of my worthy friend Dr: Jo: Cosin; deane of Peterborow, a pretty neate Coll: & delicate Chapell: next to Sidny, a fine College, Kathrine-hall, though meane structure, yet famous for the learned B: Andrews once Master: then to Emanuel Coll: that zealous house, where to the Hall, they have a Parler for the fellows: The Chapell is reform'd *ab origine*, built N. & South, meanely built, as is the Librarie: Thence to Jesus Coll: one of the best built, but in a Melancholy situation: next to Christ Coll. very nobly built, especialy the modern part, built without the Quadrangle towards the Gardens, of exact Architecture: The Schooles are very despicable, & publique Librarie but meane though somewhat improved by the Wainscoting and Books lately added by the Bishop Bancrofts Library & M.SS: They shew'd us little of antiquity: onely K: Jamess Works, being his owne gift, and kept very reverently and was the onely rarity shewd us. The Mercat place of Chambridg is very ample and remarkable for old Hobsons the pleasant Carriers beneficence of a fountaine: But the whole Towne situated in a low dirty unpleasant place, the streetes ill paved, the aire thick, as infested by the fenns; nor are its Churches (of which St. Maries is the best) anything considerable in compare to Oxford which is doubtlesse the noblest Universitie now in the whole World.

[1655] 30 (December) I went to Lond: where Dr. Wild (at St. Greg) preached the funeral Sermon of Preaching, this being the last day, after which Cromwells Proclamation was to take place, that none of the Ch: of England should dare either to Preach, administer Sacraments, Teach Schoole &c. on paine of Imprisonment or Exile; so this was the mournfullest day that in my life I had seene, or the Church of Eng: her selfe, since the Reformation: to the greate rejoicing of both Papist & Presbyter: The Text was 2. Cor: 13. 9. That however persecution dealt with the Ministries of Gods word, They were still to pray for the flock, & wish their perfection, as it was the flocks, to pray for & assist their Pastors, by the example of St. Paule &c: So pathetic was his discourse, as drew many teares from the auditory: My selfe, Wife, & some of our family received the H. Communion, God make me Thankfull, who hath hithertoo provided for us the foode of our Soules, as well as bodys. So return'd home the Evening: The Lord Jesus pitty our distressed Church, & bring back the Captivity of Sion.

[1656] Mar: 4: This night I was invited by Mr. Rog: L'Estrange to heare the incomperable Lubicer on the Violin, his variety upon a few notes & plaine ground with that wonderfull dexterity, as was admirable, & though a very young man, yet so perfect & skillfull as there was nothing so crosse & perplext, which being by our Artists, brought to him, which he did not at first sight, with ravishing sweetnesse, & improvements, play off, to the astonishment of our best Masters: In Summ, he plaid on that single Instrument a full Consort, so as the rest, flung-downe their Instruments, as acknowledging a victory: As to my owne particular, I stand to this houre amaz'd that God should give so greate perfection to so young a person: There were at that time as excellent in that profession as any were thought in Europ: Paule Wheeler, Mr. Mell and others, 'til this prodigie appeared & then they vanish'd, nor can I any longer question, the effects we read of in Davids harp, to charme maligne spirits, & what is said some particular notes produc'd in the Passions of Alexander & that King of Denmark —5. I return'd home:

[1657] Aprill: 1 Came Sir Tho: Hanmer of Hanmer in Wales to visite me: 2: I went about buisinesse to the Commissioners of the Sewers. 5: our Parson—on 4: Eph: 19.20: as formerly, & on the 12th, proving the Scriptures to be the Word of God, so on the 19th That Truth made us most to resemble God: 21 I went to Lond: to consult Dr. Bate about taking preventing Physick: Thence to Visite my Lord Hatton, with whom I dined; at my returne I step'd into Bedlame, where I saw nothing extraordinarie, besides some miserable poore Creatures in chaines, one was mad with making Verses: & also visited the Charter-house, formerly belonging to the Carthusians; now an old neate, fresh solitarie Colledge for decaied Gent: It has a grove, bowling-greene, Garden: Chapell, hall &c where they eate in common: I likewise saw Christ-Church & Hospital, a very goodly building, Gotic: also the Hall, Schoole, Lodgings, in greate order, for the bringing up many hundreds of poore Children of both sexes, & is an exemplary Charity: There is a large picture at one end of the Hall, representing the Governors, founders, & Institution: so on the 23d I returned home: 25. To Lond, return'd that Evening. I had a dangerous fall out of the Coach in Covent Garden, going to my Bro: but without harme, The Lord be praised:

25 (Dec) I went with my Wife &c: to Lond: to celebrate

Christmas day. Mr. Gunning preaching in Excester Chapell on 7: Micha 2. Sermon Ended, as he was giving us the Holy Sacrament, The Chapell was surrounded with Souldiers: All the Communicants and Assembly surpriz'd & kept Prisoners by them, some in the house, others carried away: It fell to my share to be confined to a roome in the house, where yet were permitted to Dine with the master of it, the Countesse of Dorset, Lady Hatton & some others of quality who invited me: In the afternoone came Collonel Whaly, Goffe & others from White-hall to examine us one by one, & some they committed to the Martial, some to Prison, some Committed: When I came before them they tooke my name & aboad, examind me, why contrarie to an Ordinance made that none should any longer observe the superstitious time of the Nativity (so esteem'd by them) I durst offend, & particularly be at Common prayers, which they told me was but the Masse in English, & particularly pray for Charles stuard, for which we had no Scripture: I told them we did not pray for Cha: Steward but for all Christian Kings, Princes & Governors: They replied, in so doing we praied for the K. of Spaine too, who was their Enemie, & a Papist, with other frivolous & insnaring questions, with much threatning, & finding no colour to detaine me longer, with much pitty of my Ignorance, they dismiss'd me: These were men of high flight, and above Ordinances: & spake spitefull things of our B: Lords nativity: so I got home late the next day blessed be God: These wretched miscreants, held their muskets against us as we came up to receive the Sacred Elements, as if they would have shot us at the Altar, but yet suffering us to finish the Office of Communion, as perhaps not in their Instructions what they should do in case they found us in that Action:

[1658] 27 (Jan) After six fitts of a Quartan Ague it pleased God to visite my deare Child Dick with fitts so extreame, especiale one of his sides, that after the rigor was over & he in his hot fitt, he fell into so greate & intollerable a sweate, that being surpriz'd with the aboundance of vapours ascending to his head, he fell into such fatal Symptoms, as all the help at hand was not able to recover his spirits, so as after a long & painefull Conflict, falling to sleepe as we thought, & coverd too warme, (though in midst of a severe frosty season) and by a greate fire in the roome; he plainely expird, to our unexpressable griefe & affliction. We sent for Physitians to Lond, whilst there was yet life in him; but the river was frozen up, & the Coach brake by the way ere it got a mile from the house; so as all artificial help failing, & his natural strength exhausted, we lost the prettiest, and dearest Child, that ever parents had, being but 5 yeares & 3 days old in years but even at that tender age, a prodigie for Witt, & understanding; for beauty of body a very Angel, & for endowments of mind, of incredible & rare hopes. To give onely a little tast of some of them, & thereby glory to God (who out of the mouths of Babes & Infants dos sometimes perfect his praises) At 2 yeare & halfe old he could perfectly reade any of the English, Latine, french or Gottic letters; pronouncing the three first languages exactly: He had before the 5t yeare or in that yeare not onely skill to reade most written hands, but to decline all the Nounes, Conjugate the verbs, regular, & most of the irregular; learned out *Puerilis*, got by heart almost the intire Vocabularie of Latine & french primitives & words, could make congruous Syntax, turne English into Lat: & vice versa, construe & prove what he read & did, the government & use of Relatives, Verbs Transitive, Substantives &c: Elipses & many figure & tropes, & made a considerable progresse in Commenius's *Janua*; began himselfe to write legibly, & had a strange passion for Greeke: the number of Verses he could recite was prodigious, & what he remembred of the parts of playes, which he would also act: & when seeing a Plautus in ones hand, he asked what booke it was, & being told it was Comedy &c, & too difficult for him, he wept for sorrow: strange was his apt & ingenious application of Fables & Morals, for he had read Aesop, & had a wonderfull disposition to Mathematics, having by heart, divers propositions of Euclid that were read to him in play, & he would make lines, & demonstrate them: As to his Piety, astonishing were his applications of Scripture upon occasion, & his sense of God, he had learn'd all his Catechisme early, & understood the historical part of the Bible & N. Test: to a wonder, & how Christ came to redeeme Mankind &c: & how comprehending these necessarys, himselfe, his Godfathers &c were discharged of their promise: These and the like illuminations, far exceeding his age & experience, considering the prettinesse of his addresse & behaviour, cannot but leave impressions in me at the memory of him: When one told him how many dayes a certaine Quaker had fasted in Colchester, he replied, that was no wonder; for Christ had sayd, That Man should not live by bread alone, but by the word of God: He would of himselfe select the most pathetical Psalmes, & Chapters out of Jobe, to read to his Mayde, during his sickness, telling her (when she pittied him) that all Gods Children must suffer affliction: He declaim'd against the Vanities of the World, before he had seene any: often he would desire those who came to see him, to pray by him, & before he fell sick a yeare, to kneele and pray with him alone in some Corner: How thankfully would he receive admonition, how soone be reconciled! how indifferent, continualy cherefull: Grave advise would he be giving his brother John, beare with his impertinences, & say he was but a Child: If he heard of, or saw any new thing, he was unquiet till he was told how it was made, & brought us all difficulties that he found in booke, to be expounded: He had learn'd by heart divers Sentences in Lat: & Greeke which on occasion he would produce even to wonder: In a word he was all life, all prettinesse, far from morose, sullen, or childish in any thing he said or did: The last time he had ben at Church, (which was at Greenewich) according to costome, I asked him what he remembred of the Sermon: Two good-things Father, replys he: *Bonum Gratiae*, & *Bonum Gloriae* with a just account of what the preacher said: The day before he died, he cald to me, & in a more serious manner than usualy, Told me, That for all I loved him so dearely, I would give my house, land & all my fine things to his Bro: Jack, he should have none of them, & next morning when first he found himselfe ill, & that I perswaded him to keepe his hands in bed, he demanded, whither he might pray to God with his hands un-joyn'd, & a little after, whilst in great agonie, whither he should not offend God, by using his holy name so oft, calling for Ease: What shall I say of his frequent pathetical ejaculations utter'd of himselfe, Sweete Jesus save me, deliver me, pardon my sinns, Let thine Angels receive me &c: so early knowledge, so much piety & perfection; but thus God having dressed up a Saint fit for himselfe, would not permit him longer with us, unworthy of the future fruites of this incomparable hopefull blossome: such a Child I never saw; for such a child I blesse God, in whose boosome he is: May I & mine become as this little child, which now follows the Child Jesus, that Lamb of God, in a white robe whithersoever he gos. Even so Lord Jesus, *fiat Voluntas tua*, Thou gavest him to us, thou hast taken him from us, blessed be the name of the Lord, That I had anything acceptable to thee, was from thy Grace alone, since from me he had nothing but sinn; But that thou hast pardon'd, blessed be my God for ever Amen:

15 (Feb) The afflicting hand of God being still upon us, it pleased him also to take away from us this morning my other youngest sonn George now 7 weekes languishing at Nurse, breeding Teeth, & ending in a Dropsie: Gods holy will be don: he was buried in Deptford Church the 17th following:

22 (Nov) To Lond, to visite my Bro: & the next day saw the superb Funerall of the Protectors: He was carried from Somerset-house in a velvet bed of state drawn by six horses houss'd with the same: The Pall held-up by his new Lords: Oliver lying in Effigie in royal robes, & Crown'd with a Crown, scepter, & Mund, like a King: The Pendants, & Guidons were carried by the Officers of the Army, The Imperial banners,

Atchivements &c by the Heraulds in their Coates, a rich caparizon'd Horse all embroidred over with gold: a Knight of honour arm'd Cap a pe & after all his Guards, Souldiers & innumerable Mourners: In this equipage they proceeded to Westminster μετ' πολλῆς φαντασιας &c: but it was the joyfullest funerall that ever I saw, for there was none that Cried, but dogs, which the souldiers hooted away with a barbarous noise; drinking, & taking Tobacco in the streetes as they went: I went not home til the 17th.

[1659] 25 (April) A wonderfull & suddaine change in the face of the publique: The new Protector Richard slighted, severall pretenders, & parties strive for the Government, all Anarchy and confusion; Lord have mercy on us.

5 (May) I went to visite my Bro; & next day to see a new Opera after the Italian way in Recitative Music & Sceanes, much inferior to the Italian composure & magnificence: but what was prodigious, that in a time of such a publique Consternation, such a Vanity should be kept up or permitted; I being ingag'd with company, could not decently resist the going to see it, though my heart smote me for it: I returned home:

10 (Dec) I treated privately with Coll: Morley (then Lieutenant of the Tower, & in greate trust & power) concerning delivering it to the King, and the bringing of him in, to the greate hazard of my life; but the Colonel had ben my Schole-fellow & I knew would not betray me:

[1660] 10 (Feb) Now were the Gates of the Citty broken-downe by Gen: Monke, which exceedingly exasperated the Citty; the Souldiers marching up and downe as triumphing over it, and all the old Army of the phanatics put out of their posts, & sent out of Towne. 11 I visited Mr. Boyle, where I met the Earle of Corke. A signal day: Monk perceiving how infamous & wretched a pack of knaves would have still usurped the

Supreme power, & having intelligence that they intended to take away his commission, repenting of what he had don to the Citty, & where he & his forces quarterd; Marches to White hall, dissipates that nest of robbers, & convenes the old Parliament, the rump-parliament (so cal'd as retaining some few rotten members of the other) being dissolved; and for joy wheroff, were many thousands of rumps, roasted publiquely in the Streetes at the Bonfires this night, with ringing of bells, & universal jubilee: this was the first good omen.

3 (May) Came the most happy tidings of his Majesties gracious Declaration, & applications to the Parliament, Generall, & People &c and their dutifull acceptance & acknowledgement, after a most bloudy & unreasonable Rebellion of neere 20 yeares. Praised be forever the Lord of heaven, who onely dost wondrous things, because thy mercys indure forever.

29 (May) This day came in his Majestie Charles the 2d to London after a sad, & long Exile, and Calamitous Suffering both of the King & Church: being 17 yeares: This was also his Birthday, and with a Triumph of above 20,000 horse & foote, brandishing their swords and shouting with unexpressable joy: The wayes straw'd with flowers, the bells ringing, the streetes hung with Tapissry, fountaines running with wine: The Major, Aldermen, all the Companies in their liveries, Chaines of Gold, banners; Lords & nobles, Cloth of Silver, gold & vellvet every body clad in, the windos & balconies all set with Ladys, Trumpets, Musick, & myriads of people flocking the streetes & was as far as Rochester, so as they were 7 houres in passing the Citty, even from 2 in the afternoone 'til nine at night: I stood in the strand, & beheld it, & blessed God: And all this without one drop of bloud, & by that very army, which rebell'd against him: but it was the Lords doing, *et mirabile in oculis nostris*: for such a Restauration was never seene in the mention of any history, antient or modern, since the returne of the Babylonian Captivity, nor so joyfull a day,

& so bright, ever seene in this nation: this hapning when to expect or effect it, was past all humane policy.

17 (Oct) This day were executed those murderous Traytors at Charing-Crosse, in sight of the place where they put to death their natural Prince, & in the Presence of the King his sonn, whom they also sought to kill: taken in the trap they laied for others. The Traytors executed were Scot, Scroope, Cook, Jones. I saw not their execution, but met their quarters mangld & cutt & reaking as they were brought from the Gallows in baskets on the hurdle: ô miraculous providence of God; Three days before suffered Axtel, Carew, Clements, Hacker, Hewson & Peeters for reward of their Iniquity: I returned:

[1661] (Jan. 6) I was now chosen (& nominated by his Majestie for one of that Council) by Suffrage of the rest of the Members, a Fellow of the Philosophic Society, now meeting at Gressham Coll: where was an assembly of divers learned Gent: It being the first meeting since the returne of his Majestie in Lond: but begun some years before at Oxford, & interruptedly here in Lond: during the Rebellion: This morning was another rising of the Phanatics in which some were slaine: his Majestie being absent; til the 10th. 12 I returnd home: 16 I went to the Philosophic Club: where was examin'd the Torricellian experiment: I presented my Circle of Mechanical Trades, & had recommended to me the publishing what I had written of Chalcography:

30 (Jan) Was the first Solemn Fast & day of humiliation to deplore the sinns which so long had provoked God against this Afflicted Church & people: orderd by Parliament to be annualy celebrated, to expiate the Gilt of the Execrable Murder of the late King Char: 1, our Viccar preaching on 21. Deut: 7. 8. on which he made a very pious, & proper discourse: This day (ô the stupendious, & inscrutable Judgements of God) were the Carkasses of that arch-rebell Cromewell, Bradshaw the Judge

who condemn'd his Majestie & Ireton, sonn in law to the Usurper, draged out of their superbe Tombs (in Westminster among the Kings), to Tyburne, & hanged on the Gallows there from 9 in the morning til 6 at night, & then buried under that fatal & ignominious Monument, in a deepe pit: Thousands of people (who had seene them in all their pride & pompous insults) being spectators: looke back at November 22: 1658, & be astonish'd—And fear God, & honor the King, but meddle not with them who are given to change.

23 (April) Was the Coronation of his Majesty Charles the Second in the Abby-Church of Westminster at all which Ceremonie I was present: The King & all his Nobility went to the Tower, I accompanying my L: Vicount Mordaunt part of the Way: This was on Sunday: 22: but indeede his Majestie went not 'til Early this morning, & proceeded from thence to Westminster in this order: first went the Duke of Yorks Horse guards, Messengers of the Chamber. 136 Esquires to the knights of the Bath, each having two: most richly habited: The knight Harbinger, Searjeant Porter, Sewers of the Chamber, . . . This magnificent Traine on horseback, as rich as Embroidery, velvet, Cloth of Gold & Sil: & Jewells could make them & their pransing horses, proceeded thro the streetes, strew'd with flowers, houses hung with rich Tapissry, Windos & Balconies full of Ladies, The Lond: Militia lining the ways, & the sevrrall Companies with their Banners & Loud musique ranked in their orders: The Fountaines runing wine, bells ringing, with Speeches made at the severall Triumphal Arches: At that of the Temple Barre (neere which I stood) The Lord Major was received by the Baylife of Westminster who in a Scarlet robe made a Speech: Thence with joyfull acclamations his Majestie passed to White-hall: Bonfires at night & the next day being st. Georges he went by Water to Westminster Abby: when his Majestie was entered, the Deane & Prebends brought all the Regalia, & deliverd them to severall Noble-men, to beare before the King, who met them at the West dore of the

church singing an Antheme, to the Quire: Then came the Peres in their Robes & Coronets &c in their hands, til his Majestie was placed in a Throne elevated before the Altar: Then the Bish: of Lond (the A Bishop of Canterbury being sick) went to every side of the Throne to present the King to the People, asking if they would have him for their King, & do him homage, at which they shouted 4 Times God Save K. Ch: the 2d: Then an Anthem sung: Then his Majesty attended by 3 Bishops went up to the Altar, & he offerd a pall, & a pound of Gold: Then sate he downe in another chaire during the sermon, which was preachd by Dr. Morley then B: of Worcester: after Sermon the K: tooke his Oath before the Altar, to maintaine the Religion, Mag: Charta & Laws of the Land: Then the Hymn *Veni S. Sp.*, then the Leitany by 2 Bish. Then the L: AB: of Cant (present but much indisposd & weake) said, Lift-up your hearts: Then rose up the King, & put off his robes & upper garments; & was in a Wastcoate so opened in divers places as the A: Bishop might commodiously anoint him, first in the palmes of his hands, then was sung an Anthem & prayer, Then his breast, & twixt the shoulders, bending of both armes, & lastly on the crowne of the head: with apposite hymns & prayers at each anoynting: Then closed & buttned up the Wastcoate, which was don by the Deane: . . . Then he received the H: Sacrament, & so disrobed, yet with the Crowne Imperial on his head, accompanied with all the nobility in the former order, he went on foote upon blew cloth, which was spread & reachd from the West dore of the Abby, to Westminster Stayres where he tooke Water in a Triumphal barge to White-hall where was extraordinary feasting:

24 I presented his Majestie with his Panegyric in the Privy Chamber, which he was pleasd most graciously to accept: &c. also to the L. Chancelor & most of the noble men who came to me for it, & dined at the Marq: of Ormonds now made Duke, where was a magnificent feast, & many greate persons:

25 I went to the Society where were divers Experiments in

Mr. Boyls Pneumatique Engine. We put in a Snake but could not kill it, by exhausting the aire, onely made it extreamly sick, but the chick died of Convulsions out right, in a short space:

13 (May) I heard, & saw such Exercises at the Election of Scholars at Westminster Schoole, to be sent to the Universitie, both in Lat: Gr: & Heb: Arabic &c in Theames & extemporary Verses, as wonderfully astonish'd me, in such young striplings, with that readinesse, & witt, some of them not above 12 or 13 years of age: & pitty it is, that what they attaine here so ripely, they either not retaine, or improve more considerably, when they come to be men: though many of them do: & no lesse is to be blamed their odd pronouncing of Latine, so that out of England no nation were able to understand or endure it:

13 (Sept) To Lond: 14. I presented my *Fumifugium* dedicated to his Majestie who was pleased I should publish it by his special Command; being much pleasd with it:

26 (Nov) I saw *Hamlet Pr: of Denmark* played: but now the old playe began to disgust this refined age; since his Majestie being so long abroad:

3 (Dec) By universal suffrage of our Philosophic Assembly, an order was made, & registred, that I should receive their Publique Thanks for the honorable mention I made of them by the name of Royal Society, in my Epistle Dedicatory to the Lord Chancellor, before my Traduction of Naudeus: Too greate an honour for a trifle:

[1662] 6 (Jan) Epiphanie one Dr. Lamb (a prebend) on 1. Matt: 1. of the Geneologie of Christ: I din'd at the Comptrollers. This evening (according to costome) his Majestie opned the Revells of that night, by throwing the Dice himselfe, in the Privy Chamber, where was a table set on purpose, & lost his 100 pounds: the yeare before he won 150 pounds: The

Ladys also plaied very deepe: I came away when the Duke of Ormond had won about 1000 pounds & left them still at passage, Cards &c: at other Tables, both there and at the Groome-porters, observing the wiccked folly vanity & monstrous excesse of Passion amongst some loosers, & sorry I am that such a wretched Custome as play to that excesse should be countenanc'd in a Court, which ought to be an example of Virtue to the rest of the kingdome.

16 (Jan) Having notice of his R. Highnesse the Duke of Yorks intention to visite my poore habitation and Garden this day, I returned; where he was pleased to do me that honour of his owne accord: and to stay some time viewing such things as I had to entertaine his curiosity; after which he caused me to dine with him at the Treasurer of the Navys house, & to sit with him coverd at the same table: There were with his Highnesse The Duke of Ormond & severall Lords: Then they viewed some of my Ground, about a project of a Sasse or receptacle for ships to be moored in; which was laied aside, as a fancy of Sir Nic: Crisp &c: After this I accompanied the Duke to an East India vessel that lay at Black-Wall, where we had Entertainment of several curiosities: among other spiritous drinks, as Punch &c, they gave us Canarie that had been carried to, & brought back from the Indies, which was indeede incomparably good: So I returned to Lond, with his highnesse. This night was acted before his Majestie *The Widow*, a lewd play:

18 (Jan) I came home to be private a little, not at all affecting the life & hurry of Court.

[1664] 26 (March) It pleased God to take-away my sonn Richard, being now a moneth old, yet without any sicknesse of danger perceivable, being to all appearance a most likely child; so as we suspected much the Nurse had over-layne him to our extreame sorrow, being now againe reduc'd to one: Gods will be don: 27: After evening prayer was my child buried neere the rest of his brothers, my deare children:

28 (Oct) Being casualy in the Privy Gallery at White-hall, his Majestie gave me thanks (before divers Lords & noble men) for my *Book of Architecture* & *Sylva* againe: That they were the best designd & usefull for the matter & subject, the best printed & designd (meaning the *Tallè doucès* of the Paralelles) that he had seene: then caused me to follow him alone to one of the Windows, he asked me if I had any paper about me un-written, & a Crayon; I presented him with both, & then laying it on the Window stoole, he with his owne hands, designed to me the plot for the future building of White-hall, together with Roomes of State, & other particulars, which royal draft, though not so accurately don, I reserve as a rarity by me: After this he talked with me of severall matters, & asking my advice, of many particulars, in which I find his Majestie had an extraordinary talent, becoming a magnificent Prince: The same day, at Council (there being Commissioners to be made, to take care of such sick & Wounded, & Prisoners at War, as might be expected upon occasion of a succeeding Warr, and Action at sea; a War being already declared against the Hollanders) his Majestie was pleasd to nominate me to be one; amongst three other Gent: of quality, Parliament Men:

[1665] 16 (July) To Hampton-Court againe, hearing a fragment of a sermon there by Dr. Turner: There died of the Plague in Lond: this Weeke 1100: 23. our Curat on 8. Rom: 18. concerning Afflictions, & how not be valued to the joys to be received: There perished this weeke above 2000, & now were two houses shut up in our parish:

13 (Aug) There perished this Weeke 5000: 20 our Doctor on 1. Cor: 11.28. preparatorie to the L. Supper: The Plage still increasing:

28 The Contagion growing now all about us, I sent my

Wife & whole family (two or three of my necessary Servants excepted) to Wotton to my Brothers, being resolved to stay at my house myselfe, & to looke after my Charge, trusting in the providence & goodnesse of God.

7 (Sept) Came home, there perishing now neere ten-thousand poore Creatures weekely: however I went all along the Citty & suburbs from Kent streete to St. James's, a dismal passage & dangerous, to see so many Cofines exposd in the streetes & the streete thin of people, the shops shut up, & all in mournefull silence, as not knowing whose turne might be next: I went to the D: of Albemarle for a Pest-ship, to waite on our infected men, who were not a few:

31 (Dec) Now blessed be God, for his extraordinary mercies & preservations of me this Yeare when thousands & ten thousands perish'd & were swept away on each side of me: There dying in our Parish this yeare 406 of the Pestilence:

[1666] January 1 I beged the Protection of Almighty God, for the ensuing yeare: &c:

2 I supped in None-such house (whither the Office of the Exchequer was transferrd during the Plague) at my good friends Mr. Packer: & tooke an exact view of the Plaster Statues & Bass-relievos inserted twixt the timbers & poincons of the outside walles of the Court, which must needes have ben the work of some excellent Italian: admire I did much how it had lasted so well & intire as since the time of Hen: 8 exposd, as they are to the aire, & pitty it is they are not taken out, & preserved in some dry place, a gallerie would become them: there are some Mezzo relievi as big as the life, & the storie is of the heathen Gods, Emblems, Compartiments, &c.

The Palace concists of two Courts, of which the first is of stone Castle like, by the Lord Lumlies (of whom 'twas purchas'd) the other of Timber a Gotique fabric, but these walls incomparably beautified: I also observed that the appearing timber punchions, entretices &c were all so covered with Scales of Slate, that it seemed carved in the Wood, & painted, the Slat fastned on the timber in pretty figures, that has preserved it from rotting like a coate of armour: There stand in the Garden two handsome stone Pyramids, & the avvenue planted with rows of faire Elmes, but the rest of those goodly Trees both of this & of Worcester-Park adjoyning were fell'd by those destructive & avaritious Rebells in the late Warr, which defac'd one of the stateliest seates his Majestie had.

After much, & indeede extraordinary mirth & cheere, all my Brothers, our Wives & Children being together, & after much sorrow & trouble during this Contagion, which separated our families, as well as others, I returned to my house, but 12 my Wife went back to Wotton, I not as yet willing to adventure her, the Contagion, though exceedingly abated, not as yet wholy extinguish'd amongst us:

14 our Doctor preached on 1: Isa: To us a sonn is borne: of the benefit of Christs Incarnation &c.

17 I went to Lond: about his Majesties buisinesse, returnd: 18 I went againe, returnd, & so the 19th dined with the D: of Albemarle. 21 Mr. Plume at Greenewich on . . . And put on the new man &c. Afternoone his Curate 11. Eccles: 8. preparation to death, the Plague not yet ceased: 24. Lond: Din'd with the Lord Gen: with much Companie: 28 our Doctor on the same Text, shewing Gods free-grace in Christ:

29 I went to waite on his Majestie (now return'd from Oxford to Hampton Court) where the Duke of Albemarle presenting me to him, he ran towards me, & in most gracious manner gave me his hand to kisse, with many thanks for my Care, & faithfullnesse in his service, in a time of that greate danger, when every body fled their Employments; he told me he was much oblig'd to me, & said he was severall times concern'd for me, & the peril I underwent & did receive my service most acceptably: Though in truth I did but what was my duty, & ô that I had perform'd it as I ought: After this his Majestie was pleas'd to talke with me alone neere an houre, of

severall particulars of my Employment, & ordred me to attend him againe the thursday following at White-hall: Then the Duke came towards me & embrac'd me with much kindnesse, & told me, if he had but thought my danger would have ben so greate, he would not have sufferd his Majestie to employ me in that Station: then came to salute me, my L. of St. Albans, L. Arlington, Sir William Coventrie & severall greate persons, after which I got home, not being very well in health. The Court was now in deepe Mourning for the French Queene-mother. 30. our Doctor (being the Anniversary of the Ks. Martyrdome) preach'd on 4 Threnae 20, describing the vile treatchery of his late Majesties Enemies, through the simple meaning of some, & abominable treason & malice of others: That no pretence of doing good, by evil meanes was justifiable, this he proved exceedingly well:

June: 1. Being in my Garden & hearing the Greate gunns go thick off: I immediately tooke horse, & rod that night to Rochester it being 6 at Evening when I set out: 2 Thence next day towards the Downes & Sea-Coast: but meeting with the Lieutennant of the *Hantshire* fregat, who told me what pass'd, or rather not pass'd, I returned to Lond: (there being no noise, nor appearance at Deale or that Coast of any engagement) this recounting to his Majestie (whom I found at St. Jams's Park impatiently expecting) & I knowing that Prince Rupert was loose, about 3 at St. Hellens point at N. of Wight, it greately rejoic'd him; but was astonish'd when I asur'd him they heard nothing of the Gunns in the Downes, nor the Lieutennant who landed there by five that morning.

3: Whitsonday: Dr. Cartwrite *coram rege* 'if ye love me keepe my Commandments'; after sermon came newes, that the Duke of Albemarle was still in fight & all Saturday; & cap: Harmans ship (the *Henrie*) like to be burnt: Then a letter from Mr. Bertie that Pr: Rupert was come up with his Squadron (according to my former advice of his being loose & in the way) & put new courage into our fleete now in a manner yeilding ground; so as now we were chasing the chacers: That the D: of Alb: was slightly wounded, & the rest in greate danger 'til now; so having ben much wearied with my journey, I slip'd home, the Gunns still roaring very fiercely:

5 I went this morning to Lond: where came severall particulars of the fight: 6: came Sir Dan: Harvey from the Generall & related the dreadfull encounter, upon which his Majestie commanded me to dispatch away an extraordinary Physitian, & more Chirurgions: 'Twas on the solemn fast day, when the newes came, his Majestie being in the Chapell made a suddaine Stop, to heare the relation, which being with much advantage on our side, his Majestie commanded that Publique Thanks should immediately be given as for a Victory; The Deane of the Chapell going downe to give notice of it to the other Deane officiating; & so notice was likewise sent to St. Paules and Westminster abby: But this was no sooner over, but newes came that our losse was very greate both in ships & men: That the *Prince* fregat was burnt & so a noble vessel of 90 brasse Guns lost: together with the taking of Sir Geo: Ayscue & exceeding shattring of both fleetes, so as both being obstinate, both parted rather for want of amunition & tackle than Courage, our Generall retreating like a Lyon, which exceedingly abated of our former jolitie: There was however order given for bone-fires & bells, but God knows, it was rather a deliverance than a Triumph: so much it pleased God to humble our late over Confidence, that nothing could withstand the Duke of Albemarle: who in good truth made too forward a reckoning of his successe, now, because he had once beaten the Dutch in another quarrell: & being ambitious to out-do the Earle of Sandwich, whom he had prejudice to as defective of Courage:

A Doctor preached on 'Call me in time of trouble': I supped at the Groome-porters;

7 I sent more Chirurgions, linnen, medicaments &c: to the severall ports in my District: din'd at my L: Cornburies, returned home with my Wife: 8. Dined with me Sir Alex:

Frasier (prime Physitian to his Majestie) after dinner went on board his Majesties pleasure-boate where I saw the *London* fregate launched (a most statly ship built by the Cittie, to supply that which was burnt by accident some time since) The King: L. Major & Sherifes being there, with a greate Banquet: I presented my Sonn to his Majestie:

10 our Viccar on: 8 Rom: 11. The effects of Prayer by the Spirit, how that gift differ'd from the common presbyters extemporaries: I received the H: Comm: 11. Trinity Moneday he preached before the fraternity on Psal: 'Blessed are they who put their trust in him' &c applied to the remeeting of that Corporation after the late raging & wasting Pestilence: I dined with them in their new roome in Deptford, the first time after it was new built:

12 To Lond: to our Commission. 13 To the R: Society, where was brought the new Pendulum:

14 Went home: 15 I went to Chattham: 16 in the *Jemmy* Yach't (an incomparable sailer) to sea, arived by noone at the Fleete in the B of Nore, dined with Pr: Rupert & Generall: 17: came his Majestie, Duke, & many Noblemen; after Council, we went to Prayers: having dispatch'd my buisinesse, I return'd to Chattham having layne but one night at sea, in the *Royal Charles*, we had a tempestuous sea; I went on shore at Sheere-Nesse, where they were building an Arsenal for the Fleete, & designing a royal Fort, with a receptable for greate ships to ride at Anker; but here I beheld that sad spectacle, namely more than halfe of that gallant bulwark of the Kingdome miserably shatterd, hardly a Vessell intire, but appearing rather so many wracks & hulls, so cruely had the Dutch mangled us: when the losse of the *Prince* (that gallant Vessell) had ben a losse to be universaly deplor'd, none knowing for what reason we first ingaged in this ungratefull warr: we lost besids 9 or 10 more, & neere 600 men slaine, & 1100 wounded 2000 Prisoners, to balance which perhaps we might destroy 18 or 20 of the Enemies ships & 7 or 800 poore men: 18 weary of this sad sight I returned home: 19 came Sir Rob: Cotton, my Lady

Morice (wife to the Secretarie of State) to dine with me. 20: Came to visite me my old Italian acquaintance Dr. Croydon, Waldrond, Clark, Quartermaine to dine with me: 24: Our Viccar as formerly: 26 To Lond: 27: To Our Society: 28 Din'd at my L: Chancelors: 30: returned home:

July. 1 Our Curate preachd on 18 Matt 29, the dutie of Mercifullnesse: 2. Came Sir Jo: Duncomb & Mr. Tho: Chichley both Privy Councellers & Commissioners of his Majesties Ordinance to give me a visite, & to let me know his Majestie had in Council nominated me to be one of the Commissioners for regulating the farming & making of Salt-peter through the whole Kingdome, & that we were to sit in the Tower the next day &c: When they were gon, came to see me Sir. Jo: Cotton (heire to the famous Antiquarie Sir Robert) a pretended greate Gretian, but had by no meanes the parts or genius of his Grandfather: with him were severall other knights & Gent:

3 I went to sit with the Commissioners at the Tower of Lond, where our Commiss: being read, we made some progresse in buisinesse: Sir G: Wharton being our Secretary, that famous Mathematitian, & who writ the yearely Almanac, during his Majesties troubles:

Thence to Painter hall to our other Commiss: & dined at my L: Majors: 4: Doctor Megot preached the solemn fast day *coram rege* on 26: Esay: 8 an excellent discourse on the terror of Gods Judgements: After Sermon I waited on my L: A: Bish: of Cant and B: of Winchester; where the Deane of Westminster spake to me about putting into my hands the disposal of 50 pounds which the Charitable people at Oxford had sent to be distributed among the sick & wounded seamen &c: since the battaile: Thence I went to my L: Chancellor to joy him of his Royal Highnesse second sonne now born at St. James's, and to desire the use of the Star-chamber for our Commissioners to meete in, painters hall not being so convenient. 5. I met at Painters hall, thence went home. 8. our Viccar on 17: Gen: 1. of Gods omnipotency to reward &

punish: Afternoone to Greenewich where Dr. Harding deane of Rochester on 4. Amos 11. Exciting to repentance by reason of the Judgements of God begun &c: 10. To the Tower about the salt-peter Commiss: thence to the Court of Wards: &c: 11. To Sir William Coventrie to explaine certaine orders of his R: Highnesse: din'd at my Lord Fitz Hardings, Afterwards to the R: Society, where was an experiment of vibrating two concave Globes fill'd with sand, of severall dimensions, to represent the motion of the Earth & Moone about it, which the sand issuing out of the bottome described on the floore: Triall againe of the saddle Charriot, & fountaine to water Gardens & tops of tallest trees: &c: 12: We sate the first time at the Star-Chamber: There was added to the Commission now Sir Geo: Downing (one that had ben a greate . . . against his Majestie but now insinuated into favour, & from a pedagoge & fanatic preacher, not worth a groate, becoming excessive rich) to inspect the Hospitals, & treate about Prisoners: so I return'd this night:

14 To Lond: Sat at Tower, with Sir J: Duncomb & L Berkeley to signe Deputations for Undertakers to furnish their proportions of Salt-peter, returnd: 15 our Curate on 8: Matt: 26. Pomerid: 68. Psal: 1. 17. To Lond: to prepare for the next Engagement of the Fleetes now gotten to sea againe: Sir Robert Murray brought in severall Minerals & Marcasites to the R: SO: out of Walles, with divers Medailes: 18: home: 20: sat at the Tower.

22 I went to Greenewich to Prayers: our Parish still exceedingly infected with the Contagion:

24 To Lond: 25 The Fleetes ingaged: I din'd at L. Berkeleys at St. James's where dined my Lady Harriette Hyde, L: Arlington, Sir Jo: Duncomb &c: 26. returned:

28 At The Tower about the Salt-peter Commiss: & immediately returnd home:

29 The Pestilence now a fresh increasing in our Parish, I forebore going to Church: In the Afternoon came tidings of our Victorie over the Hollanders, sinking some, and driving

others on ground, & into their ports: 31. To Lond: to the Star-Chamber:

Aug: 1 Being pub: fast: Dr. Gunning on Psal: . . . shewing how the Angels had the custody of Good men: &c: In the afternoone I went to Dr. Keffler who married the daughter of the famous Chymist Drebbell inventor of the Bow-dyed Scarlet: I went to see his Yron Ovens made portable formerly for the Pr: of Oranges Armie &c: I supped at the Rhenish Wine-house with divers Scots Gentlemen: 2: return'd home. 5 our Viccar on former text: That the perfection & uprightnesse of God require not our following or imitation of the most perfect of good men, without bringing their actions & practis to the rule of Gods Word: the contrary having ben a stumbling block to many: I received the H: Sacrament.

6. To Lond: din'd with Mr. Povy, & then went with him, to see a Country house he had bought neere Brainford, returning by Kensington, which house I saw standing to a very gracefull avenue of trees; but tis an ordinary building, especialy one part. I returnd to Lond:

8 Dined at Sir Stephen Foxes, & came home: 10 To Lond: din'd with Mr. Odart Secretary of the Latine tongue: 12 The pestilence still raging in our Parish, I durst not go to Church. 14 came with my Wife to Lond: sat with the Commissioners: passd the Evening at Hide-park. 10 Went to Parsone greene. 17 Din'd with L: Chancellor whom I intreated to visite the Hospital of the Savoy, & reduce it (after the greate abuse had ben continued) to its original institution, for the benefit of the poore, which he promised to do: 18 din'd at Sir Arthyr Ingrams in the Citty at a greate feast, & returnd home: 19: went not to church by reason of the Contagion. 21. To star-Chamber. 22. Din'd at Sir Will: Morices (sec: of state) having ben in the morning at Sir W: Coventries about baile for some Captaines my Prisoners: Afternoone at our Society: 23. Sat at Star-Chamber, Din'd at Sir William D'Oylies now recovered as it were miraculously: In the afternoone Visited the Savoy Hospital, where I staied to see the miserably dismembred &

wounded men dressed & gave some necessary orders: Then to my L: Chancelor, who had (with the Bish: of Lond & others in Commission) chosen me one of the three Surveyors of the repaires of Paules, & to consider of a model for the new building, or (if it might be) repairing of the Steeple, which was most decayd: & so I returned home.

26 Contagion still continuing, we had the Church Office at home &c:

27 I went to St. Paules Church in Lond: where with Dr. Wren, Mr. Prat, Mr. May, Mr. Tho: Chichley, Mr. Slingsby, the Bish: of Lond., the Deane of S. Paule & severall expert Workmen, we went about, to survey the generall decays of that antient & venerable Church, & to set down the particulars in writing, what was fit to be don, with the charge thereof: giving our opinion from article to article: We found the maine building to receede outward: It was Mr. Chichleys & Prats opinion that it had ben so built *ab origine* for an effect in Perspective, in reguard of the height; but I was with Dr. Wren quite of another judgement, as indeede ridiculous, & so we entered it: We plumbed the Uprights in severall places: When we came to the Steeple, it was deliberated whither it were not well enought to repaire it onely upon its old foundation, with reservation to the 4 Pillars: This Mr. Chichley & Prat were also for; but we totaly rejected it & persisted that it requird a new foundation, not onely in reguard of the necessitie, but for that the shape of what stood was very meane, & we had a mind to build it with a noble Cupola, a forme of church building, not as yet knowne in England, but of wonderfull grace: for this purpose we offerd to bring in a draught & estimate, which (after much contest) was at last assented to, & that we should nominate a Committè of able Workemen to examine the present foundation: This concluded we drew all up in Writing, and so going with my L: Bishop to the Deanes, after a little refreshment, went home.

28 To Lond: Sate at Star-Chamber: next day to the R: So: where one Mercator an excellent Mathematician produced his

* Almost Miltonic.

rare Clock & new motion to performe the aequations, & Mr. Rooke his new Pendulum: 30: Went home: 31: Mr. Henshaw came with one Mr. Garret to dine with me.

September 2: This fatal night about ten, began that deplorable fire, neere Fish-streete in Lond: 2: I had pub: prayers at home: after dinner the fire continuing, with my Wife & Sonn took Coach & went to the bank side in Southwark, where we beheld that dismal speectaccle, the whole City in dreadfull flames neere the Water side, & had now consumed all the houses from the bridge all Thames Streete & up-wards towards Cheape side, downe to the three Cranes, & so returned exceedingly astonishd, what would become of the rest: 3 The Fire having continud all this night (if I may call that night, which was as light as day for 10 miles round about after a dreadfull manner) when conspiring with a fierce Eastern Wind, in a very drie season, I went on foote to the same place, when I saw the whole South part of the City burning from Cheape side to the Thames, & all along Cornehill (for it likewise kindled back against the Wind, as well as forward) Tower-Streete, Fenchurch-streete, Gracious Streete, & so along to Bainard Castle, and was now taking hold of St. Paules-Church, to which the Scaffalds contributed exceedingly: The Conflagration was so universal, & the people so astonish'd, that from the beginning (I know not by what desponding or fate), they hardly stirr'd to quench it, so as there was nothing heard or seene but crying out & lamentation, & running about like distracted creatures, without at all attempting to save even their goods; such a strange consternation there was upon them, so as it burned both in breadth & length, The Churches, Publique Halls, Exchange, Hospitals, Monuments, & ornaments, leaping after a prodigious manner from house to house & streete to streete, at greate distance one from the other, for the heate (with a long set of faire & warme weather) had even ignited the aire, & prepared the materials to conceive the fire, which devoured after a(n) incredible manner, houses, furniture & everything: Here we saw the Thames covered with goods floating, all the barges &

+ Another almost false, stylistic parentheses.

boates laden with what some had time & courage to save, as on the other, the Carts &c carrying out to the fields, which for many miles were strewed with moveables of all sorts, & Tents erecting to shelter both people &c what goods they could get away: ô the miserable & calamitous speectacle, such as happly the whole world had not seene the like since the foundation of it, nor to be out don, 'til the universal Conflagration of it, all the skie were of a fiery aspect, like the top of a burning Oven, & the light seene above 40 miles round about for many nights: God grant mine eyes may never behold the like, who now saw above ten thousand houses all in one flame, the noise & crakling & thunder of the impetuous flames, the shreeking of Women & children, the hurry of people, the fall of towers, houses & churches was like an hideous storme, & the aire all about so hot & inflam'd that at the last one was not able to approach it, so as they were force'd to stand still, and let the flames consume on which they did for neere two whole miles in length and one in breadth: The Clowds also of Smoke were dismall, & reached upon computation neere 50 miles in length: Thus I left it this afternoone burning, a resemblance of Sodome, or the last day: It call'd to mind that of 4 Heb: *non enim hic habemus stabilem Civitatem;* the ruines resembling the picture of Troy; London was, but is no more: Thus I return'd:

4 The burning still rages; I went now on horse back, & it was now gotten as far as the Inner Temple; all Fleetestreete, old baily, Ludgate hill, Warwick Lane, Newgate, Paules Chaine, Wattling-streete now flaming & most of it reduc'd to ashes, the stones of Paules flew like granados, the lead mealting downe the streetes in a streame, & the very pavements of them glowing with fiery rednesse, so as nor horse nor man was able to tread on them, & the demolitions had stopped all the passages, so as no help could be applied; the Eastern Wind still more impetuously driving the flames forewards: Nothing but the almighty power of God was able to stop them, for vaine was the help of man: on the fift it crossed towards White-hall, but ô the Confusion was then at that Court: It pleased his Majestie

to command me among the rest to looke after the quenching of fetter-lane end, to preserve (if possible) that part of Holborn, whilst the rest of the Gent: tooke their several posts, some at one part, some at another, for now they began to bestirr themselves, & not 'til now, who 'til now had stood as men interdict, with their hands a crosse, & began to consider that nothing was like to put a stop, but the blowing up of so many houses, as might make a wider gap, than any had yet ben made by the ordinary method of pulling them downe with Engines; This some stout Seamen proposd early enought to have saved the whole Citty; but some tenacious & avaritious Men, Aldermen &c. would not permitt, because their houses must have ben of the first: It was therefore now commanded to be practised, & my concerne being particularly for the Hospital of st. Bartholomeus neere Smithfield, where I had many wounded & sick men, made me the more diligent to promote it: nor was my care for the Savoy lesse: So as it pleased Almighty God by abating of the Wind, & the industrie of people, now when all was lost, infusing a new Spirit into them (& such as had if exerted in time undoubtedly preserved the whole) that the furie of it began sensibly to abate, about noone, so as it came no farther than the Temple West-ward, nor than the enterance of Smithfield North; but continued al this day & night so impetuous toward Cripple-Gate, & The Tower, as made us even all despaire; It also brake out againe in the Temple: but the courage of the multitude persisting, & innumerable houses blown up with Gunpowder, such gaps & desolations were soone made, as also by the former three days consumption, as the back fire did not so vehemently urge upon the rest, as formerly: There was yet no standing neere the burning & glowing ruines neere a furlongs Space; The Coale & Wood wharfes & magazines of Oyle, rozine, chandler &c: did infinite mischiefe; so as the invective I but a little before dedicated to his Majestie & publish'd, giving warning what might probably be the issue of suffering those shops to be in the Citty, was lookd on as prophetic: but there I left this smoking & sulltry heape, which mounted up in dismall clowds night & day, the poore Inhabitans dispersd all about St. Georges, Moore filds, as far as higate, & severall miles in Circle, Some under tents, others under miserable Hutts and Hovells, without a rag, or any necessary utinsils, bed or board, who from delicatnesse, riches & easy accommodations in stately & well furnishd houses, were now reduc'd to extreamest misery & poverty: In this Calamitous Condition I returnd with a sad heart to my house, blessing & adoring the distinguishing mercy of God, to me & mine who in the midst of all this ruine, was like Lot, in my little Zoar, safe and sound:

6 Thursday, I represented to his Majestie the Case, of the French Prisoners at War in my Custodie, & besought him, there might be still the same care of Watching at all places contiguous to unseized houses: It is not indeede imaginable how extraordinary the vigilance & activity of the King & Duke was, even labouring in person, & being present, to command, order, reward, and encourage Workemen; by which he shewed his affection to his people, & gained theirs: Having then disposed of some under Cure at the Savoy, I return'd to white hall, where I dined at Mr. Offleys, Groome-porter, who was my relation, together with the Knight Martial, where I also lay that night.

7 I went this morning on foote from White hall as far as London bridge, thro the Late fleete streete, Ludgate hill, by St. Paules, Cheape side, Exchange, Bishopsgate, Aldersgate, & out to Morefields, thence thro Cornehill, &c: with extraordinary difficulty, clambring over mountaines of yet smoking rubbish, & frequently mistaking where I was, the ground under my feete so hott, as made me not onely Sweate, but even burnt the soles of my shoes, & put me all over in Sweate: In the meane time his Majestie got to the Tower by Water, to demolish the houses about the Graft, which being built intirely about it, had they taken fire, & attaq'd the white Towre, where the Magazines of Powder lay, would undoubtedly have not onely beaten downe & destroyed all the bridge, but sunke & torne all the vessels in the river, & rendred the demolition beyond all expres-

sion for severall miles even about the Country at many miles distance: At my returne I was infinitly concern'd to find that goodly Church St. Paules now a sad ruine, & that beautifull Portico (for structure comparable to any in Europ, as not long before repaird by the late King) now rent in pieces, flakes of vast Stone Split in sunder, & nothing remaining intire but the Inscription in the Architrave which shewing by whom it was built, had not one letter of it defac'd: which I could not but take notice of: It was astonishing to see what imense stones the heate had in a manner Calcin'd, so as all the ornaments, Columns, freezes, Capitels & projectures of massie Portland stone flew off, even to the very roofe, where a Sheete of Leade covering no lesse than 6 akers by measure, being totaly mealted, the ruines of the Vaulted roofe, falling brake into St. Faithes, which being filled with the magazines of bookes, belonging to the Stationers, & carried thither for safty, they were all consumed burning for a weeke following: It is also observable, that the lead over the Altar at the East end was untouch'd; and among the divers monuments, the body of one Bishop, remaind intire. Thus lay in ashes that most venerable Church one of the antientest Pieces of early Piety in the Christian World, beside neere 100 more; The lead, yronworke, bells, plate &c mealted; the exquisitely wrought Mercers Chapell, the Sumptuous Exchange, the august fabricque of Christ church, all the rest of the Companies Halls, sumptuous buildings, Arches, Enteries, all in dust. The fountaines dried up & ruind, whilst the very waters remained boiling; the Voragos of subterranean Cellars Wells & Dungeons, formerly Warehouses, still burning in stench & dark clowds of smoke like hell, so as in five or six miles traversing about, I did not see one loade of timber unconsum'd, nor many stones but what were calcind white as snow, so as the people who now walked about the ruines, appeard like men in some dismal desart, or rather in some greate Citty, lay'd wast by an impetuous & cruel Enemy, to which was added the stench that came from some poore Creaturs bodys, beds, & other combustible goods: Sir Tho: Gresshams Statue, though falln to the ground from its nich in the Ro: Exchange remain'd intire, when all those of the Kings since the Conquest were broken to pieces: also the Standard in Cornehill, & Q: Elizabeths Effigies, with some armes on Ludgate continud with but little detriment, whilst the vast yron Chaines of the Cittie streetes, vast hinges, barrs & gates of Prisons were many of them mealted, & reduc'd to cinders by the vehement heats: nor was I yet able to passe through any of the narrower streetes, but kept the widest, the ground & aire, smoake & fiery vapour, continud so intense, my haire being almost seinged, & my feete unsufferably surbated: The bielanes & narrower streetes were quite fill'd up with rubbish, nor could one have possibly knowne where he was, but by the ruines of some church, or hall, that had some remarkable towre or pinacle remaining: I then went towards Islington, & high-gate, where one might have seene two hundred thousand people of all ranks & degrees, dispersed, & laying along by their heapes of what they could save from the *Incendium*, deploring their losse, & though ready to perish for hunger & destitution, yet not asking one penny for reliefe, which to me appeard a stranger sight, than any I had yet beheld: His Majestie & Council indeeade tooke all imaginable care for their reliefe, by Proclamation, for the Country to come in & refresh them with provisions: when in the middst of all this Calamity & confusion, there was (I know not how) an Alarme begun, that the French & Dutch (with whom we were now in hostility) were not onely landed, but even entring the Citty; there being in truth, greate suspicion some days before, of those two nations joyning, & even now, that they had ben the occasion of firing the Towne: This report did so terrifie, that on a suddaine there was such an uprore & tumult, that they ran from their goods, & taking what weapons they could come at, they could not be stop'd from falling on some of those nations whom they casualy met, without sense or reason, the clamor & perill growing so excessive, as made the whole Court amaz'd at it, & they did with infinite paines, & greate difficulty reduce & apease the people, sending Guards & troopes of souldiers, to cause them to retire into the fields againe, where they were watched all this night when I left them pretty quiet, & came home to my house, sufficiently weary and broken: Their spirits thus a little sedated, & the affright abated, they now began to repaire into the suburbs about the Citty, where such as had friends or opportunitie got shelter & harbour for the Present; to which his Majesties Proclamation also invited them. Still the Plage, continuing in our parish, I could not without danger adventure to our Church. 10: I went againe to the ruines, for it was now no longer a Citty: 11 Sat at Star Chamber, on the 13, I presented his Majestie with a Survey of the ruines, and a Plot for a new Citty, with a discourse on it, whereupon, after dinner his Majestie sent for me into the Queenes Bed-chamber, her Majestie & the Duke onely present, where they examind each particular, & discoursd upon them for neere a full houre, seeming to be extreamly pleasd with what I had so early thought on: The Queene was now in her Cavaliers riding habite, hat & feather & horsemans Coate, going to take the aire; so I tooke leave of his Majestie & visiting the Duke of Albemarle, now newly return'd from Sea, I went home. 15 To Lond: & dined with my L: Brounchar president of our Society, where was also the Earle of Clancarne, Sir Rob: Murray, & Dr. Christopher Wrenn. 16 Pomeridiano I went to Greene-wich church, when Mr. Plume preached very well on Pet: 'Seing therefore all these things must be disolvd' &c: takeing occasion from the late unparalell'd Conflagration, to mind us, how we ought to walke more holilie, in all manner of Conversation: 19: To Star-Chamber, returned at night; 23: To Greene-wich, where the Minister proceeded on his former Text: 25 To Lond: to Star: cha: 26. Din'd at Sir W: Boremans. 27: at Sir William D'Oylies with that worthy Gent: Sir Jo: Holland of Suffolck, & Mr. Scaven, sat with our Commissioners for sick & Wounded, & returned home. 29 Michaelmas-day, I went to visite my Bro: Richard, who was now indisposed in his health:

October 2: I gave my Bro: of Wotton a Visite, being myselfe

also not well, & returnd the 4th, so as I entred into a Course of Steele, against the Scorbut:

10 This day was indicted a Generall fast through the nation, to humble us, upon the late dreadfull Conflagration, added to the Plage & Warr, the most dismall judgments could be inflicted, & indeede but what we highly deserved for our prodigious ingratitude, burning Lusts, disolute Court, profane & abominable lives, under such dispensations of Gods continued favour, in restoring Church, Prince, & people from our late intestine calamities, of which we were altogether unmindfull even to astonishment: This made me resolve to go to our Parish Assemblie, where our Doctor preached on 19 Luke: 41 &c: piously applying it to the occasion, after which followd a Collection for the poore distressd loosers in the late fire, & their present reliefe. 14: He preachd on 9: Dan: 14, shewing the justnesse of Gods judgments, & how for time, place & kind, they frequently met offenders &c:

18 To Lond: Star-Chamber: thence to Court, it being the first time of his Majesties putting himselfe solemnly into the Eastern fashion of Vest, changing doublet, stiff Collar, bands & Cloake &c: into a comely Vest, after the Persian mode with girdle or shash, & Shoe strings & Garters, into bouckles, of which some were set with precious stones, resolving never to alter it, & to leave the French mode, which had hitherto obtained to our greate expense & reproch: upon which divers Courtiers & Gent: gave his Majesty gold, by way of Wager, that he would not persist in this resolution: I had some time before indeede presented an Invectique against that unconstancy, & our so much affecting the french fashion, to his Majestie in which I tooke occasion to describe the Comelinesse & usefullnesse of the Persian clothing in the very same manner, his Majestie clad himselfe; This Pamphlet I intituled *Tyrannus or the mode*, & gave it his Majestie to reade; I do not impute the change which soone happn'd to this discourse, but it was an identitie, that I could not but take notice of: This night was acted my Lord Brahals Tragedy cal'd *Mustapha* before their Majesties &c: at Court: at which I was present, very seldom

at any time, going to the publique Theaters, for many reasons, now as they were abused, to an atheisticall liberty, fowle & undecent; Women now (& never 'til now) permitted to appeare & act, which inflaming severall young noble-men & gallants, became their whores, & to some their Wives, wittnesse the Earle of Oxford, Sir R: Howard, Pr: Rupert, the E: of Dorset, & another greater person than any of these, who fell into their snares, to the reproch of their noble families, & ruine both of body & Soule: I was invited to see this Tragedie, exceedingly well writ, by my Lord Chamberlain, though in my mind, I did not approve of any such passe time, in a season of such Judgements & Calamitie: 19 I return'd home;

21 Our Viccar on his former subject: This season (after so long & extraordinary a drowth in September, & Aug: as if preparatory for the dreadfull fire) was so very wett & rainy, as many feared an ensuing famine: 23. To Star-Chamber.

24 I din'd at my L. Corneberies; 25 at Star-chamb. return'd: 28 our Viccar as before, shewing what were presumptuous sinns, & the misery of making Conscience our accuser & enemy, which is the Tribunal of God in every man, & our best friend to admonishe: Pomerid: 1 Rom: 18 of the severity of Gods Judgement against sinners: That it was the L. Jesus, the 2d Person in Trinity: who overthrew Sodom for dishonoring the nature he was to assume &c: The Pestilence now through Gods mercy, began now to abate in our Towne considerably. 30 To Lond to our Office, & now had I on the Vest, & Surcoate, or Tunic as 'twas cald, after his Majestie had brought the whole Court to it; It being a comely, & manly habite: too good to hold, it being impossible for us to leave the Monsieurs Vanitys in good earnest long: 31 I heard pleaded the signal Cause of my L: Cleavelands pleaded by the Solicitor before the House of Lords, & was this day 46 yeares of age, wonderfully protected by the mercies of God, for which I render him immortal thanks: & return'd to my house:

November 4 our Doctor as formerly on the 1. Rom: shewing the dreadfullnesse & degrees of the wroth of God against sinners: I received the blessed Communion; & went in the afternoone to Greenewich to prayers: 5. our Viccar on 116 Psal: 1. of the many obligations we had to glorifie & praise Almighty God: 8. I went to Woodcot, to visite my Bro: who having now a sore leg, was much indisposd, my Wife accompanying me, returned that evening: 9: To Lond: & returnd: 10. Came my Bro: in Law Glanvill to visite us: 11 our Viccar as formerly, against the unreasonablenesse of Atheisme: In the afternoone to Greenewich wher Mr. Plume on 91 Psal: 11. concerning Tutelar Angels &c:

14 I went my Winter Circle through my district, Rochester & other places wher I had men quartered & in Custody: 15. To Leedes Castle. 16 I musterd them being about 600 Dutch & French, ordred their proportion of Bread to be augmented, & provided cloths & fuell: Monsieur Colbert Ambassador at the Court of England, having also this day sent mony from his Master the French King to every Prisoner of that nation under my Guards: I lay at Chilston at my Co: Hales's. 17: I return'd to Chattham, my Charriot overturning on the steepe of Boxley-hill, wounded me in two places in the head, but slightly, my sonn Jack being with me, & then but newly out of long Coates, was like to have ben Worse cutt, by the Glasse, of the Charriot dores, but I thank God, we both escaped without much hurt, though not without exceeding danger. 18. one of the Prebends of Rochester preach'd in the Cathedral on 13. Gen: 8. & in the Afternoone Mr. Loton (who had formerly ben Curate at our Parish) on: 11. Matt. 12. by what violence even heaven itselfe might be taken; 19 I got home:

22 To Lond: 23. I heard an extraordinary Case before a Comittè of the whole house of Commons, in the Commons house of Parliament, betweene one Cap: Taylor, & my Lord Vicount Mordaunt; where after the Lawyers had pleaded, & the Witnesses examin'd, such foule & dishonorable things were producd against his Lordship of Tyrannie during his government of Windsore Castle, of which he was Constable, Incontinence & suborning, of which last one Sir Rich: Breames

was most concerned, that I was exceedingly concerned for his Lordship, who was my special friend, and husband of the most virtuous Lady in the world: We sate 'till neere ten at night, & yet but halfe the Council had don, on behalfe of the plaintife: The question then was put, for the bringing in of lights to sit longer, which lasted so long a time before it was determind, & raisd such a confused noise among the Members, that a stranger would have been astonished at it: & I admire, that there is not a Rationale to regulate such trifling accidents, which yet I find consume a world of time, & is a reproch to the gravity of so greate an Assembly of sober men: 24 I went home. 26 To Lond: 27: Sate in Star: cha: 27: Sir Hugh Pollard Comptroller of the household died at W: Hall, & his Majestie Conferred the White-Staffe on my bro: Commissioner for Sick & Wounded, on Sir Tho: Clifford, (since Lord high Treasurer of England) a bold young Gent: of a meane fortune in Devon: but advanc'd by my L: Arlington Sec: of State: to the greate astonishment of all the Court: This Gent: was some what related to me, by the marriage of his mother, to my neerest Kindsman Greg: Coale, & was ever my noble friend; a valiant & daring person, but by no meanes fit for a soupple & flattering Courtier: I dined at my L: Jo: Berkeleys. 28 Sate at star-Chamber: din'd with L. Cornberie, afterward went to see Clarendon house (since quite demolished) now almost finish'd, a goodly pile to see too, but had many defects as to the Architecture, though placed most gracefully: After this I waited on my L: Chancellor who was now at Berkshire house since the burning of London. 30 I returned home.

December 2 our Viccar as formerly: 2 dind with me Monsieur Kiviet a Dutch Gent: Pensioner of Roterdam, who came over hither for protection, being of the Prince of Oranges party, now not wellcome in Holland: The King knighted him for some merit in the princes behalfe: he should (if caught) have been beheaded with Monsieur Buat, & was brother in Law to Van Tromp, the Sea Generall &c: with him came downe Mr. Gab: Sylvius, & Mr. Williamson, Secretarie to my L. Arlington: Sir Kiviet came downe to examine, whither the soile about the river of Thames would be proper to make Clinkar brick with & to treate with me about some accommodations in order to it: 9: To Lond: & returned the 14: 16 our Doctor as before, against deceite, & detraction: 17 To Lond: about severall affaires. 20 Visited my L. Duke of Albemarle, returned home:

25 Our Doctor on 2. Cor: 8. 9. shewing the exceeding povertie & exinanition of our B: Saviour for our Sakes: I received the blessed Communion, being Christmas day: 26 Divers Neighbours dined with me, according to costome: & so the next day:

30: Dr. Dolben deane of Westminster, & now made Bishop of Rochester our Diocesse, preached at our Parish-Church his first sermon on 1. Tim: 3. 16, of the wonder of our B:S: Incarnation &c: after sermon Confirmed many young children, solemnly prepar'd the weeke before, among whom my sonn John was brought, and then his Lordship dined at my house. 31. Blessed God for his Protection of me & mine this past yeare:

[1667] 11 (June): To Lond: alarm'd by the Dutch, who were falln on our Fleete, at Chattam by a most audacious enterprise entering the very river with part of their fleete, doing us not onely disgrace, but incredible mischiefe in burning severall of our best Men of Warr, lying at Anker & Moored there, & all this thro the unaccountable negligence of our negligence in setting out our fleete in due time: This alarme caused me (fearing the Enemie might adventure up the Thames even to Lond, which with ease they might have don, & fired all the Vessels in the river too) to send away my best goods, plate &c: from my house to another place; for this alarme was so greate, as put both County and Citty in to a panique feare & consternation, such as I hope I shall never see more: for every body were flying, none knew why or whither: Now then were Land forces dispatched with Lord Duke of Albemarle, L: Midleton, Pr: Rupert & the Duke to hinder the Dutch comming to Chattham, fortifying Upnore Castle, & Laying chaines & bombs, but the resolute Enemy brake through all, & set fire on our ships, & retreated in spight, stopping up the Thames, the rest of their Fleete lying before the mouth of it: 14: I went to see the Work at Woolwich, a batterie for to defend them from coming up to Lond: which Pr: Rupert comanded, & sunk some ships in the river. 16: Our Viccar on 13. Hosea. 9.

17 This night about 2 a clock, some chipps & combustible matter prepared for some fireships, taking flame, in Deptford yard, made such a blace, and caused such an uprore in the Towne, it being given out that the Dutch fleet were come up, & had landed their men, & fired the Towne, as had like to have don much mischiefe before people would be perswaded to the Contrary, & believe the accident: every body went to their armes, & all my family alarm'd with the extraordinarie light, & confusion &c: These were sad, & troublesome times.

18 To Lond, & returned the 20th: 23: our Doctor as formerly. 24 I was before the Council (the Dutch fleete still continuing to stop up the river of Thames, so as nothing could stirr out, or come in) and commanded by his Majestie that I with some others, should search about the invirons of the Citty, now exceedingly distressed for want of fuell, whither there could be any Peate or turfe, fit for use, could be found: & the next day I went, & found enough, & made my report, that there might be found a greate deale, &c: but nothing was now farther don in it: so on the 28 I went to Chattham, and thence to view not onely what Mischiefe the Dutch had don, but how triumphantly their whole Fleete, lay within the very mouth of the Thames, all from North-foreland, Mergate, even to the Buoy of the Noore, a Dreadfull Spectacle as ever any English men saw, & a dishonour never to be wiped off: Those who advised his Majestie to prepare no fleete this Spring, deserv'd I know what! but——

20 (Aug): There was now a very gallant horse to be baited

to death with doggs, but he fought them all, so as the fiercest of them, could not fasten on him, til they run him thro with their swords; This wiccked and barbarous sport, deserv'd to have been published in the cruel Contrivers, to get mony, under pretence the horse had killed a man, which was false: I would not be perswaded to be a Spectator:

[1669] 10 (June): Came my Lord Cornbery, Sir William Poultny & others to visite me; I went that evening to Lond: to carry Mr. Pepys to my Bro: (now exceedingly afflicted with the Stone in the bladder) who himselfe had ben successfully cut; & carried the Stone (which was as big as a tenis-ball) to shew him, and encourage his resolution to go thro the operation.

[1670] March: 3 Finding my brother in such exceeding torture, & that he now began to fall into Convulsion fits, I solemnly set the next-day a part, to beg of God to mitigate his sufferings, & prosper the onely meanes which yet remained for his recovery; or if otherwise; that it would please Almighty God to prepare him for himselfe, he not onely being very much wasted, but exceedingly, & all along averse from being cut, which he was advised to undergo from time to time, with extraordinary probability of successe: but when it came to the operation, & all things prepared, his spirit & resolution failed, & there was now lesse hopes than ever. 5. I went to visite my poore afflicted brother, whom I found almost in the last agonies:

6 Dr. Patric in Covent Garden Church, on his former Text, of fraternal Correption. I participated of the blessed Sacrament, recomending the deplorable condition of my bro: his agonies still increasing: In the Afternoone, a stranger made an excellent sermon against Atheists: &c. I watched late with my Bro: this night, yet not imagining his end to be so neere; but so it pleased God, to deliver him out of this miserable life, towards five this moneday morning, to my unspeakable griefe & sorrow, being a Bro: whom I most dearely loved for many

Virtues; & that was but two yeares Younger than my-selfe, a sober, prudent, & worthy Gent: he had married a greate fortune, and left one onely daughter, & a most noble seate, at Woodcot neere, Epsom in Surrey &c:

16 (June) I was forc'd to accompanie some friends to the Bear-garden &c: Where was Cock fighting, Beare, Dog-fighting, Beare & Bull baiting, it being a famous day for all these butcherly Sports, or rather barbarous cruelties: The Bulls did exceedingly well but the Irish Wolfe dog exceeded, which was a tall Gray-hound, a stately creature in deede, who beate a cruell Mastife: One of the Bulls tossd a Dog full into a Ladys lap, as she sate in one of the boxes at a Considerable height from the Arena: There were two poore dogs killed; & so all ended with the Ape on horse-back, & I most heartily weary, of the rude & dirty passetime, which I had not seene I think in twenty yeares before:

[1671] 18 (Jan) I this day first acquainted his Majestie with that incomparable young man, Gibson, whom I had lately found in an Obscure place, & that by meere accident, as I was walking neere a poore solitary thatched house in a field in our Parish neere Says-Court: I found him shut in, but looking into the Window, I perceiv'd him carving that large Cartoone or Crucifix of Tintorets, a Copy of which I had also my selfe brought from Venice, where the original Painting remaines: I asked if I might come in, he opned the doore civily to me, & I saw him about such a work, as for the curiosity of handling, drawing, & studious exactnesse, I never in my life had seene before in all my travells: I asked why he worked in such an obscure & lonesome place; he told me, it was that he might apply himselfe to his profession without interruption; & wondred not a little how I came to find him out: I asked if he were unwilling to be made knowne to some Greate men; for that I believed it might turne to his profit; he answerd, he was yet but a beginner; but would yet not be sorry to sell off that piece; I asked him the price, he told me 100 pounds. In good earnest the very frame was worth the mony, there being nothing even in nature so tender, & delicate as the flowers & festoones about it, & yet the worke was very strong; but in the Piece above 100 figures of men &c: I found he was likewise Musical, & very Civil, sober & discreete in his discourse: There was onely an old Woman in the house; so desiring leave to visite him sometimes, I tooke my leave: Of this Young Artist, together with my manner of finding him out, I acquainted the King, and beged of his Majestie that he would give me leave to bring him & his Worke to White-hall, for that I would adventure my reputation with his Majestie that he had never seene any thing approch it, & that he would be exceedingly pleased, & employ him: The King sayd, he would himselfe go see him: This was the first notice his Majestie ever had of Mr. Gibbons.

Mar: 1. I caused Mr. Gibbon to bring to Whitehall his excellent piece of Carving where being come, I advertised his Majestie who asked me where it was, I told him, in Sir R: Brownes (my F. in Laws) Chamber, & that if it pleased his Majestie to appoint whither it should be brought (for 'twas large, and though of Wood, yet heavy) I would take care for it: No says the King; shew me the Way, Ile go to Sir Richards Chamber: which his Majestie immediately did, walking all along the Enteries after me as far as the Ewrie til he came up into the rome where I also lay: & no sooner was he entred, & cast his eye on the Worke, but he was astonish'd at the curiositie of it, & having considred it a long time, & discoursed with Mr. Gibbon, whom I brought to kisse his hand; he commanded it should be immediately carried to the Queenes side to shew her Majestie, so it was carried up into her bed-chamber, where she and the King looked on & admired it againe, the King thus leaving us with the Queene being now caled away, I think to Council, believing that she would have bought it, it being a Crucifix; but when his Majestie was gon, a French pedling woman, one Madame de boord, that used to bring peticoates &

fanns & baubles out of France to the Ladys, began to find faults with severall things in the worke, which she understood no more than an Asse or Monky; so as in a kind of Indignation, I caused the porters who brought it, to carry it to the Chamber againe, finding the Queene so much govern'd by an ignorant french woman: and this imcomparable Artist had the labour onely for his paines, which not a little displeased me; so he was faine to send it downe to his cottage againe, though he not long after sold it for 80 pounds, which was realy, (even without the frame) worth an hundred: Sir Geo: Viner buying it of him, as his first Essay, and his Majesties Surveyor Mr. Wren faithfully promising me to employ him for the future; I having bespoke his Majestie also for his Worke at Windsore which my friend Mr. May (the Architect there) was going to alter and repaire universaly: for on the next day, I had a faire opportunity of talking to his Majestie about it, in the Lobby next the Queenes side, where I presented him with some Sheetes of my historie, & thence walked with him thro St. James's Parke to the Garden, where I both saw and heard a very familiar discourse betweene . . . & Mrs. Nellie as they cal'd an impudent Comedian, she looking out of her Garden on a Terrace at the top of the Wall, & . . . standing on the greene Walke under it: I was heartily sorry at this scene:

17 (Oct) My Lord: Henry Howard coming this night to visite my Lord Chamberlain, & staying a day, would needes have me go along with him to Norwich; promising to convey me back againe after a day or two; This as I could not refuse, so I was not hardly perswaded to, having a desire to see that famous Scholar & Physition Dr. T. Browne author of *Religio Medici* & *Vulgar Errors* &c: now lately knighted: . . .

Being come to the Ducal Palace, my Lord made very much of me, but I had little rest, so exceedingly desirous he was to shew me the contrivances he had made, for the entertainement of their Majesties & whole Court not long before, & which, though much of it, but temporary appartments fram'd of boards &c onely, were yet standing: As to the Palace, tis an old wretched building, & that part of it, newly built of brick, is very ill understood; so as I was of opinion, it had ben much better to have demolish'd all, & set it in a better place than to proceede any farther; for it stands in the very Market place, & though neere a river, yet a very narrow muddy one & without any extent: here before we went to bed, my Lord fell-out with his Carpenter, about measuring of a roome, & grew into such a passion, as in my life, I had never seene any mortal man; so much beneath his dignitie, & for so wretched a trifle; my Lord saying the dimension was so many foote, the Workman so many: This conflict lasting from 8 till 1 at night, was grievous to me:

Next morning I went to see Sir Tho: Browne (with whom I had sometime corresponded by Letters tho never saw before) whose whole house & Garden being a Paradise & Cabinet of rarities, & that of the best collection, especially Medails, books, Plants, natural things, did exceedingly refresh me after last nights confusion: Sir Thomas had amongst other curiosities, a collection of the Eggs of all the foule & birds he could procure, that Country (especialy the promontorys of Norfolck) being (as he said) frequented with severall kinds, which seldom or never, go farther into the Land, as Cranes, Storkes, Eagles &c: & variety of Waterfoule: He likewise led me to see all the remarkable places of this antient Citty, being one of the largest, & certainely (after London) one of the noblest of England, for its venerable Cathedrall, number of Stately Churches, Cleanesse of the streetes; & buildings of flint, so exquisitely headed & Squared, as I was much astonish'd at; Sir Tho: told me they had lost the art, of squaring the flint, which once they were so excellent in: & of which the Churches, best houses, & Walls are built: . . . One thing I observ'd of remarkable in this Citty, that most of the Church-yards (though some of them large enough) were filled up with earth, or rather the congestion of dead bodys one upon another, for want of Earth &c to the very top of the Walls, & many above the wales, so as the Churches seem'd to be built in pitts:

[1672] 24 (March): I din'd with Mr. Commissioner Cox having seene that morning my Chirurgeon cut off a poore creaturs Leg, a little under the knee, first cutting the living & untainted flesh above the Gangreene with a sharp knife, and then sawing off the bone in an instant; then with searing & stoopes stanching the blood, which issued aboundantly; the stout & gallant man, enduring it with incredible patience, & that without being bound to his chaire, as is usual in such painefull operations, or hardly making a face (or crying oh): I had hardly courage enough to be present, nor could I endure to se any more such cruel operations.

The leg was so rotten & gangreen'd, that one might have run a straw through it; but neither did this the cure, for it not being amputated high-enough, the gangreene prevaild upon the knee, & so a second amputation of the Thigh, cost the poore Creature his life, to my very greate sorrow: I do not remember that ever in my life I smelt so intollerable a stink as what issu'd from the part was cut off, & which I ordered should immediatly be buried in the Garden: Lord, what miseries are mortal men obnoxious to, & what confusion & mischiefe dos the avarice, anger, and ambition of Princes cause in the world, who might be happier with halfe they possesse: This stoute man, was but a common sailer.

31 (May). I received another Command to repaire to the sea-side againe, so I went to Rochester, where I found many both Wounded, sick, and Prisoners newly put on shore, after the Engagement of the 28, in which the Earle of Sandwich, that incomparable person, & my particular friend & divers more whom I loved, were lost:

7 (June) I went to see Upnore Castle, which I found pretty well defended, but of no greate moment: Next day I sailed to the Fleete now riding at the buoy of the Noore, where I met his Majestie, the Duke, L. Arlington & all the greate men in the *Charles*, lying miserably shattered; but the misse of my

Lord Sandwich redoubled the losse to me, as well as the folly of hazarding so brave a fleete, & loosing so many good men, for no provocation in the World but because the Hollander exceeded us in Industrie, & all things else but envy:

[1679] 4 (June). To Lond: Din'd with Mr. Pepys at the Tower, whither he was committed by the house of Commons, for misdemeanors in the Admiralty, where he was Secretary; but I believe unjustly: Here I saluted my Lord Stafford & Peters who were also committed for the Popish Plot:

18 (July) I went early to the old-Baily Sessions-house to the famous Trial of Sir Geo: Wakeman (one of the Queenes Physitians) & 3 Benedictine Monkes; The first (whom I was well acquainted with, & take to be a worthy gent: abhorring such a fact) for intending to poyson the King: The other as complices to carry on the Plott, to subvert the Government, & introduce Poperie: the Bench was crowded with the Judges, Lo: Major, Justices, & innumerable spectators: The chiefe Accusers Dr. Oates (as he called himselfe) and one Bedlow, a man of inferior note; but their testimony were not so pregnant, & I feare much of it from heare-say, but sworne positively to some particulars, which drew suspicion upon their truth; nor did Circumstances so agree, as to give either the bench or Jurie so intire satisfaction as was expected: After therefore a long & tedious tryal of 9 houres, the Jury brought them in not guilty to the extraordinary triumph of the Papists, & not without sufficient disadvantage & reflections on the Witnesses, especialy Oates & Bedlow: And this was an happy day for the Lords in the Tower, who expecting their Triall (had this gon against the Prisoners at the barr) would all of them have ben in uttmost hazard: For my part, I do looke on Oates as a vaine, insolent man, puff'd up, with the favour of the Commons, for having discovered something realy true; as more especialy detecting the dangerous intrigue of Coleman, proved out of his owne letters: & of a generall designe, which the Jesuited party of the Papists,

ever had, & still have to ruine the Church of England; but that he was trusted with those greate seacrets he pretended, or had any solid ground for what he accused divers noble men of, I have many reasons to induce my contrary beliefe; That amongst so many Commissions as he affirm'd he delivered to them from P: Oliva & the Pope, he who made no scrupule of opening all other Papers, letters & seacrets, should not onely, not open any of those pretended Commissions, but not so much as take any Copy, or Witnesse, of any one of them, is almost miraculous: But the Commons (some leading persons I meane of them) had so exalted him, that they tooke for Gospell all he said, & without more ado, ruin'd all whom he nam'd to be Conspirators, nor did he spare whomsoever came in his way; But indeed the Murder of Sir Ed: Godferie (suspected to have been compassed by the Jesuite party, for his intimacy with Coleman (a buisy person whom I also knew) & the feare they had he was able to have discovered some thing to their prejudice) did so exasperate, not onely the Commons, but all the nation; That much of these sharpnesses against even the more honest Ro: Catholicks who lived peaceably, is to be imputed to that horrid fact: The Sessions ended I dined, or rather indeede supped, (so late it was) with the Judges, in the large roome annexed to the Place, & so returned to my house: And though it was not my Custome or delight, to be often present at any Capital Trials, we having them commonly, so exactly published, by those who take them in short hand; Yet I was inclined to be at this signal one, that by the occular view of the carriages, & other Circumstances of the Manegers & parties concerned I might informe my selfe, and regulate my opinion of a Cause that had so alarm'd the whole Nation, & filled it with such expectations:

[1680] 13 (May): I was at the funerall of old Mr. Shish Master Shipwrite of the Kings Yard here in this Parish, an honest and remarkable man, & his death a publique losse, for his excellent successe in building Ships, (though illiterate altogether) & for the breeding up so many of his Children to be able Artists: I held up the Pall, with three knights who did him that honour, & he was worthy of it: our Viccar preaching on a Text of the good-mans choice out of 12 Isa: 2. shewing his Trust, and faith in God, & thankfullnesse for his mercies: It was the Costome of this good man, to rise in the night, and to pray kneeling in his owne Cofin; which many yeares he had lying by him: he was borne that famous yeare of the Gunpowder Plot 1605:

30 (Oct) I went to Lond: to be private: My Birth-day being the next; & I now arived to the sixtieth yeare of Age; upon which, I began a more solemn survey of my whole Life, in order to the making, and confirming my peace with God, by an accurate Scrutinie of all my actions past, as far as I was able to call them to min'd: And oh, how difficult, & uncertaine, yet most necessarie worke; The Lord be mercifull to me & accept me. Who can tell how oft he offendeth? Teach me therefore so to Number my daies, that I may apply my heart to wisdome, make my calling & election sure: Amen Lord Jesus: I spent this whole day in Exercise &c:

12 (December) Our Viccar & Curate proceeded on their former Texts: This Evening looking out of my Chamber Window towards the West. I first saw a Meteor, (or what ever other Phaenomenon it was) of an obscure bright Colour (if so I may call it without a solecisme) resembling the brightnesse of the Moone when under a thin Clow'd, very much in shape like the blade of a sword, whose point to the starrs in appearance, bending Northwards towards London, not seeming at the Horizon to be above a yard in bredth, & so pyramidal, the rest of the skie, very serene & cleere; The Moone new, but not appearing, the Weather exceeding sharp, hard frost with some snow falling 2 daies before: What this may Portend (for it was very extraordinarie) God onely knows; but such another Phaenomenon I remember I saw, which went from North to South, & was much brighter, & larger, but not so Ensiforme in

the yeare 1640, about the Triall of the greate Earle of Strafford, praeceeding our bloudy Rebellion: I pray God avert his Judgments; we have had of late severall Comets, which though I believe appeare from natural Causes, & of themselves operate not, yet I cannot despise them; They may be warnings from God, as they commonly are for-runners of his Annimadversions: After some daies this plainly appeared to be headed with a small hazy-starr distant from Venus 23°-58′ & the bright st: of Aquila 28-15-½-5°-09 Latitude-9°-44 South, the taile or point extending to the middle of Sagitta above a degree broad, & was 35 deg: long.

[1681] 24 (Nov). I was at the Audience of the Russia Ambassador which was befor both their Majesties in the Banqueting-house: The presents were carried before them, held up by his followers standing in two rankes towards the Kings state, & consisted of Tapissry (one suit of which was doubtlesse brought from France as being of that fabric, this Ambassador having passed through that Kingdom as he came out of Spaine) a large Persian Carpet, Furrs of Sable & Ermine &c: but nothing was so splendid & exotick, as the Ambassador Who came soone after his Majesties restauration: This present Ambassador was exceedingly offended that his Coach was not permited to come into the Court; til being told that no Kings Ambassadors did, he was pacified, yet requiring an attestation of it under Sir Ch: Cotterells the Master of the Ceremonies hand; being it seemes afraid he should offend his Master if he omitted the least puntillo: 'Twas reported he condemn'd his sonn to loose his head, for shaving off his beard, & putting himselfe in the French mode at Paris, & that he had executed it, had not the french King interceeded: of this *quaere*:

[1682] 27 (Jan). This Evening Sir St. Fox acquainted me againe with his Majesties resolutions of proceeding in his Erection of a Royal Hospital for Emerited Souldiers on that spot of ground The Ro: Society had sold his Majestie for 1300 pounds & that he would settle 5000 pounds per Annum on it, & build to the value of 20000 pounds for the reliefe & reception of 4 Companies, viz. 400 men, to be as in a Coledge or Monastrie: I was therefore desired by Sir Stephen (who had not onely the whole menaging of this, but was (as I perceiv'd) himselfe to be a grand benefactor, as well it became him, who had gotten so vast an Estate by the Souldiers &c) to assist him & Consult what Method to Cast it in, as to the Government: So in his Study, we set downe the Governor, Chaplaine, Steward, Housekeeper, Chirurgion, Cooke, Butler, Gardner, Porter & other Officers, with their severall salaries & entertainements: I would needes have a Librarie, & mentioned severall books &c. since some souldiers might possibly be studious, when they were at this leasure to recolect: Thus we made the first Calculations, & set down our thoughts to be considered & digested better to shew his Majestie & the Archbishop: He also engaged me to consider of what Laws & Orders were fit for the Government, which was to be in every respect as strickt as in any religious Convent &c: After supper, came in the famous Trebble Mr. Abel newly return'd from Italy, & indeede I never heard a more excellent voice, one would have sworne it had been a Womans it was so high, & so well & skillfully manag'd: being accompanied with Signor Francesco on the Harpsichord:

28 Mr. Pepys (late Sec: to the Admiralty) shewed me a large folio containing the whole Mechanic part, & art of Building royal ships & Men of Warr; made by Sir Anth: Deane, being so accurate a Piece, from the very keele to the lead block, rigging, Gunns, Victualing, Manning, even to every individual Pin & naile, in a Method so astonishing & curious; with the draughts both Geometrical, & in Perspective, & severall sections; That I do not think the Whole World can shew the like; I esteeme this one booke above any of the Sybillas, & it is an extraordinary Jewel: hence I returned home.

7 (Feb). I went home: My Daughter Mary now first

began to learne Musick of Signor Bartholomeo, & Dauncing of Monsieur Isaac, both reputed the best Masters &c: I continu'd ill for 2 fitts after, and then bathing my leggs to the knees in Milk made as hott as I could endure it, & sitting so in it, in a deepe Churn or Vessell, Covered with blanquets & drinking Carduus posset, then going to bed & sweating, I not onely missed that expected fit, but had no more; onely continued so weake that I could not go to church 'til Ash-wednesday, which I had not missed I think so long in twenty yeares, so long had God ben gracious to me:

After this Warning & admonition, I now began to looke-over & methodize all my Writings, Accompts, Letters, Papers &c: Inventoried the goods &c of the house, & to put things into the best order I could; & also new made my Will: That growing now in yeares, I might have none of these secular things & Concernes, to distract me, whensoever it should please Almighty God to call me from this transitorie life: And with this prepared me some special Meditations & devotions for the time of sicknesse: The Lord Jesus grant them Salutary for my poore Soule at that day, that I may obtaine Mercy & acceptance.

22 (March): I dined with severall of the R: Society (as frequently we did on the meeting daies) & the President being absent, I was voted into the Chaire: Severall letters from abroad were red, & answers ordered to them: There was shewed a live Scorpion found in an Oyle-shop in Lond: Also were presented divers faire pieces of Amber from the Duke of Brandenburg, in one of which was a large spider, in another a gnat, both very intire & rare: The experiment for the day, was the Anatomical demonstration of Dr. Tysons, of the decussations of the optic-nerves, so as to cause the sight to be single, & not double, from the paralelle fibres on the Retina, exactly answering one-the-other, which being by any accident distorted, caused Squinting, & indirect Vision &c: Then follow'd a discourse in Latine, endeavoring to shew how much wider the pores of Gold were than Silver; & affirm'd to be the occasion

of the operation of *Aqua regalis* upon it, insinuating more easily; which being reasoned upon, was rejected: Also there was a discourse of the tinging of Glasse, especialy with red, & the difficulty of finding any red colour effectual, to penetrate glasse among the glasse-painters; That the most diaphanous as blew, yellow &c did not enter into the substance of what was ordinarily painted, but very shallowly, unlesse incorporated in the mettal itselfe, other redds & whites, not at all farther than to the superficies onely: &c:

30 (Oct) Being my Birth-day, and I now entering my greate Climacterical of 63, after serious Recollection of the yeares past, giving Almighty God thanks for all his mercifull preservations & forbearance; beging pardon for my sinns & unworthinesse, & his blessing & mercy on me the Yeare entering: I went with my Lady Fox, to survey her Building, and give some direction for the Garden at Chiswick: The Architect is Mr. May, somewhat heavy & thick; & not so well understood: The Garden much too narrow, the place without water, neere an high way, & another greate house of my Lord Burlingtons; little Land about it; so as I wonder at the expence; but Women will have their Will.

[1683] 16 (March) I went to see Sir Josiah Childs prodigious Cost in planting of Walnut trees, about his seate, & making fish-ponds, for many miles in Circuite, in Eping-forest, in a Cursed & barren spot; as commonly these over growne & suddainly monied men for the most part seate themselves: He from an ordinary Merchants Apprentice, & managements of the E. India Comp: Stock, being arived to an Estate of (tis said) 200000 pounds: & lately married his daughter to the Eldest sonn of the Duke of Beaufort, late Marques of Worcester, with 30000 pounds portion at present, & various expectations: This Merchant, most sordidly avaricious &c:

17 (June). I visited my Lady Arlington Groome of the

Stoole to her Majestie, who being hardly set downe to supper, word was brought her, that the Queene was going into the Park, to walke, it being now neere Eleaven at night; The alarme caused this Countesse to rise in all hast, leave her supper to us; by which one may take an estimate of the extreame slavery & subjection that Courtiers live in, who have not time to eate & drinke at their pleasure; & put me in mind of Horace's Mouse, & to blesse God for my owne private Condition.

15 (July) A stranger preached on 6. Jer: 8: The not harkning to Instruction, portentous of desolation to a people: The old man preached much after Bish: Andrews's method, full of Logical divisions, in short, & broken periods, & latine sentences, now quite out of fashion in the pulpet, grown into a far more profitable way, of plaine & practical, of which sort this Nation nor any other ever had greater plenty, & more profitable (I am confident) since the Apostles time: so much has it to answer for thriving no better on it:

Pomerid: our Curate on 11: Matt: 28. The sweete Invitation of Christ to over laden sinners:

The whole Nation was now in greate Consternation, upon the late Plot & Conspiracy; his Majestie very Melancholic, & not stirring without redoubled Guards, all the Avenues & private dores about White-hall & the Park shut up; few admitted to walke in it: The Papists in the meane while very jocond, & indeede they had reason, seeing their owne plot brought to nothing, & turn'd to ridicule & now a Conspiracy of Protestants, as they cald them: The Turk likewise in hostility against the German Emperor, almost Master of the upper Hungarie & drawing towards Vienna; on the other side the French (who tis believed brought in the Infidel) disturbing their Spanish, & Dutch Neighbours, & almost swallowed, all Flanders, pursuing his ambition of a fift & Universal Monarchy; & all this blood, & dissorder in Christendome had evidently its rise from our defections at home, in a Wanton peace, minding nothing but Luxurie, Ambition, & to procure Mony for our Vices: To this add our irreligion & Atheisme, greate ingratitude & selfe Interest: the Apostacie of some, & the Suffering the French to grow so Greate, and the Hollanders so Weake. In a word we were Wanton, madd, and surfeiting with prosperity, every moment unsettling the old foundations, & never constant to any thing. The Lord in mercy avert the sad Omen; & that we do not provoke him farther, 'til he beare it no longer:

18 (Sept) I went to Lond: to visite & waite on the Dutchesse of Grafton now greate with Child, a most vertuous & beautifull Lady, & dining with her at my Lord Chamberlains met my Lo: of St. Albans, now growne so blind, that he could not see to the taking his meate: It is incredible how easy a life this Gent: has lived, & in what plenty even abroad, whilst his Majestie wàs a sufferer; nor lesse, the immense summs he has lost at play, which yet at about 80 yeares old he continues, having one that sets by him to name the spot in the Chards: He eate & dranke with extraordinary appetite. He is with all this a prudent old Courtier, & much inrich'd since his Majesties returne.

After dinner I walked to survey the sad demolitions of Clarendon house that costly & onely sumptuous Palace of the late L. Chancelor Hydes, where I have often ben so cherefull with him, & so sad; hapning to make him a visite but the day before he fled from the angry Parliament, accusing him of maladministration, & envious at his grandure, who from a private lawyer, came to be fatherinlaw to the Duke of York; &, as some would suggest, designing his Majesties marriage with the Infanta of Portugal, not apt to breede; To this they imputed much of our unhappinesse, & that being sole Minister & favorite at his Majesties Restauration he neglected to gratifie his Majesties suffering party, for the rewards he received of his richer, & disloyal subjects, who were the cause of our troubles: But perhapps as many of these were injuriously laied to his charge; so he kept the Government far steadier than since it has proved: I could name some others who I thinke contributed greately to his ruine, The bouffones, and the Misses to whom he was an Eye sore: 'Tis true he was of a jolly temper, after the old English fashion; but France had now the ascendant, & we become quite another nation.

[1684] 24 (Jan) The frost still continuing more & more severe, the Thames before London was planted with bothes in formal streetes, as in a Citty, or Continual faire, all sorts of Trades & shops furnished, & full of Commodities, even to a Printing presse, where the People & Ladys tooke a fansy to have their names Printed & the day & yeare set down, when printed on the Thames: This humour tooke so universaly, that 'twas estimated the Printer gained five pound a day, for printing a line onely, at six-pence a Name, beside what he gott by Ballads &c: Coaches now plied from Westminster to the Temple, & from severall other staires too & froo, as in the streetes; also on sleds, sliding with skeetes; There was likewise Bull-baiting, Horse & Coach races, Pupet-plays & interludes, Cookes & Tipling, & lewder places; so as it seem'd to be a bacchanalia, Triumph or Carnoval on the Water, whilst it was a severe Judgement upon the Land: the Trees not onely splitting as if lightning-strock, but Men & Cattell perishing in divers places, and the very seas so locked up with yce, that no vessells could stirr out, or come in: The fowle Fish & birds, & all our exotique Plants & Greenes universaly perishing; many Parks of deere destroied, & all sorts of fuell so deare that there were greate Contributions to preserve the poore alive; nor was this severe weather much lesse intense in most parts of Europe even as far as Spaine, & the most southern tracts: London, by reason of the excessive coldnesse of the aire, hindring the ascent of the smoke, was so filld with the fuliginous steame of the Sea-Coale, that hardly could one see crosse the streete, & this filling the lungs with its grosse particles exceedingly obstructed the breast, so as one could scarce breath: There was no water to be had from the Pipes & Engines, nor could the Brewers, and divers other

Tradesmen work, & every moment was full of disastrous accidents &c:

13 (Feb) Dr. Tenison communicating to me his intention of Erecting a Library in St. Martines parish, for the publique use, desird my assistance with Sir Chr: Wren about the placing & structure thereof: a worthy & laudable designe: He told me there were 30 or 40 Young Men in Orders in his Parish, either, Governors to young Gent: or Chaplains to Noble-men, who being reprov'd by him upon occasion, for frequenting Taverns or Coffè-houses, told him, they would study & employ their time better, if they had books: This put the pious Doctor upon this designe, which I could not but approve of, & indeede a greate reproch it is, that so great a Citty as Lond: should have never a publique Library becoming it: There ought to be one at S. Paules, the West end of that Church (if ever finish'd), would be a convenient place:

12 (June) I went to advise & give directions about the building of two streetes in Berkeley Gardens, reserving the house, & as much of the Garden as the breadth of the house; in the meane time I could not but deplore that sweete place (by farr the most pleasant & noble Gardens Courts and Accommodations, statly porticoes &c any where about the Towne) should so much of it be streitned & turn'd into Tennements; but that magnificent pile & Gardens contiguous to it (built by the late L. Chancellor Hyde with so vast cost) being all demolish'd, & design'd for piazzas & buildings, was some excuse for my Lady Berkleys resolution of leting out her ground also, for so excessive a price as was offerd, advancing her revenue neere 1000 pounds per Ann: in meere Ground rents; to such a mad intemperance the age was come of building about a Citty, by far too disproportionat already to the Nation, I having in my time seene it almost as large more than it was within my memorie. I return'd home this evening.

22 (Oct) At the same time I went to see a living Crocodile, brought from some of the W: Indian Ilands, in every respect resembling the Egyptian Crocodile, it was not yet fully 2 yards from head to taile, very curiously scaled & beset with impenetrable studds of a hard horny substance, & most beautifully ranged in works especialy on the ridge of the back & sides, of a dusky greene Colour, save the belly, which being tender, & onely vulnerable, was of a lively & lovely greene, as lizards are, whose shape it exactly kept: The Eyes were sharp & piercing, over which it could at pleasure draw up a thin cobweb skinn: The rictus was exceeding deepe set with a tirrible rank of sharp & long teeth: We could not discerne any tongue, but a small lump of flesh at the very bottome of its throate, which I suppose helped his swallowing: the feete were divided into long fingers as the Lizards, & he went forward wadling, having a chaine about the neck: seemed to be very tame; I made its keeper take up his upper jaw which he affirmed did onely move, & so Pliny & others confidently report; but it did not appeare so plaine to me, whither his keeper did not use some dexterity in opening his mouth & placing his head so as to make it seeme that the upper chap, was loose; since in that most ample & perfect sceleton in our Repositarie at the R: Society, it is manifestly fixed to the neck & Vertebrae: the neither jaw onely loose: They kept the beast or Serpent in a longish Tub of warme Water, & fed him with flesh &c: If he grow, it will be a dangerous Creature.

December. St. Andrews day being on the Sonday, our Election & meeting of the R: Society was on Moneday, when I brought the Duke of Norfolck & Earle of Clarendon to the Society, who being first ballotted & chosen, tooke their places, & were after chosen also of the Council for this yeare, as was also myselfe: Mr. Pepys, Secretary of the Admiralty elected President.

[1685] 4 (Feb) I went to Lond, hearing his Majestie had

ben the noneday before surpriz'd in his bed chamber with an Apoplectical fit, & so, as if by Gods providence, Dr. King (that excellent chirurgeon as well as Physitian) had not ben accidentaly present to let him bloud with his lancet in his pocket his Majestie had certainely died that moment, which might have ben of direfull consequence, there being no body else with the King save this doctor & one more, as I am assured: It was a mark of the extraordinary dexterity, resolution & presentnesse of Judgment in the Doctor to let him bloud in the very paroxysme, without staying the coming of other physitians, which regularly should have ben done, & the not doing so, must have a formal pardon as they tell me: This rescued his Majestie for that instant, but it prov'd only a reprieve for a little time; he still complain'd & was relapsing & often fainting & sometimes in Epileptical symptoms 'til Wednesday, for which he was cupp'd, let bloud againe in both jugularies, had both vomit & purges &c: which so relieved him, that on the Thursday hops of recovery were signified in the publique Gazett; but that day about noone the Physitians conjectur'd him somewhat feavorish; This they seem'd glad of, as being more easily alaied, & methodicaly to be dealt with, than his former fits, so as they prescrib'd the famous Jesuits powder; but it made his Majestie worse; and some very able Doctors present, did not think it a feavor, but the effect of his frequent bleeding, & other sharp operations used by them about his head: so as probably the powder might stop the Circulation, & renew his former fitts, which now made him very weake: Thus he pass'd Thursday night with greate difficulty, when complaining of a paine in his side, they drew 12 ounces more of blood from him, this was by 6 in the morning on friday, & it gave him relief, but it did not continue; for being now in much paine and strugling for breath, he lay doz'd, & after some conflicts, the Physitians despairing of him, he gave up the Ghost at halfe an houre-after Eleaven in the morning, being the 6 of Feb: in the 36t yeare of his reigne, & 54 of his age: 'Tis not to be express'd the teares & sorrows of Court, Citty & Country: Prayers were solemnly made in all the Churches, especialy in both the Court Chapells, where the Chaplaines relieved one another every halfe quarter of an houre, from the time he began to be in danger, til he expir'd: according to the forme prescribed in the Church office: Those who assisted his Majesties devotion were the A: Bish: of Cant: of London, Durrham & Ely; but more especialy the B: of Bath & Wells. It is sayd they excedingly urged the receiving the H: Sacrament but that his Majestie told them he would Consider of it, which he did so long, 'til it was too late: others whispered, that the Bishops being bid withdraw some time the night before, (except the Earls of Bath, & Feversham), Hurlston the priest, had presum'd to administer the popish Offices; I hope it is not true; but these buisie emissaries are very forwarde upon such occasions: He gave his breeches & Keys to the Duke, who was almost continualy kneeling by his bed side, & in teares; he also recommended to him the care of his natural Children, all except the D: of Monmoth, now in Holland, & in his displeasure; he intreated the Queene to pardon him, (nor without cause) who a little before had sent a Bishop to excuse her not more frequently visiting him, in reguard of her excessive griefe, & with all, that his Majestie would forgive it, if at any time she had offended him: He spake to the Duke to be kind to his Concubines the DD: of Cleveland, & especialy Portsmouth, & that Nelly might not sterve; I do not heare he said any thing of the Church or his people, now falling under the government of a Prince suspected for his Religion, after above 100 yeares the Church & Nation had ben departed from Rome: Thus died K. Charles the 2d, of a Vigorous & robust constitution, & in all appearance capable of a longer life. A prince of many Virtues, & many greate Imperfections, Debonaire, Easy of accesse, not bloudy or Cruel: his Countenance fierce, his voice greate, proper of person, every motion became him, a lover of the sea, & skillfull in shipping, not affecting other studys, yet he had a laboratory and knew of many Empyrical Medicines, & the easier Mechanical Mathematics: Loved Planting, building, & brought in a politer way of living, which passed to Luxurie &

intollerable expense: He had a particular Talent in telling stories & facetious passages of which he had innumerable, which made some bouffoones and vitious wretches too presumptuous, & familiar, not worthy the favours they abused: He tooke delight to have a number of little spaniels follow him, & lie in his bed-Chamber, where often times he suffered the bitches to puppy & give suck, which rendred it very offensive, & indeede made the whole Court nasty & stinking: An excellent prince doubtlesse had he ben lesse addicted to Women, which made him uneasy & allways in Want to supply their unmeasurable profusion, & to the detriment of many indigent persons who had signaly serv'd both him & his father: Easily, & frequently he changed favorites to his greate prejudice &c: As to other publique transactions and unhappy miscarriages, 'tis not here I intend to number them; but certainely never had King more glorious opportunities to have made himselfe, his people & all Europ happy, & prevented innumerable mischiefs, had not his too Easy nature resign'd him to be menag'd by crafty men, & some abandoned & prophane wretches, who corrupted his otherwise sufficient parts, disciplin'd as he had ben by many afflictions, during his banishment: which gave him much experience, & knowledge of men & things: but those wiccked creatures tooke him off from all application becoming so greate a King: the History of his Reigne will certainely be the most wonderfull for the variety of matter & accidents above any extant of many former ages: The sad tragical death of his father, his banishment, & hardships, his miraculous restauration, conjurations against him; Parliaments, Warrs, Plagues, Fires, Comets; revolutions abroad happning in his time with a thousand other particulars: He was ever kind to me & very gracious upon all occasions, & therefore I cannot without ingratitude but deplore his losse, which for many respects (as well as duty) I do with all my soule: . . . (I am never to forget the unexpressable luxury, & prophanesse, gaming, & all dissolution, and as it were total forgetfullnesse of God (it being Sunday Evening) which this day sennight, I was witnesse of; the King, sitting & toying with his Concubines Portsmouth, Cleaveland, & Mazarine: &c: A french boy singing love songs, in that glorious Gallery, whilst about 20 of the greate Courtiers & other dissolute persons were at Basset round a large table, a bank of at least 2000 in Gold before them, upon which two Gent: that were with me made reflexions with astonishment, it being a sceane of uttmost vanity; and surely as they thought would never have an End: six days after was all in the dust.)

14 (Feb) The King was this night very obscurely buried in a Vault under Hen: 7th Chapell in Westminster, without any manner of pomp, and soone forgotten after all this vainity, & the face of the whole Court exceedingly changed into a more solemne and moral behaviour: The new King affecting neither Prophanesse, nor bouffonry: All the Greate Officers broke their white-Staves on the Grave &c: according to forme:

7th (May): I was in Westminster Hall when Oates (who had made such a stirr in the whole Kingdome, (upon his revealing a plot of the Papists) as alarm'd several Parliaments, & had occasion'd the execution of divers persons, priests, noble men &c:) was tried for Perjurie at the Kings-bench; but it being exceedingly tedious, I did not much endeavor to see the issue of it, considering that it would certainely be publish'd. Aboundance of R: Cath: were now in the Hall, in expectation of the most gratefull conviction & ruine of a person who had ben so obnoxious to them; & as I verily believe had don much mischiefe & greate injurie to several by his violent & ill grounded proceedings, whilst he was at first so unreasonably blowne-up, & encourag'd, that his insolence was no longer sufferable:

16 (May) Was sentenc'd Oates to be whip'd & pilloried with uttmost severity: &c:

15 (July): This day was Monmoth brought to Lond: examin'd before the King to whom he made great submission,

acknowledg'd his seduction by Fergusson the Scot, whom he named the bloudy Villain: thence sent to the Tower, had an enterview with his late Dutchesse, whom he received coldly, having lived dishonestly with the Lady Hen: Wentworth for two yeares; from obstinatly asserting his conversation with that debauched woman to be no sin, seing he could not be perswaded to his last breath, the Divines, who were sent to assist him, thought not fit to administer the holy Communion to him: for the rest of his faults he professed greate sorrow, and so died without any apparent feare, would make use of no cap, or other circumstance but lying downe bid the fellow do his office better than to my late Lord Russell, & gave him gold: but the wretch made five Chopps before he had his head off, which so incens'd the people, that had he not ben guarded & got away they would have torne him in pieces: He made no Speech on the Scaffold (which was on Tower-hill) but gave a paper (containing not above 5 or 6 lines) for the King, in which he disclaimes all Title to the Crowne, acknowledges that the late King (his Father) had indeede told him, he was but his base sonn, & so desire'd his Majestie to be kind to his Wife & Children: This Relation I had from the Mouth of Dr. Tenison Rector of St. Martines, who with the Bishops of Ely & Bath & Wells, was one of the divines his Majestie sent to him, & were at the execution: Thus ended this quondam Duke, darling of his Father, and the Ladys, being extraordinarily handsome, and adroit: an excellent souldier, & dauncer, a favorite of the people, of an Easy nature, debauched by lust, seduc'd by crafty knaves who would have set him up onely to make a property; tooke this opportunity of his Majestie being of another Religion, to gather a party of discontented; failed of it, and perished: He was a lovely person, had a vertuous & excellent Lady that brought him greate riches & a second Dukedome in Scotland; Was Master of the Horse, Gen. of the K. his fathers Army, Gent: of the Bed chamber: Knight of the Garter, Chancellor of Camb: in a Word had accumulations without end: Se what Ambition and want of principles brought him to.

20 (July) The Trinity Company met this day, as it should have indeede don on the moneday after Trinity Sonday, which was put off til now, by reason of the royal Charter, which being exceeding large could not be ready before: some other immunities superadded: Mr. Pepys (Secretary of the Admiralty) was a second time chosen Master: present the Duke of Grafton, & Lord of Dartmouth Master of the Ordnance, the Commissioners of the Navy & breathren of that Corporation:

27 (July) This night when we were all asleepe went my Daughter Eliz: away, to meete a young fellow, nephew to Sir Jo: Tippet (Surveyor of the Navy: & one of the Commissioners) whom she married the next day being Tuesday; without in the least acquainting either her parents, or any soule in the house: I was the more afflicted & astonish'd at it, in reguard, we had never given this Child the least cause to be thus dissobedient, and being now my Eldest, might reasonably have expected a double Blessing: But it afterward appeared, that this Intrigue had been transacted by letters long before, & when she was with my Lady Burton in Licester shire, and by private meetings neere my house: She of all our Children had hitherto given us least cause of suspicion; not onely for that she was yet young, but seemed the most flattering, souple and observant; of a silent & particular humor; in no sort betraying the levity & Inclination which is commonly apparent in Children who fall into these snares; having ben bred-up with the uttmost Circumspection, as to principles of severest honour & Piety: But so far it seemes, had her passion for this Young fellow made her forget her duty, and all that most Indulgent Parents expected from her, as not to consider the Consequence of her folly & dissobedience, 'til it was too late: This Affliction went very neere me & my Wife, neither of us yet well compos'd for the untimely losse of that incomparable & excellent Child, which it pleased God to take from us by the small pox a few moneths before: But this farther Chastizement was to be humbly submitted to, as a part of the burden God was pleased to lay farther

upon us; in this yet the lesse afflictive, That we had not ben wanting in giving her an Education every way becoming us: We were most of all astonish'd at the suddainesse of this action, & the privatenesse of its manegement; the Circumstances also Consider'd & quality, how it was possible she should be flattered so to her dissadvantage: He being in no condition sortable to hers, & the Blessing we intended her: The thing has given us much disquiet, I pray God direct us, how to govern our Resentments of her dissobedience; and if it be his will, bring good out of all this Ill:

16 (August) Came newes to us that my undutifull daughter was visited with the small-pox, now universaly very contagious: I was yet willing my Wife should go visite & take care of her:

28 (August) My poore unhappy Daughters sickness increasing, a violent feavor succeeding when her other distemper appeared to be past danger; I went up againe to see, & comfort her, together with our Minister: My disconsolate Wife I left with her, who had ben almost all her sicknesse with her; so I return'd home in greate doubt how God would deale with her, whom the next morning he was pleased to take out of this vale of misery, I humbly trust, to his infinite mercy, though to our unspeakable affliction, loosing another Child in the flower of her age, who had never 'til now given us cause of any displeasure, but many hopes of Comfort: & thus in lesse than 6 moneths were we depriv'd of two Children for our unworthinesse, & causes best known to God, whom I beseech from the bottome of my heart that he will give us grace to make that right use of all these chastisements that we may become better, and intirely submitt in all things to his infinite wise disposal. She departed this life on Saturday 29: Aug: at 8 in the Morning: fell sick & died on the same day of the weeke, that my other most deare & dutifull daughter did, and as also one of my servants (a very pious youth) had don the yeare before: I

beseech God of his mercy Sanctifie this and all other Afflictions & dispensations to me. His holy will be don Amen.

The 3 of Sep: I went to Lond, being sent to by a Letter from my Lord Clarendon (Lord privy-seale) to let me know that his majestie being pleased to send him Lord Lieutennant into Ireland, was also pleased to Nominate me one of the Commissioners to execute the office of Privy-Seale during his Lieutenancy there: It behoving me 4 to waite upon his Majestie & to give him thanks for his greate honor (returning home that Evening) I accompanied his Lordship 5 the next morning to Windsore (dining by the way at Sir Hen: Capels at Cue) where his Majestie receiving me with extraordinary kindnesse, I kissed his hands: I told him how sensible I was of his Majesties gracious favour to me: that I would endeavour to serve him with all sincerity, dilligence & loyalty, not more out of my duty, than Inclinations: He said, he doubted not of it, & was glad he had this opportunity to shew the kindnesse he had for me:

15 (Sept) I went to Lond: accompanied Mr. Pepys (Secretary of the Admiralty) to Portsmouth, Whither his Majestie was going the first time since his coming to the Crowne, to see in what state the Fortifications were:

28 (Oct) I went to the R: Society, being the first meeting after our Summer recesse, & was very full: An Urn full of bones, was presented, for the repository, dug up in an high way, by the repairers of it: in a field in Camberwell in Surry: This Urn & cover was found intire among many others; believed to be truely Roman & antient: Sir Ri: Bulkeley, described to us a model of a Charriot he had invented, which it was not possible to overthrow, in whatsoever uneven way it was drawn: giving us a stupendious relation, of what it had perform'd in that kind; for Ease, expedition, & Safty: There was onely these inconveniences yet to be remedied; that it would not containe above one person; That it was ready to fire every 10 miles, & being

plac'd & playing on no fewer than 10 rollers, made so prodigious noise, as was almost intollerable: These particulars the Virtuosi were desir'd to excogitate the remedies, to render the Engine of extraordinary Use: &c:

5 (Nov) It being an extraordinary wett morning, & I indisposed by a very greate rheume, I could not go to Church this day, to my greate sorrow, it being the first Gunpowder conspiracy Anniversary, that had ben kept now this 80 yeares, under a Prince of the Roman Religion: Bonfires forbidden &c: What dos this portend?

[1686] 12 (March) There was a doquett to be sealed importing a Lease of 21 yeares to one Hall, who styled himselfe his Majesties Printer (& lately turn'd Papist) for the printing Missals, Offices, Lives of Saints, Portals, Primers &c: books expressly forbidden to be printed or sold, &c by divers Acts of Parliament: which I refused to put the seale to, & made my exceptions against, so it was laied by:

26 (Nov) I dine'd at my L. Chancelors, where being 3 other Serjants at Law, after dinner being cherefull & free, they told their severall stories, how long they had detained their clients in tedious processes, by their tricks, as if so many highway thieves should have met & discovered the severall purses they had taken: This they made but a jeast of: but God is not mocked:

[1687] 13 (March) I went this Evening to see the order of the Boys & children at Christs hospital, there was neere 800 of them, Boys & Girles: so decently clad, cleanely lodged, so wholesomly fed, so admirably taught, some the Mathematics, Especialy the 40 of the late Kings foundation; that I was plainly astonished to see the progresse some little youths of 13 & 14 years of age, had made: I saw them at supper, visited their dormitories, admired the order, Oeconomie, & excellent government of this most charitable seminary: The rest, some are tought for the Universitie, others designed for seamen, all for Trades & Callings: The Girles instructed in all such worke as became their Sex, & as might fit them to make good Wives, Mistresses, & a blessing to their generation: They sung a Psalme before they sat downe to supper, in the greate hall, to an Organ which played all the time, & sung with that cherefull harmony, as seem'd to me a vision of heavenly Angels: & I came from the place with infinite Satisfaction, having never in my life seene a more noble, pious, & admirable Charity: All these consisting of Orphans onely:

[1688] 8 (June) This day were the Arch-Bishop of Canterbery together with the Bishops of Ely, Chichester, St. Asaph, Bristol, Peterborow & Bath & Wells, sent from the Privy Council, Prisoners to the Tower, for refusing to give baile for their appearance (upon their not reading the Declaration for Liberty of Conscience) because in giving baile, they had prejudiced their Peerage: Wonderfull was the concerne of the people for them, infinite crowds of people on their knees, beging their blessing & praying for them as they passed out of the Barge; along the Tower wharfe &c:

10 A young Prince borne &c. (which will cost dispute.)

8 (Nov) I went to Lond: heard the newes of the Prince of Oranges being landed at Tor-bay, with a fleete of neere 700 saile, so dreadfull a sight passing through the Channell with so favorable a Wind, as our Navy could by no meanes intercept or molest them: This put the King & Court into greate Consternation, now employed in forming an Army to incounter their farther progresse: for they were gotten already into Excester, & the season, & wayes very improper for his Majesties forces to march so greate a distance:

2 (Dec) Visited my L. Godolphin, then going with the Marquis of Halifax, & E: of Notingham as Commissioner to

the Prince of Orange: He told me, they had little power: Plymouth declared for the Prince & L: Bath: Yorke, Hull, Bristoll, all the eminent nobility & persons of quality throout England declare for the Protestant Religion & Laws, & go to meete the Prince; who every day sets forth new declarations &c: against the Papists: The Greate favorits at Court, priests & Jesuites, flie or abscond: Every thing (til now conceiled) flies abroad in publique print, & is Cryed about the streetes: Expectations of the Pr: coming to Oxon: Pr: of Wales & greate Treasure sent daily to Portsmouth, Earle of Dover Governor: Addresse from the Fleete not gratefull to his Majestie: The Popists in offices lay down their Commissions & flie: Universal Consternation amongst them: it lookes like a Revolution: Herbert beates a french fleete:

18 (Dec) The Pr: comes to St. James, fills W-hall (the King taking barge to Gravesend at 12 a Clock) with Dutch Guard: A Council of Peres meete about an Expedient to call a parliament: Adjourne to the House of Lords: The Chancelor, E. of Peterbor, & divers Priests & other taken: E: of Sunderland flies & divers others, Sir E: Hales, Walker & other taken & secured: All the world go to see the Prince at St. Jamess where is a greate Court, there I saw him & severall of my Acquaintance that come over with him: He is very stately, serious, & reserved: The Eng: souldiers &c. sent out of Towne to distant quarters: not well pleased: Divers reports & opinions, what all this will end in; Ambition & faction feared:

24 (Dec) The King passes into France, whither the queen & child wer gon a few days before.

[1689] I saw the new Queene & King, so proclaim'd, the very next day of her coming to White-hall, Wednesday 13. Feb. with wonderfull acclamation & general reception, Bonfires, bells, Gunns &c: It was believed that they both, especialy the Princesse, would have shewed some (seeming) reluctancy at least, of assuming her Fathers Crowne & made some Apologie, testifying her regret, that he should by his misgoverment necessitat the Nation to so extraordinary a proceeding, which would have shewed very handsomly to the world, (and according to the Character given of her piety &c) & consonant to her husbands first Declaration, that there was no intention of Deposing the King, but of Succoring the Nation; But, nothing of all this appeared; she came into W-hall as to a Wedding, riant & jolly, so as seeming to be quite Transported: rose early on the next morning of her arival, and in her undresse (as reported) before her women were up; went about from roome to roome, to see the Convenience of White-hall: Lay in the same bed & appartment where the late Queene lay: & within a night or two, sate downe to play at Basset, as the Q. her predecessor us'd to do: smiled upon & talked to every body; so as no manner of change seem'd in Court, since his Majesties last going away, save that the infinite crowds of people thronged to see her, & that she went to our prayers: This carriage was censured by many: she seemes to be of a good nature, & that takes nothing to heart whilst the Pr: her husband has a thoughtfull countenance, is wonderfull serious & silent, seemes to treate all persons alike gravely:

16 (June) K: James's declaration was now dispersed, offring pardon to all if upon his landing or 20 days after, they should returne to their obedience:

Our Fleete, not yet at sea, & thro some prodigious sloth, & mens minding only their present Interest: The French riding master at Sea, taking many great prises, to our wonderfull Reproch: No certaine newes from Ireland, various reports of Scotland, discontents at home: The K. of Denmark at last joyning with the Confederates: & the two Northern Princes reconciled:

The E. India Company like to be disolv'd by the Parliament for many arbitrarie actions:

Oates acquitted of perjurie to all honest mens admiration.

8 (July) To Lond: 9 I sat for my Picture to Mr. Kneller, for Mr. Pepys late Secretary of the Admiralty, holding my *Sylva* in my right hand: It was upon his long and earnest request; & is plac'd in his Library: nor did Kneller ever paint better & more masterly work:

31 (Oct): My Birthday, being now 69 years old: Blessed Father who hast prolonged my years to this greate Age, & given me to see so greate & wonderfull Revolutions, preserved me amidst them, to this moment; accept I beseech thee the continuance of my Prayers & thankfull acknowledgements, and graunt to me the Grace to be working out my Salvation, & redeeme the Time, that thou mayst be glorified by me here, & my immortal Soule saved, when ever thou shall call for it, to perpetuate thy prayes to all eternity, in that heavenly Kingdome, where there is no more Changes, nor Vicissitudes, but rest & peace, & Joy & consummate felicity for ever: Grant this ô heavenly Father, for the sake of the L. Jesus, thyne onely Sonn & our Saviour: Amen:

[1690] 10 (June) I went to Lond: Mr. Pepys read to me his Remonstrance, shewed with what malice & injustice he was suspected, with Sir Ant: Deane, about the Timber of which the 30 ships were built by a late Act of Parliament: with the exceeding danger the present Fleet would be shortly in by reason of the Ignorance & incompetency of those who now manag'd the Admiralty & affaires of the Navy, of which he gave an accurate state, & shewed his greate abillitie.

24 (June) Dined with & Visited me Mr. Pepys, Mr. Stuart & other friends. Mr. P: sent the next day to the Gate-house, & severall greate persons to the Towre, on suspicion of being affected to K. James: amongst which was my Lord Earle of Clarendon, unkle to the Queene.

[1692] 25 [July] We went to Mr. Hewers's to Clappham,

who has a very excellent, usefull & Capacious House upon the Common: built by Sir Den: Gauden, & by him sold to Mr. Ewers, who got a very Considerable Estate in the Navy, in which, (from being Mr. Pepys's Cleark) he came to be one of the principal Officers, but was put out of all Employment upon the Revolution, as were all the best Officers, upon suspicion of being no friends to the change: & such put in their place, as were most shamefully Ignorant: & unfit: Mr. Hewers lives very handsomly and friendly to every body &c.

[1694] May 4th. I went this day, with my Wife & 3 Servants from Says-Court, & removing much furniture of all sorts, books, Pictures, Hangings, bedding &c: to furnish the Appartment my Brother assign'd me; & now after more than 40 yeares, to spend the rest of my dayes with him at Wotton, where I was borne; leaving my House, & 3 servants at my house at Deptford (full furnished) to my Son in Law Draper, to passe the summer in & what longer time he thought good to make use of it: I pray God this solemn Remove may be to the Glory of his mercy, & the good of my family:

[1703] 26 (May) This day dyed Mr. Sam: Pepys, a very worthy, Industrious, & curious person, none in England exceeding him in the Knowledge of the Navy, in which he had passed thro all the most Considerable Offices, Clerk of the Acts, & Secretary to the Admiralty, all which he performed with greate Integrity: when K: James the 2d went out of England he layed down his Office, & would serve no more: But withdrawing himselfe from all publique Affairs, lived at Clapham with his partner (formerly his Cleark) Mr. Hewer, in a very noble House & sweete place, where he injoyed the fruit of his labours in greate prosperity, was universaly beloved, Hospitable, Generous, Learned in many things, skill'd in Musick, a very greate Cherisher of Learned men, of whom he had the Conversation. His Library & other Collections of Curiositys was one of the most Considerable; The models of Ships expecialy &c.

Beside what he boldly published of an Account of the Navy, as he found & left it, He had for divers years under his hand the History of the Navy, or, *Navalia* (as he call'd it) but how far advancd & what will follow of his, is left I suppose to his sisters son Mr. Jackson, a young Gent: whom his Unkle had educated in all sorts of usefull learning, Travell abroad, returning with extraordinary Accomplishments, & worthy to be his Heire: Mr: Pepys had ben for neere 40 years, so my particular Friend, that he now sent me Compleat Mourning: desiring me to be one to hold up the Pall at his magnificent Obsequies; but my present Indisposition, hindred me from doing him this last Office:

[1706] Jan: 1 Making up my Accompts for the past yeare, payed Wages, Bills, New years Gifts according to Custome, &c: Tho much Indisposed, & in so advanced an Age I went to our Chapell to give God publique Thanks: Beseeching Almighty God, to assist me with his Mercy & protection to me & my Family the Ensuing yeare, if he should yet Continue my Pilgrimage here, & bring me at last to a better life with him in his heavenly Kingdom.

Divers of our Friends & Relations dined with us this day.

6 Epiphany Exceedingly Indispos'd: I could not go to church, which I believe in very many yeares I have not omitted: And this whole Weeke, I had 3 fits of a shaking-fit, and feavor, with greate paines in the Kidneys, which much afflicted me: Some Snow & sharp dayes:

13 I got to church in the Afternoone, but was exceeding drowsy: A Chap of the Bishop of Lond 2 Ephes: 17.

House of Comm, settling the Regency, in Case of the Q. death; & about admitting no officers Members in the future Elections.

I was much Indisposed most of this weeke:

20 A Lecturer in the morning on 7 Ecles: 14. The goodnesse of God, in giving us time to Consider of our ways & life in Affiiction; the Infinite folly & madnesse to protract it, whilst in

health & prosperity, since Affliction one way or other will or may befalle us here.

The holy Sacrament followed, at which I received, The Lord make me mindfull.

Afternoone, another, on 11 Matt. 6: Christs being the Messias, doubted of by Johns disciples, & others, were sent to our B. Saviour to be convinced by his Miracles &c that he was the true Messias, which by reason of his meane appearance, they questioned: whilst John himselfe firmly believed & affirmed, from the moment of the Voice & dove sent on him at his Baptism. The inference was, that the humility of our B. Lord, should teach us to Imitate his Grace in whomsoever, & not to be Scandalized or be offended upon such Circumstances in the faithfull: I was exceeding drowsy, which God in mercy pardon, for the rest better than before:

No Intelligence publique:

27 The Raine and a Thaw upon a deepe Snow, hindred me from going to Church.

My Infirmitys increasing, I was exceeding ill this whole weeke.

Feb. 3. A stranger at our Chapell on 19 Levit: 17, the necessity of warning a Brother or Christian, & method of Admonition, when we find any go astray or do amisse, with the Rules to be observed, according to the danger and natur of the fault &c.

Afternoon, a Scotchman, on 'Let every one that names the L. Jesus depart from Evill, & increase in love of that profession.'

EVELYN'S EPITAPH

Here lies the Body
of JOHN EVELYN Esq.
of this place second son
of RICHARD EVELYN Esq.
who having served ye Publick
in several employments, of which that
of Com'issioner of ye Privy Seal in ye
Reign of K. James ye 2d was most
Honourable: & perpetuated his fame
by far more lasting Monuments than
those of Stone, or Brass, his Learned
& usefull works fell asleep ye 27th day
of February 170$\frac{5}{6}$ being ye 86th Year
of his age in a full hope of a glorious
resurrection thro' faith in Jesus Christ.
Living in an age of extraordinary
events, & revolutions he learn't
(as himself asserted) this truth
which pursuant to his intention
is here declared
That all is vanity wch is not honest,
& that there's no solid Wisdom
but in real Piety.
Of five Sons, & three Daughters
borne to him from his most
vertuous, & excellent Wife
MARY sole daughter, & heiress
of Sr RICHd BROWNE of Sayes
Court near Deptford in Kent
onely one daughter SUSANNA
married to WILLm DRAPER
Esq. of Adscomb in this County
survived him, ye two others

dying in ye flower of their
age & all ye Sons very young
except one nam'd JOHN, who
deceasd ye 24th of March $169\frac{8}{9}$
in ye 45th year of his age,
leaving one son JOHN, & one
daughter ELIZABETH.

EXTRACTS FROM THE DIARY OF SAMUEL PEPYS

[1660] Blessed be God, at the end of the last year I was in very good health, without any sense of my old pain, but upon taking of cold. I lived in Axe Yard, having my wife, and servant Jane, and no more in family than us three.

The condition of the State was thus; viz. the Rump, after being disturbed by my Lord Lambert, was lately returned to sit again. The officers of the Army all forced to yield. Lawson lies still in the river, and Monk is with his army in Scotland. Only my Lord Lambert is not yet come into the Parliament, nor is it expected that he will without being forced to it. The new Common Council of the City do speak very high; and had sent to Monk their sword-bearer, to acquaint him with their desires for a free and full Parliament, which is at present the desires, and the hopes, and expectation of all. Twenty-two of the old secluded members having been at the House-door the last week to demand entrance, but it was denied them; and it is believed that neither they nor the people will be satisfied till the House be filled. My own private condition very handsome, and esteemed rich, but indeed very poor; besides my goods of my house, and my office, which at present is somewhat uncertain. Mr. Downing master of my office.

January 1st (Lord's day). This morning (we living lately in the garret,) I rose, put on my suit with great skirts, having not lately worn any other clothes but them. Went to Mr. Gunning's chapel at Exeter House, where he made a very good sermon upon these words:—"That in the fulness of time God sent his Son, made of a woman," &c.; showing, that, by "made under the law," is meant his circumcision, which is solemnized this day. Dined at home in the garret, where my wife dressed the remains of a turkey, and in the doing of it she burned her hand. I staid at home all the afternoon, looking over my accounts;

then went with my wife to my father's, and in going observed the great posts which the City have set up at the Conduit in Fleet-street. Supt at my father's, where in came Mrs. The. Turner and Madam Morrice, and supt with us. After that my wife and I went home with them, and so to our own home.

January 16th. In the morning I went up to Mr. Crew's, and at his bedside he gave me direction to go to-morrow with Mr. Edward to Twickenham, and likewise did talk to me concerning things of state; and expressed his mind how just it was that the secluded members should come to sit again. I went from thence, and in my way went into an alehouse and drank my morning draft with Matthew Andrews and two or three more of his friends, coachmen. And of one of them I did hire a coach to carry us to-morrow to Twickenham. From thence to my office, where nothing to do; but Mr. Downing he came and found me all alone; and did mention to me his going back into Holland, and did ask me whether I would go or no, but gave me little encouragement, but bid me consider of it; and asked me whether I did not think that Mr. Hawly could perform the work of my office alone or no. I confess I was at a great loss, all the day after, to bethink myself how to carry this business. At noon, Harry Ethall came to me and went along with Mr. Maylard by coach as far as Salsbury Court, and there we set him down, and we went to the Clerks, where we came a little too late, but in a closet we had a very good dinner by Mr. Pinkny's courtesy, and after dinner we had pretty good singing, and one, Hazard, sung alone after the old fashion, which was very much cried up, but I did not like it. Thence we went to the Green Dragon, on Lambeth Hill, both the Mr. Pinkney's, Smith, Harrison, Morrice, that sang the bass, Sheply and I, and there we sang of all sorts of things, and I ventured with good success upon things at first sight, and after that I played on my flageolet, and staid there till nine o'clock, very merry and drawn on with one song after another till it came to be so late. After that Sheply, Harrison and myself, we went towards Westminster on foot, and at the Golden Lion, near Charing Cross, we went in and drank a pint of wine, and so parted, and thence home, where I found my wife and maid a-washing. I staid up till the bell-man came by with his bell just under my window as I was writing of this very line, and cried, "Past one of the clock, and a cold, frosty, windy morning." I then went to bed, and left my wife and the maid a-washing still.

March 25th (Lord's day). About two o'clock in the morning, letters came from London by our coxon, so they waked me, but I would not rise but bid him stay till morning, which he did, and then I rose and carried them in to my Lord, who read them a-bed. Among the rest, there was the writ and mandate for him to dispose to the Cinque Ports for choice of Parliament-men. There was also one for me from Mr. Blackburne, who with his own hand superscribes it to S.P.Esq., of which God knows I was not a little proud. After that I wrote a letter to the Clerk of Dover Castle, to come to my Lord about issuing of those writs. About ten o'clock Mr. Ibbott, at the end of the long table, begun to pray and preach and indeed made a very good sermon, upon the duty of all Christians to be stedfast in faith. After that Captain Cuttance and I had oysters, my Lord being in his cabin not intending to stir out to-day. After that up into the great cabin above to dinner with the Captain, where was Captain Isham and all the officers of the ship. I took place of all but the Captains; after dinner I wrote a great many letters to my friends at London. After that, sermon again, at which I slept, God forgive me! After that, it being a fair day, I walked with the Captain upon the deck talking. At night I supped with him and after that had orders from my Lord about some business to be done against to-morrow, which I sat up late and did and then to bed.

October 13th. To my Lord's in the morning, where I met with Captain Cuttance, but my Lord not being up I went out to Charing Cross, to see Major-general Harrison hanged, drawn, and quartered; which was done there, he looking as cheerful as any man could do in that condition. He was presently cut down, and his head and heart shown to the people, at which there was great shouts of joy. It is said, that he said that he was sure to come shortly at the right hand of Christ to judge them that now had judged him; and that his wife do expect his coming again. Thus it was my chance to see the King beheaded at White Hall, and to see the first blood shed in revenge for the blood of the King at Charing Cross. From thence to my Lord's, and took Captain Cuttance and Mr. Sheply to the Sun Tavern, and did give them some oysters. After that I went by water home, where I was angry with my wife for her things lying about, and in my passion kicked the little fine basket, which I bought her in Holland, and broke it, which troubled me after I had done it. Within all the afternoon setting up shelves in my study. At night to bed.

[1661] January 19th. To the Comptroller's, and with him by coach to White Hall; in our way meeting Venner and Pritchard upon a sledge, who with two more Fifth Monarchy men were hanged to-day, and the two first drawn and quartered. Where we walked up and down, and at last found Sir G. Carteret, whom I had not seen a great while, and did discourse with him about our assisting the Commissioners in paying off the Fleet, which we think to decline. Here the Treasurer did tell me that he did suspect Thos. Hater to be an informer of them in this work, which we do take to be a diminution of us, which do trouble me, and I do intend to find out the truth. Hence to my Lady, who told me how Mr. Hetley is dead of the small-pox going to Portsmouth with my Lord. My Lady went forth to dinner to her father's, and so I went to the Leg in King Street and had a rabbit for myself and my Will, and after dinner I sent him home and myself went to the Theatre, where I saw *The Lost Lady*, which do not please me much. Here I was troubled to be seen by four of our office clerks, which sat in the half-crown box and I in the 1s. 6d. From thence by link, and bought two mouse traps of Thomas Pepys, the Turner, and so went and drank a cup of ale with him, and so home and wrote by post to Portsmouth to my Lord and so to bed.

January 28th. At the office all the morning; dine at home, and after dinner to Fleet Street, with my sword to Mr. Brigden (lately made Captain of the Auxiliaries) to be refreshed, and with him to an ale-house, where I met Mr. Davenport, and after some talk of Cromwell, Ireton and Bradshaw's bodies being taken out of their graves to-day, I went to Mr. Crew's and thence to the Theatre, where I saw again *The Lost Lady*, which do now please me better than before; and here I sitting behind in a dark place, a lady spit backward upon me by a mistake, not seeing me, but after seeing her to be a very pretty lady, I was not troubled at it at all. Thence to Mr. Crew's, and there met Mr. Moore, who came lately to me, and went with me to my father's, and with him to Standing's, whither came to us Dr. Fairbrother who I took and my father to the Bear and gave a pint of sack and a pint of claret. He do still continue his expressions of respect and love to me, and tells me my brother John will make a good scholar. Thence to see the Doctor at his lodging at Mr. Holden's, where I bought a hat, cost me 35s. So home by moonshine, and by the way was overtaken by the Comptroller's coach, and so home to his house with him. So home and to bed. This noon I had my press set up in my chamber for papers to be put in.

March 31st (Sunday). At church, where a stranger preached like a fool. From thence home and dined with my wife, she staying at home, being unwilling to dress herself, the house being all dirty. To church again, and after sermon I walked to my father's, and to Mrs. Turner's, where I could not woo The. to give me a lesson upon the harpsicon and was angry at it. So home and finding Will abroad at Sir W. Batten's talking with the people there (Sir W. and my Lady being in the country), I took occasion to be angry with him, and so to prayers and to bed.

April 22nd. KING'S GOING FROM Y TOWER TO WHITE HALL

Up early and made myself as fine as I could, and put on my velvet coat, the first day that I put it on, though made half a year ago. And being ready, Sir W. Batten, my Lady, and his two daughters and his son and wife, and Sir W. Pen and his son and I, went to Mr. Young's, the flag-maker, in Corne-hill; and there we had a good room to ourselves, with wine and good cake, and saw the show very well. In which it is impossible to relate the glory of this day, expressed in the clothes of them that rid, and their horses and horses-clothes, among others, my Lord Sandwich's. Embroidery and diamonds were ordinary among them. The Knights of the Bath was a brave sight of itself; and their Esquires, among which Mr. Armiger was an Esquire to one of the Knights. Remarquable were the two men that represent the two Dukes of Normandy and Aquitane. The Bishops come next after Barons, which is the higher place; which makes me think that the next Parliament they will be called to the House of Lords. My Lord Monk rode bare after the King, and led in his hand a spare horse, as being Master of the Horse. The King, in a most rich embroidered suit and cloak, looked most noble. Wadlow, the vintner, at the Devil, in Fleet-street, did lead a fine company of soldiers, all young comely men, in white doublets. There followed the Vice-Chamberlain, Sir G. Carteret, a company of men all like Turks; but I know not yet what they are for. The streets all gravelled, and the houses hung with carpets before them, made brave show, and the ladies out of the windows, one of which over against us I took much notice of, and spoke of her, which made good sport among us. So glorious was the show with gold and silver, that we were not able to look at it, our eyes at last being so much overcome with it. Both the King and the Duke of York took notice of us, as he saw us at the window. The show being ended, Mr. Young did give us a dinner, at which we were very merry, and pleased above imagination at what we have seen. Sir W. Batten going home, he and I called and drunk some mum and laid our wager about my Lady Faulconbridge's name, which he says not to be Mary, and so I won above 20s. So home, where Will and the boy staid and saw the show upon Towre Hill, and Jane at T. Pepys's, The. Turner, and my wife at Charles Glassecocke's in Fleet Street. In the evening by water to White Hall to my Lord's, and there I spoke with my Lord. He talked with me about his suit, which was made in France, and cost him £200, and very rich it is with embroidery. I lay with Mr. Shepley, and

CORONAC̄ON DAY

April 23rd. About 4 I rose and got to the Abbey, where I followed Sir J. Denham, the Surveyor, with some company that he was leading in. And with much ado, by the favour of Mr. Cooper, his man, did get up into a great scaffold across the North end of the Abbey, where with a great deal of patience I sat from past 4 till 11 before the King came in. And a great pleasure it was to see the Abbey raised in the middle, all covered with red, and a throne (that is a chair) and footstool on the top of it; and all the officers of all kinds, so much as the very fiddlers, in red vests. At last comes in the Dean and Prebends of Westminster, with the Bishops (many of them in cloth of gold copes), and after them the Nobility, all in their Parliament robes, which was a most magnificent sight. Then the Duke, and the King with a scepter (carried by my Lord Sandwich) and sword and mond before him, and the crown too. The King in his robes, bare-headed, which was very fine. And after all had placed themselves, there was a sermon and the service; and then in the Quire at the high altar, the King passed through all the ceremonies of the Coronac̄on, which to my great grief I and most in the Abbey could not see. The crown being put upon his head, a great shout begun, and he came forth to the throne, and there passed more ceremonies: as taking the oath, and having things read to him by the Bishop; and his lords (who put on their caps as soon as the King put on his crown) and bishops come, and kneeled before him. And three times the King at

Arms went to the three open places on the scaffold, and proclaimed, that if any one could show any reason why Charles Stewart should not be King of England, that now he should come and speak. And a Generall Pardon also was read by the Lord Chancellor, and meddalls flung up and down by my Lord Cornwallis, of silver, but I could not come by any. But so great a noise that I could make but little of the musique; and indeed, it was lost to every body. But I went out a little while before the King had done all his ceremonies, and went round the Abbey to Westminster Hall, all the way within rayles, and 10,000 people, with the ground covered with blue cloth; and scaffolds all the way. Into the Hall I got, where it was very fine with hangings and scaffolds one upon another full of brave ladies; and my wife in one little one, on the right hand. Here I staid walking up and down, and at last upon one of the side stalls I stood and saw the King come in with all the persons (but the soldiers) that were yesterday in the cavalcade; and a most pleasant sight it was to see them in their several robes. And the King came in with his crown on, and his sceptre in his hand, under a canopy borne up by six silver staves, carried by Barons of the Cinque Ports, and little bells at every end. And after a long time, he got up to the farther end, and all set themselves down at their several tables; and that was also a brave sight: and the King's first course carried up by the Knights of the Bath. And many fine ceremonies there was of the Heralds leading up people before him, and bowing; and my Lord of Albemarle's going to the kitchen and eat a bit of the first dish that was to go to the King's table. But, above all, was these three Lords, Northumberland, and Suffolk, and the Duke of Ormond, coming before the courses on horseback, and staying so all dinner-time, and at last to bring up Dymock the King's Champion, all in armour on horseback, with his spear and targett carried before him. And a Herald proclaims "That if any dare deny Charles Stewart to be lawful King of England, here was a Champion that would fight with him;" and with these words, the Champion flings down his gauntlet, and all this he do three times in his going up towards the King's table. At last when he is come, the King drinks to him, and then sends him the cup which is of gold, and he drinks it off, and then rides back again with the cup in his hand. I went from table to table to see the Bishops and all others at their dinner, and was infinitely pleased with it. And at the Lords' table, I met with William Howe, and he spoke to my Lord for me, and he did give me four rabbits and a pullet, and so I got it and Mr. Creed and I got Mr. Michell to give us some bread, and so we at a stall eat it, as every body else did what they could get. I took a great deal of pleasure to go up and down, and look upon the ladies, and to hear the musique of all sorts, but above all, the 24 violins. About six at night they had dined, and I went up to my wife, and there met with a pretty lady (Mrs. Frankleyn, a Doctor's wife, a friend of Mr. Bowyer's), and kissed them both, and by and by took them down to Mr. Bowyer's. And strange it is to think, that these two days have held up fair till now that all is done, and the King gone out of the Hall; and then it fell a-raining and thundering and lightening as I have not seen it do for some years: which people did take great notice of; God's blessing of the work of these two days, which is a foolery to take too much notice of such things. I observed little disorder in all this, but only the King's footmen had got hold of the canopy, and would keep it from the Barons of the Cinque Ports, which they endeavoured to force from them again, but could not do it till my Lord Duke of Albemarle caused it to be put into Sir R. Pye's hand till to-morrow to be decided. At Mr. Bowyer's; a great deal of company, some I knew, others I did not. Here we staid upon the leads and below till it was late, expecting to see the fire-works, but they were not performed to-night: only the City had a light like a glory round about it with bonfires. At last I went to King-street, and there sent Crockford to my father's and my house, to tell them I could not come home to-night, because of the dirt, and a coach could not be had. And so after drinking a pot of ale alone at Mrs. Harper's I returned to Mr. Bowyer's, and after a little stay more I took my wife and Mrs. Frankleyn (who I proffered the civility of lying with my wife at Mrs. Hunt's to-night) to Axe-yard, in which at the further end there were three great bonfires, and a great many great gallants, men and women; and they laid hold of us, and would have us drink the King's health upon our knees, kneeling upon a faggot, which we all did, they drinking to us one after another. Which we thought a strange frolique; but these gallants continued thus a great while, and I wondered to see how the ladies did tipple. At last I sent my wife and her bedfellow to bed, and Mr. Hunt and I went in with Mr. Thornbury (who did give the company all their wine, he being yeoman of the wine-cellar to the King) to his house; and there, with his wife and two of his sisters, and some gallant sparks that were there, we drank the King's health, and nothing else, till one of the gentlemen fell down stark drunk, and there lay spewing; and I went to my Lord's pretty well. But no sooner a-bed with Mr. Shepley but my head began to hum, and I to vomit, and if ever I was foxed it was now, which I cannot say yet, because I fell asleep and slept till morning. Only when I waked I found myself wet with my spewing. Thus did the day end with joy every where; and blessed be God, I have not heard of any mischance to any body through it all, but only to Serjt. Glynne, whose horse fell upon him yesterday, and is like to kill him, which people do please themselves to see how just God is to punish the rogue at such a time as this; he being now one of the King's Serjeants, and rode in the cavalcade with Maynard, to whom people wish the same fortune. There was also this night in King-street, a woman had her eye put out by a boy's flinging a firebrand into the coach. Now, after all this, I can say that, besides the pleasure of the sight of these glorious things, I may now shut my eyes against any other objects, nor for the future trouble myself to see things of state and show, as being sure never to see the like again in this world.

July 6th. Waked this morning with news, brought me by a messenger on purpose, that my uncle Robert is dead, and died yesterday; so I rose sorry in some respect, glad in my expectations in another respect. So I made myself ready, went and told my uncle Wight, my Lady, and some others thereof, and bought me a pair of boots in St. Martin's, and got myself ready, and then to the Post House and set out about eleven and twelve o'clock, taking the messenger with me that came to me, and so we rode and got well by nine o'clock to Brampton, where I found my father well. My uncle's corps in a coffin standing upon joynt-stools in the chimney in the hall; but it begun to smell, and so I caused it to be set forth in the yard all night, and watched by two men. My aunt I found in bed in a most nasty ugly pickle, made me sick to see it. My father and I lay together to-night, I greedy to see the will, but did not ask to see it till to-morrow.

September 1st (Lord's day). Last night being very rainy the rain broke into my house, the gutter being stopped, and spoiled all my ceilings almost. At church in the morning, and dined at home with my wife. After dinner to Sir W. Batten's, where I found Sir W. Pen and Captain Holmes. Here we were very merry with Sir W. Pen about the loss of his tankard, though all be but a cheat, and he do not yet understand it; but the tankard was stole by Sir W. Batten, and the letter, as from the thief, wrote by me, which makes very good sport. Here I staid all the afternoon, and then Captain Holmes and I by coach to White Hall; in our way, I found him by discourse, to be a great friend of my Lord's, and he told me there was many did seek to remove him; but they were old seamen, such as Sir J. Minnes (but he would name no more, though I do believe Sir W. Batten is one of them that do envy him), but he says he knows that the King do so love him, and the Duke of York too, that there is no fear of him. He seems to be very well acquainted with the King's mind, and with all the several factions at Court, and spoke all with so much frankness, that I do take him to be my Lord's good friend, and one able to do him great service, being a cunning fellow, and one (by his own confession to me) that can put on two several faces, and look his enemies in the face with as much love as his friends. But, good God! what an age is this, and what a world is this! that a man cannot live without playing the knave and dissimulation. At White-hall we parted, and I to Mrs. Pierce's, meeting her and Madam Clifford in the street, and there staid talking and laughing with them a good while, and so back to my mother's, and there supped, and so home and to bed.

September 29th (Lord's day). To church in the morning, and so to dinner, and Sir W. Pen and daughter, and Mrs. Poole, his kinswoman, Captain Poole's wife, came by appointment to dinner with us, and a good dinner we had for them, and were very merry, and so to church again, and then to Sir W. Pen's and there supped, where his brother, a traveller, and one that speaks Spanish very well, and a merry man, supped with us, and what at dinner and supper I drink I know not how, of my own accord, so much wine, that I was even almost foxed, and my head aked all night; so home and to bed, without prayers, which I never did yet, since I came to the house, of a Sunday night: I being now so out of order that I durst not read prayers, for fear of being perceived by my servants in what case I was. So to bed.

November 3rd (Lord's day). This day I stirred not out, but took physique, and it did work very well, and all the day as I was at leisure I did read in Fuller's *Holy Warr*, which I have of late bought, and did try to make a song in the praise of a liberall genius (as I take my own to be) to all studies and pleasures, but it not proving to my mind I did reject it and so proceeded not in it. At night my wife and I had a good supper by ourselves of a pullet hashed, which pleased me much to see my condition come to allow ourselves a dish like that, and so at night to bed.

December 1st (Lord's day). In the morning at church and heard Mr. Mills. At home dined and with me by appointment Mr. Sanchy, who should have brought his mistress, Mrs. Mary Archer, of Cambridge, but she could not come, but we had a good dinner for him. And so in the afternoon my wife went to church, and he and I stayed at home and drank and talked, and he stayed with me till night and supped with me, when I expected to have seen Jack Cole and Lem. Wagstaffe, but they did not come. We this day cut a brave collar of brawn from Winchcombe which proves very good, and also opened the glass of girkins which Captain Cocke did give my wife the other day, which are rare things. So at night to bed. There hath lately been great clapping up of some old statesmen, such as Ireton, Moyer, and others, and they say, upon a great plot, but I believe no such thing; but it is but justice that they should be served as they served the poor Cavaliers; and I believe it will oftentimes be so as long as I live, whether there be cause or no. This evening my brother Tom was with me, and I did talk again to him about Mr. Townsend's daughter, and I do intend to put the business in hand. I pray God give a good end to it.

December 31st. My wife and I this morning to the Paynter's, and there she sat the last time, and I stood by and did tell him some little things to do, that now her picture I think will please me very well; and after her, her little black dogg sat in her lap, and was drawn, which made us very merry; so home to dinner, and so to the office; and there late finishing our estimate of the debts of the Navy to this day; and it come to near £374,000. So home, and after supper, and my barber had trimmed me, I sat down to end my journell for this year, and my condition at this time, by God's blessing, is thus: my health (only upon catching cold, which brings great pain in my back as it used to be when I had the stone) is very good, and so my wife's in all respects: my servants, W. Hewer, Sarah, Nell, and Wayneman: my house at the Navy Office. I suppose myself to be worth about £500 clear in the world, and my goods of my house my own, and what is coming to me from Brampton, when my father dies, which God defer. But, by my uncle's death, the whole care and trouble of all, and settling of all lies upon me, which is very great, because of law-suits, especially that with T. Trice, about the interest of £200, which will, I hope, be ended soon. My chiefest thought is now to get a good wife for Tom, there being one offered by the Joyces, a cozen of theirs, worth £200 in ready money. I am also upon writing a little treatise to present to the Duke, about our privilege in the seas, as to other nations striking their flags to us. But my greatest trouble is, that I have for this last half year been a very great spendthrift in all manner of respects, that I am afeard to cast up my accounts, though I hope I am worth what I say above. But I will cast them up very shortly. I have newly taken a solemn oath about abstaining from plays and wine, which I am resolved to keep according to the letter of the oath which I keep by me. The fleet hath been ready to sail for Portugall, but hath lacked wind this fortnight, and by that means my Lord is forced to keep at sea all this winter, till he brings home the Queen, which is the expectation of all now, and the greatest matter of publique talk.

[1662] January 1st. Waking this morning out of my sleep on a sudden, I did with my elbow hit my wife a great blow over her face and nose, which waked her with pain, at which I was sorry, and to sleep again. Up and went forth with Sir W. Pen by coach towards Westminster, and in my way seeing that the *Spanish Curate* was acted to-day, I 'light and let him go alone, and I home again and sent to young Mr. Pen and his sister to go anon with my wife and I to the Theatre. That done, Mr. W. Pen came to me and he and I walked out, and to the stationer's, and looked over some pictures and maps for my house, and so home again to dinner, and by and by came the two young Pens, and after we had eat a barrel of oysters we went by coach to the play, and there saw it well acted, and a good play it is, only Diego the Sexton did overdo his part too much. From thence home, and they sat with us till late at night at cards very merry, but the jest was Mr. W. Pen had left his sword in the coach, and so my boy and he run out after the coach, and by very great chance did at the Exchange meet with the coach and got his sword again. So to bed.

February 2nd (Lord's day). To church in the morning, and then home and dined with my wife, and so both of us to church again, where we had an Oxford man give us a most impertinent sermon upon "Cast your bread upon the waters", &c. So home to read, supper, and to prayers, and then to bed.

February 28th. The boy failing to call us up as I commanded, I was angry, and resolved to whip him for that and many other faults, to-day. Early with Sir W. Pen by coach to Whitehall, to the Duke of York's chamber, and there I presented him from my Lord a fine map of Tangier, done by one Captain Beckman, a Swede, that is with my Lord. We staid looking it over a great while with the Duke after he was ready. Thence I by water to the Painter's, and there sat again for my face in little, and thence home to dinner, and so at home all the afternoon. Then came Mr. Moore and staid and talked with me, and then I to the office, there being all the Admiralty papers brought hither this afternoon from Mr. Blackburne's, where they have lain all this while since my coming into this office. This afternoon Mr. Hater received half a year's salary for me, so that now there is not owing me but this quarter, which will be out the next month. Home, and to be as good as my word, I bade Will get me a rod, and he and I called the boy up to one of the upper rooms of the Comptroller's house towards the garden, and there I reckoned all his faults, and whipped him soundly, but the rods were so small that I fear they did not much hurt to him, but only to my arm, which I am already, within a quarter of an hour, not able to stir almost. After supper to bed.

July 9th. Up by four o'clock, and at my multiplicacion-table hard, which is all the trouble I meet withal in my arithmetique. So made me ready and to the office, where all the morning busy, and Sir W. Pen came to my office to take his leave of me, and desiring a turn in the garden, did commit the care of his building to me, and offered all his services to me in all matters of mine. I did, God forgive me! promise him all my service and love, though the rogue knows he deserves none from me, nor do I intend to show him any; but as he dissembles with me, so must I with him. Dined at home, and so to the office again, my wife with me, and while I was for an hour making a hole behind my seat in my closet to look into the office, she was talking to me about her going to Brampton, which I would willingly have her to do but for the cost of it, and to stay here will be very inconvenient because of the dirt that I must have when my house is pulled down. Then to my business till night, then Mr. Cooper and I to our business, and then came Mr. Mills, the minister, to see me, which he hath but rarely done to me, though every day almost to others of us; but he is a cunning fellow, and knows where the good victuals is, and the good drink, at Sir W. Batten's. However, I used him civilly, though I love him as I do the rest of his coat. So to supper and to bed.

July 21st. Up early, and though I found myself out of order and cold, and the weather cold and likely to rain, yet upon my promise and desire to do what I intended, I did take boat and down to Greenwich, to Captain Cocke's, who hath a most pleasant seat, and neat. Here I drank wine, and eat some fruit off the trees; and he showed a great rarity, which was two or three of a great number of silver dishes and plates, which he bought of an embassador that did lack money, in the edge or rim of which was placed silver and gold medalls, very ancient, and I believe wrought, by which, if they be, they are the greatest rarity that ever I saw in my life, and I will show Mr. Crumlum them. Thence to Woolwich to the Rope-yard; and there looked over several sorts of hemp, and did fall upon my great survey of seeing the working and experiments of the strength and the charge in the dressing of every sort; and I do think have brought it to so great a certainty, as I have done the King great service in it: and do purpose to get it ready against the Duke's coming to town to present to him. I breakfasted at Mr. Falconer's well, and much pleased with my inquiries. Thence to the dock, where we walked in Mr.

Shelden's garden, eating more fruit, and drinking, and eating figs, which were very good, and talking while the *Royal James* was bringing towards the dock, and then we went out and saw the manner and trouble of docking such a ship, which yet they could not do, but only brought her head into the Dock, and so shored her up till next tide. But, good God! what a deal of company was there from both yards to help to do it, when half the company would have done it as well. But I see it is impossible for the King to have things done as cheap as other men. Thence by water, and by and by landing at the riverside somewhere among the reeds, we walked to Greenwich, where to Cocke's house again and walked in the garden, and then in to his lady, who I find is still pretty, but was now vexed and did speak very discontented and angry to the Captain for disappointing a gentleman that he had invited to dinner, which he took like a wise man and said little, but she was very angry, which put me clear out of countenance that I was sorry I went in. So after I had eat still some more fruit I took leave of her in the garden plucking apricots for preserving, and went away and so by water home, and there Mr. Moore coming and telling me that my Lady goes into the country to-morrow, I carried my wife by coach to take her leave of her father, I staying in Westminster Hall, she going away also this week, and thence to my Lady's, where we staid and supped with her, but found that my Lady was truly angry and discontented with us for our neglecting to see her as we used to do, but after a little she was pleased as she was used to be, at which we were glad. So after supper home to bed.

November 27th. At my waking, I found the tops of the houses covered with snow, which is a rare sight, that I have not seen these three years. Up, and put my people to perfect the cleaning of my house, and so to the office, where we sat till noon; and then we all went to the next house upon Tower Hill, to see the coming by of the Russia Embassador; for whose reception all the City trained-bands do attend in the streets, and the King's life-guards, and most of the wealthy citizens in their black velvet coats, and gold chains (which remain of their gallantry at the King's coming in), but they staid so long that we went down again home to dinner. And after I had dined, I heard they were coming, and so I walked to the Conduit in the Quarrefowr, at the end of Gracious-street and Cornhill; and there (the spouts thereof running very near me upon all the people that were under it) I saw them pretty well go by. I could not see the Embassador in his coach; but his attendants in their habits and fur caps very handsome, comely men, and most of them with hawkes upon their fists to present to the King. But Lord! to see the absurd nature of Englishmen, that cannot forbear laughing and jeering at every thing that looks strange. So back and to the office, and there we met and sat till seven o'clock, making a bargain with Mr. Wood for his masts of New England, and then in Mr. Coventry's coach to the Temple, but my cozen Roger Pepys not being at leisure to speak to me about my business, I presently walked home, and to my office till very late doing business, and so home, where I found my house more and more clear and in order, and hope in a day or two now to be in very good condition there and to my full content. Which God grant! So to supper and to bed.

December 25th (Christmas Day). Up pretty early, leaving my wife not well in bed, and with my boy walked, it being a most brave cold and dry frosty morning, and had a pleasant walk to White Hall, where I intended to have received the Communion with the family, but I came a little too late. So I walked up into the house and spent my time looking over pictures, particularly the ships in King Henry the VIIIth's Voyage to Bullen; marking the great difference between their build then and now. By and by down to the chappell again where Bishop Morley preached upon the song of the Angels, "Glory to God on high, on earth peace, and good will towards men." Methought he made but a poor sermon, but long, and reprehending the mistaken jollity of the Court for the true joy that shall and ought to be on these days, he particularized concerning their excess in plays and gaming, saying that he whose office it is to keep the gamesters in order and within bounds, serves but for a second rather in a duell, meaning the groom-porter. Upon which it was worth observing how far they are come from taking the reprehensions of a bishop seriously, that they all laugh in the chappell when he reflected on their ill actions and courses. He did much press us to join these publique days of joy, and to hospitality. But one that stood by whispered in my ear that the Bishop himself do not spend one groat to the poor himself. The sermon done, a good anthem followed, with vialls, and then the King came down to receive the Sacrament. But I staid not, but calling my boy from my Lord's lodgings, and giving Sarah some good advice, by my Lord's order, to be sober and look after the house, I walked home again with great pleasure, and there dined by my wife's bed-side with great content, having a mess of brave plum-porridge and a roasted pullet for dinner, and I sent for a mince-pie abroad, my wife not being well to make any herself yet. After dinner sat talking a good while with her, and then to see Sir W. Pen a little, and so to my office, practising arithmetique alone and making an end of last night's book with great content till eleven at night, and so home to supper and to bed.

[1663] January 6th (Twelfth Day). Up and Mr. Creed brought a pot of chocolate ready made for our morning draft, and then he and I to the Duke's, but I was not very willing to be seen at this end of the town, and so returned to our lodgings, and took my wife by coach to my brother's, where I set her down, and Creed and I to St. Paul's Church-yard, to my bookseller's, and looked over several books with good discourse, and then into St. Paul's Church, and there finding Elborough, my old schoolfellow at Paul's, now a parson, whom I know to be a silly fellow, I took him out and walked with him, making Creed and myself sport with talking with him, and so sent him away, and we to my office and house to see all well, and thence to the Exchange, where we met with Major Thomson, formerly of our office, who do talk very highly of liberty of conscience, which now he hopes for by the King's declaration, and that he doubts not that if he will give him, he will find more and better friends than the Bishops can be to him, and that if he do not, there will many thousands in a little time go out of England, where they may have it. But he says that they are well contented that if the King thinks it good, the Papists may have the same liberty with them. He tells me, and so do others, that Dr. Calamy is this day sent to Newgate for preaching, Sunday was se'nnight, without leave, though he did it only to supply the place; when otherwise the people must have gone away without ever a sermon, they being disappointed of a minister: but the Bishop of London will not take that as an excuse. Thence into Wood Street, and there bought a fine table for my dining-room, cost me 50s.; and while we were buying it, there was a scare-fire in an ally over against us, but they quenched it. So to my brother's, where Creed and I and my wife dined with Tom, and after dinner to the Duke's house, and there saw *Twelfth Night* acted well, though it be but a silly play, and not related at all to the name or day. Thence Mr. Battersby the apothecary, his wife, and I and mine by coach together, and setting him down at his house, he paying his share, my wife and I home, and found all well, only myself somewhat vexed at my wife's neglect in leaving of her scarf, waistcoat, and night-dressings in the coach to-day that brought us from Westminster, though, I confess, she did give them to me to look after, yet it was her fault not to see that I did take them out of the coach. I believe it might be as good as 25s. loss or thereabouts. So to my office, however, to set down my last three days' journall, and writing to my Lord Sandwich to give him an account of Sir J. Lawson's being come home, and to my father about my sending him some wine and things this week, for his making an entertainment of some friends in the country, and so home. This night making an end wholly of Christmas, with a mind fully satisfied with the great pleasures we have had by being abroad from home, and I do find my mind so apt to run to its old want of pleasures, that it is high time to betake myself to my late vows, which I will to-morrow, God willing, perfect and bind myself to, that so I may, for a great while, do my duty, as I have well begun, and increase my good name and esteem in the world, and get money, which sweetens all things, and whereof I have much need. So home to supper and to bed, blessing God for his mercy to bring me home, after much pleasure, to my house and business with health and resolution to fall hard to work again.

January 9th. Waking in the morning, my wife I found also awake, and begun to speak to me with great trouble and tears, and by degrees from one discourse to another at last it appears that Sarah has told somebody that has told my wife of my meeting her at my brother's and making her sit down by me while she told me stories of my wife, about her giving her scallop to her brother, and other things, which I am much vexed at, for I am sure I never spoke any thing of it, nor could any body tell her but by Sarah's own words. I endeavoured to excuse my silence herein hitherto by not believing anything she told me, only that of the scallop which she herself told me of. At last we pretty good friends, and my wife begun to speak again of the necessity of her keeping somebody to bear her company; for her familiarity with her other servants is it that spoils them all, and other company she hath none, which is too true, and called for Jane to reach her out of her trunk, giving her the keys to that purpose, a bundle of papers, and pulls out a paper, a copy of what, a pretty while since, she had wrote in a discontent to me, which I would not read, but burnt. She now read it, and it was so piquant, and wrote in English, and most of it true, of the retiredness of her life, and how unpleasant it was; that being wrote in English, and so in danger of being met with and read by others, I was vexed at it, and desired her and then commanded her to tear it. When she desired to be excused it, I forced it from her, and tore it, and withal took her other bundle of papers from her, and leapt out of the bed and in my shirt clapped them into the pocket of my breeches, that she might not get them from me, and having got on my stockings and breeches and gown, I pulled them out one by one and tore them all before her face, though it went against my heart to do it, she crying and desiring me not to do it, but such was my passion and trouble to see the letters of my love to her, and my Will wherein I had given her all I have in the world, when I went to sea with my Lord Sandwich, to be joyned with a paper of so much disgrace to me and dishonour, if it should have been found by any body. Having torn them all, saving a bond of my uncle Robert's, which she hath long had in her hands, and our marriage license, and the first letter that ever I sent her when I was her servant, I took up the pieces and carried them into my chamber, and there, after many disputes with myself whether I should burn them or no, and having picked up the pieces of the paper she read to-day, and of my Will which I tore, I burnt all the rest, and so went out to my office troubled in mind. Hither comes Major Tolhurst, one of my old acquaintance in Cromwell's time, and sometimes of our clubb, to see me, and I could do no less than carry him to the Mitre, and having sent for Mr. Beane, a merchant, a neighbour of mine, we sat and talked, Tolhurst telling me the manner of their collierys in the north. We broke up, and I home to dinner. And to see my folly, as discontented as I am, when my wife came I could not forbear smiling all dinner till she began to speak bad words again, and then I began to be angry again, and so to my office. Mr. Bland came in the evening to me hither, and sat talking to me about many things of merchandise, and I should be very happy in his discourse, durst I confess my ignorance to him, which is not so fit for me to do. There coming a letter to me from Mr. Pierce, the surgeon, by my desire appointing his and Dr. Clerke's coming to dine with me next Monday, I went to my wife and agreed upon matters, and at last for my honour am forced to make her presently a new Moyre gown to be seen by Mrs. Clerke, which troubles me to part with so much money, but, however, it sets my wife and I to friends again, though I and she never were so heartily angry in our lives as to-day almost, and I doubt the heart-burning will not be soon over, and the truth is I am sorry for the tearing of so many poor loving letters of mine from sea and elsewhere to her. So to my office again, and there the Scrivener brought me the end of the manuscript which I am going to get together of things of the Navy, which pleases me much. So home, and mighty friends with my wife again, and so to bed.

January 30th. A solemn fast for the King's murther, and we were forced to keep it more than we would have done, having forgot to take any victuals into the house. I to church in the forenoon, and Mr. Mills made a good sermon upon David's heart smiting him for cutting off the garment of Saul. Home, and whiled away some of the afternoon at home talking with my wife. So to my office, and all alone making up my month's accounts, which to my great trouble I find that I am got no further than £640. But I have had great expenses this month. I pray God the next may be a little better, as I hope it will. In the evening my manuscript is brought home handsomely bound, to my full content; and now I think I have a better collection in reference to the Navy, and shall have by the time I have filled it, than any of my predecessors. So home and eat something such as we have, bread and butter and milk, and so to bed.

June 13th. Up and betimes to Thames Street among the tarr men, to look the price of tarr and so by water to Whitehall thinking to speak with Sir G. Carteret, but he lying in the city all night, and meeting with Mr. Cutler the merchant, I with him in his coach into the city to Sir G. Carteret, but missing him there, he and I walked to find him at Sir Tho. Allen's in Bread Street, where not finding him he and I walked towards our office, he discoursing well of the business of the Navy, and particularly of the victualling, in which he was once I perceive concerned, and he and I parted and I to the office and there had a difference with Sir W. Batten about Mr. Bowyer's tarr, which I am resolved to cross, though he sent me last night, as a bribe, a barrel of sturgeon, which, it may be, I shall send back, for I will not have the King abused so abominably in the price of what we buy, by Sir W. Batten's corruption and underhand dealing. So from the office, Mr. Wayth with me, to the Parliament House, and there I spoke and told Sir G. Carteret all, with which he is well pleased, and do recall his willingness yesterday, it seems, to Sir W. Batten, that we should buy a great quantity of tarr, being abused by him. Thence with Mr. Wayth after drinking a cupp of ale at the Swan, talking of the corruption of the Navy, by water. I landed him at Whitefriars, and I to the Exchange, and so home to dinner, where I found my wife's brother, and thence after dinner by water to the Royall Theatre, where I resolve to bid farewell, as shall appear by my oaths to-morrow against all plays either at publique houses or Court till Christmas be over. Here we saw *The Faithfull Sheepheardesse*, a most simple thing, and yet much thronged after, and often shown, but it is only for the scenes' sake, which is very fine indeed and worth seeing; but I am quite out of opinion with any of their actings, but Lacy's, compared with the other house. Thence to see Mrs. Hunt, which we did and were much made of; and in our way saw my Lady Castlemaine, who, I fear, is not so handsome as I have taken her for, and now she begins to decay something. This is my wife's opinion also, for which I am sorry. Thence by coach, with a mad coachman, that drove like mad, and down byeways, through Bucklersbury home, everybody through the street cursing him, being ready to run over them. So home, and after writing letters by the post, home to supper and bed. Yesterday, upon conference with the King in the Banqueting House, the Parliament did agree with much ado, it being carried but by forty-two voices, that they would supply him with a sum of money; but what and how is not yet known, but expected to be done with great disputes the next week. But if done at all, it is well.

October 19th. Waked with a very high wind, and said to my wife, "I pray God I hear not of the death of any great person, this wind is so high!" fearing that the Queen might be dead. So up; and going by coach with Sir W. Batten and Sir J. Minnes to St. James's, they tell me that Sir W. Compton, who it is true had been a little sickly for a week or a fortnight, but was very well upon Friday at night last at the Tangier Committee with us, was dead—died yesterday: at which I was most exceedingly surprised, he being, and so all the world saying that he was, one of the worthyest men and best officers of State now in England; and so in my conscience he was: of the best temper, valour, abilities of mind, integrity, birth, fine person, and diligence of any one man he hath left behind him in the three kingdoms; and yet not forty years old, or if so, that is all. I find the sober men of the Court troubled for him; and yet not so as to hinder or lessen their mirth, talking, laughing, and eating, drinking, and doing every thing else, just as if there was no such thing, which is as good an instance for me hereafter to judge of death, both as to the unavoidableness, suddenness, and little effect of it upon the spirits of others, let a man be never so high, or rich, or good, but that all die alike, no more matter being made of the death of one than another, and that even to die well, the praise of it is not considerable in the world, compared to the many in the world that know not nor make anything of it, nor perhaps to them (unless to one that like this poor gentleman, who is one of a thousand, there nobody speaking ill of him) that will speak ill of a man. Coming to St. James's, I hear that the Queen did sleep five hours pretty well to-night, and that she waked and gargled her mouth, and to sleep again; but that her pulse beats fast, beating twenty to the King's or my Lady Suffolk's eleven; but not so strong as it was. It seems she was so ill as to be shaved and pidgeons put to her feet, and to have the extreme unction given her by the priests, who were so long about it that the doctors were angry. The King, they all say, is most fondly disconsolate for her, and weeps by her, which makes her weep; which one this day told me he reckons a good sign, for that it carries away some rheume from the head. This morning Captain Allen tells me how the famous Ned Mullins, by a slight fall, broke his leg at the ancle, which festered; and he had his leg cut off on Saturday, but so ill done, notwithstanding all the great chyrurgeons about the town at the doing of it, that they fear he will not live with it, which is very strange, besides the torment he was put to with it. After being a little with the Duke, and being invited to dinner to my Lord Barkeley's, and so, not knowing how to spend our time till noon, Sir W. Batten and I took coach, and to the Coffee-house in Cornhill; where much talk about the Turk's proceedings, and that the plague is got to Amsterdam, brought by a ship from Argier; and it is also carried to Hambrough. The Duke says the King purposes to forbid any of their ships coming into the river. The Duke also told us of several Christian commanders (French) gone over to the Turks to serve them; and upon inquiry I find that the King of France do by this aspire to the Empire, and so to get the Crown of Spayne also upon the death of the King, which is very probable, it seems. Back to St. James's, and there dined with my Lord Barkeley and his Lady, where Sir G. Carteret, Sir W. Batten, and myself, with two gentlemen more; my Lady, and one of the ladies of honour to the Duchesse (no handsome woman, but a most excellent hand). A fine French dinner, and so we after dinner broke up and to Creed's new lodgings in Axe-yard, which I like very well, and so with him to White Hall and walked up and down in the galleries with good discourse, and anon Mr. Coventry and Povy, sad for the loss of one of our number we sat down as a Committee for Tangier and did some business and so broke up, and I down with Mr. Coventry and in his chamber discoursing of business of the office and Sir J. Minnes and Sir W. Batten's carriage, when he most ingeniously tells me how they have carried themselves to him in forbearing to speak the other day to the Duke what they know they have so largely at other times said to him, and I told him what I am put to about the bargain for masts. I perceive he thinks of it all and will remember it. Thence took up my wife at Mrs. Harper's where she and Jane were, and so called at the New Exchange for some things for her, and then at Tom's went up and saw his house now it is finished, and indeed it is very handsome, but he not within and so home and to my office, and then to supper and to bed.

December 4th. Up pretty betimes, that is about 7 o'clock, it being now dark then, and so got me ready, with my clothes, breeches and warm stockings, and by water with Henry Russell, cold and wet and windy to Woolwich, to a hempe ship there, and staid looking upon it and giving direction as to the getting it ashore, and so back again very cold, and at home without going on shore anywhere about 12 o'clock, being fearful of taking cold, and so dined at home and shifted myself, and so all the afternoon at my office till night, and then home to keep my poor wife company, and so to supper and to bed.

[1664] January 8th. Up and all the morning at my office and with Sir J. Minnes, directing him and Mr. Turner about keeping of their books according to yesterday's work, wherein I shall make them work enough. At noon to the 'Change, and there long, and from thence by appointment took Luellin, Mount, and W. Symons, and Mr. Pierce, the chirurgeon, home to dinner with me and were merry. But, Lord! to hear how W. Symons do commend and look sadly and then talk bawdily and merrily, though his wife was dead but the other day, would make a dogg laugh. After dinner I did go in further part of kindness to Luellin for his kindness about Deering's £50 which he procured me the other day of him. We spent all the afternoon together and then they to cards with my wife, who this day put on her Indian blue gowne which is very pretty, where I left them for an hour, and to my office, and then to them again, and by and by they went away at night, and so I again to my office to perfect a letter to Mr. Coventry about Department Treasurers, wherein I please myself and hope to give him content and do the King service therein. So having done, I home and to teach my wife a new lesson in the globes, and to supper, and to bed. We had great pleasure this afternoon; among other things, to talk of our old passages together in Cromwell's time; and how W. Symons did make me laugh and wonder to-day when he told me how he had made shift to keep in, in good esteem and employment, through eight governments in one year (the year 1659, which were indeed, and he did name them all), and then failed unhappy in the ninth, viz. that of the King's coming in. He made good to me the story which Luellin did tell me the other day, of his wife upon her death-bed; how she dreamt of her uncle Scobell, and did foretell, from some discourse she had with him, that she should die four days thence, and not sooner, and did all along say so, and did so. Upon the 'Change a great talke there was of one Mr. Tryan, an old man, a merchant in Lyme-Streete, robbed last night (his man and mayde being gone out after he was a-bed), and gagged and robbed of £1,050 in money and about £4,000 in jewells, which he had in his house as security for money. It is believed by many circumstances that his man is guilty of confederacy, by their ready going to his secret till in his desk, wherein the key of his cash-chest lay.

March 18th. Up betimes, and walked to my brother's, where a great while putting things in order against anon; then to Madam Turner's and eat a breakfast there, and so to Wotton, my shoemaker, and there got a pair of shoes blacked on the soles against anon for me; so to my brother's and to church, and with the grave-maker chose a place for my brother to lie in, just under my mother's pew. But to see how a man's tombes are at the mercy of such a fellow, that for sixpence he would, (as his owne words were,) "I will justle them together but I will make room for him;" speaking of the fulness of the middle isle, where he was to lie; and that he would, for my father's sake, do my brother that is dead all the civility he can; which was to disturb other corps that are not quite rotten, to make room for him; and methought his manner of speaking it was very remarkable; as of a thing that now was in his power to do a man a courtesy or not. At noon my wife, though in pain, comes, but I being forced to go home, she went back with me, where I dressed myself, and so did Besse; and so to my brother's again: whither, though invited, as the custom is, at one or two o'clock, they came not till four or five. But at last one after another they come, many more than I bid: and my reckoning that I bid was one hundred and twenty; but I believe there was nearer one hundred and fifty. Their service was six biscuits a-piece, and what they pleased of burnt claret. My cosen Joyce Norton kept the wine and cakes above; and did give out to them that served, who had white gloves given them. But above all, I am beholden to Mrs. Holden, who was most kind, and did take mighty pains not only in getting the house and every thing else ready, but this day in going up and down to see the house filled and served, in order to mine, and their great content, I think; the men sitting by themselves in some rooms, and women by themselves in others, very close, but yet room enough. Anon to church, walking out into the streets to the Conduit, and so across the streete, and had a very good company along with the corps. And being come to the grave as above, Dr. Pierson, the minister of the parish, did read the service for buriall: and so I saw my poor brother laid into the grave; and so all broke up; and I and my wife and Madam Turner and her family to my brother's, and by and by fell to a barrel of oysters, cake, and cheese, of Mr. Honiwood's, with him, in his chamber and below, being too merry for so late a sad work. But, Lord! to see how the world makes nothing of the memory of a man, an houre after he is dead! And, indeed, I must blame myself; for though at the sight of him dead and dying, I had real grief for a while, while he was in my sight, yet presently after, and ever since, I have had very little grief indeed for him. By and by, it beginning to be late, I put things in some order in the house, and so took my wife and Besse (who hath done me very good service in cleaning and getting ready every thing and serving the wine and things to-day, and is indeed a most excellent good-natured and faithful wench, and I love her mightily), by coach home, and so after being at the office to set down the day's work home to supper and to bed.

August 13th. Up, and before I went to the office comes my Taylor with a coate I have made to wear within doors, purposely to come no lower than my knees, for by my wearing a gowne within doors comes all my tenderness about my legs. There comes also Mr. Reeve, with a microscope and scotoscope. For the first I did give him £5 10s., a great price, but a most curious bauble it is, and he says, as good, nay, the best he knows in England, and he makes the best in the world. The other he gives me, and is of value; and a curious curiosity it is to look objects in a darke room with. Mightly pleased with this I to the office, where all the morning. There offered by Sir W. Pen his coach to go to Epsum and carry my wife, I stept out and bade my wife make her ready, but being not very well and other things advising me to the contrary, I did forbear going, and so Mr. Creed dining with me I got him to give my wife and me a play this afternoon, lending him money to do it, which is a fallacy that I have found now once, to avoyde my vow with, but never to be more practised I swear, and to the new play, at the Duke's house, of *Henry the Fifth*; a most noble play, writ by my Lord Orrery; wherein Betterton, Harris, and Ianthe's parts are most incomparably wrote and done, and the whole play the most full of height and raptures of wit and sense that ever I heard; having but one incongruity, or what did not please me in it, that is, that King Harry promises to plead for Tudor to their Mistresse, Princesse Katherine of France, more than when it comes to it he seems to do; and Tudor refused by her with some kind of indignity, not with a difficulty and honour that it ought to have been done in to him. Thence home and to my office, wrote by the post, and then to read a little in Dr. Power's book of discovery by the Microscope to enable me a little how to use and what to expect from my glasse. So to supper and to bed.

December 31st. At the office all the morning, and after dinner there again, dispatched first my letters, and then to my accounts, not of the month but of the whole yeare also, and was at it till past twelve at night, it being bitter cold; but yet I was well satisfied with my worke, and, above all, to find myself, by the great blessing of God, worth £1,349, by which, as I have spent very largely, so I have laid up above £500 this yeare above what I was worth this day twelvemonth. The Lord make me for ever thankful to his holy name for it! Thence home to eat a little and so to bed. Soon as ever the clock struck one, I kissed my wife in the kitchen by the fireside, wishing her a merry new yeare, observing that I believe I was the first proper wisher of it this year, for I did it as soon as ever the clock struck one.

[1665] February 7th. Up and to my office, where busy all the morning, and at home to dinner. It being Shrove Tuesday, had some very good fritters. All the afternoon and evening at the office, and at night home to supper and to bed. This day, Sir W. Batten, who hath been sicke four or five days, is now very bad, so as people begin to fear his death; and I am at a loss whether it will be better for me to have him die, because he is a bad man, or live, for fear a worse should come.

February 9th. Up and to my office, where all the morning very busy. At noon home to dinner, and then to my office again, where Sir William Petty come, among other things to tell me that Mr. Barlow is dead; for which, God knows my heart, I could be as sorry as is possible for one to be for a stranger, by whose death he gets £100 per annum, he being a worthy, honest man; but after having considered that when I come to consider the providence of God by this means unexpectedly to give me £100 a year more in my estate, I have cause to bless God, and do it from the bottom of my heart. So home late at night, after twelve o'clock, and so to bed.

February 13th. Up and to St. James's, did our usual business before the Duke. Thence I to Westminster and by water (taking Mr. Stapely the rope-maker by the way), to his rope-ground and to Limehouse, there to see the manner of stoves and did excellently inform myself therein, and coming home did go on board Sir W. Petty's *Experiment*, which is a brave roomy vessel, and I hope may do well. So went on shore to a Dutch house to drink some mum, and there light upon some Dutchmen, with whom we had good discourse touching stoveing and making of cables. But to see how despicably they speak of us for our using so many hands more to do anything than they do, they closing a cable with 20, that we use 60 men upon. Thence home and eat something, and then to my office, where very late, and then to supper and to bed. Captain Stokes, it seems, is at last dead at Portsmouth.

March 1st. Up, and this day being the day that by a promise, a great while ago, made to my wife, I was to give her £20 to lay out in clothes against Easter, she did, notwithstanding last night's falling out, come to peace with me and I with her, but did boggle mightily at the parting with my money, but at last did give it her, and then she abroad to buy her things, and I to my office, where busy all the morning. At noon I to dinner at Trinity House, and thence to Gresham College, where Mr. Hooke read a second very curious lecture about the late Comet; among other things proving very probably that this is the very same Comet, that appeared before in the year 1618, and that in such a time probably it will appear again, which is a very new opinion; but all will be in print. Then to the meeting, where Sir G. Carteret's two sons, his owne, and Sir N. Slaning, were admitted of the society: and this day I did pay my admission money, 40s. to the society. Here was very fine discourses and experiments, but I do lacke philosophy enough to understand them, and so cannot remember them. Among others, a very particular account of the making of the several sorts of bread in France, which is accounted the best place for bread in the world. So home, where very busy getting an answer to some question of Sir Philip Warwicke touching the expense of the navy, and that being done I by coach at 8 at night with my wife and Mercer to Sir Philip's and discoursed with him (leaving them in the coach), and then back with them home and to supper and to bed.

April 1st. All the morning very busy at the office preparing a last half-year's account for my Lord Treasurer. At noon eat a bit and stepped to Sir Ph. Warwicke, by coach to my Lord Treasurer's, and after some private conference and examining of my papers with him I did return into the City and to Sir G. Carteret, whom I found with the Commissioners of Prizes dining at Captain Cocke's, in Broad Streete, very merry. Among other tricks, there did come a blind fiddler to the doore, and Sir G. Carteret did go to the doore and lead the blind fiddler by the hand in. Thence with Sir G. Carteret to my Lord Treasurer, and by and by come Sir W. Batten and Sir J. Minnes, and anon we come to my Lord, and there did lay open the expense for the six months past, and an estimate of the seven months to come, to November next: the first arising to above £500,000, and the latter will, as we judge, come to above £1,000,000. But to see how my Lord Treasurer did bless himself, crying he could do no more than he could, nor give more money than he had, if the occasion and expense were never so great, which is but a sad story. And then to hear how like a passionate and ignorant asse Sir G. Carteret did harangue upon the abuse of Tickets did make me mad almost and yet was fain to hold my tongue. Thence home, vexed mightily to see how simply our greatest ministers do content themselves to understand and do things, while the King's service in the meantime lies a-bleeding. At my office late writing letters till ready to drop down asleep with my late sitting up of late, and running up and down a-days. So to bed.

August 3rd. Up, and betimes to Deptford to Sir G. Carteret's, where, not liking the horse that had been hired by Mr. Uthwayt for me, I did desire Sir G. Carteret to let me ride his new £40 horse, which he did, and so I left my *hacquenée* behind, and so after staying a good while in their bed-chamber while they were dressing themselves, discoursing merrily, I parted and to the ferry, where I was forced to stay a great while before I could get my horse brought over, and then mounted and rode very finely to Dagenhams; all the way people, citizens, walking to and again to enquire how the plague is in the City this week by the Bill; which by chance, at Greenwich, I had heard was 2,020 of the plague, and 3,000 and odd of all diseases; but methought it was a sad question to be so often asked me. Coming to Dagenhams, I there met our company coming out of the house, having staid as long as they could for me; so I let them go a little before, and went and took leave of my Lady Sandwich, good woman, who seems very sensible of my service in this late business, and having her directions in some things, among others, to get Sir G. Carteret and my Lord to settle the portion, and what Sir G. Carteret is to settle, into land, soon as may be, she not liking that it should lie long undone, for fear of death on either side. So took leave of her, and then down to the buttery, and eat a piece of cold venison pie, and drank and took some bread and cheese in my hand; and so mounted after them, Mr. Marr very kindly staying to lead me the way. By and by met my Lord Crew returning, after having accompanied them a little way, and so after them, Mr. Marr telling me by the way how a mayde servant of Mr. John Wright's (who lives thereabouts) falling sick of the plague, she was removed to an outhouse, and a nurse appointed to look to her; who, being once absent, the mayde got out of the house at the window, and run away. The nurse coming and knocking, and having no answer, believed she was dead, and went and told Mr. Wright so; who and his lady were in great strait what to do to get her buried. At last resolved to go to Burntwood hard by, being in the parish, and there get people to do it. But they would not; so he went home full of trouble, and in the way met the wench walking over the common, which frighted him worse than before; and was forced to send people to take her, which he did; and they got one of the pest coaches and put her into it to carry her to a pest house. And passing in a narrow lane, Sir Anthony Browne, with his brother and some friends in the coach, met this coach with the curtains drawn close. The brother being a young man, and believing there might be some lady in it that would not be seen, and the way being narrow, he thrust his head out of his own into her coach, and to look, and there saw somebody look very ill, and in a sick dress, and stunk mightily; which the coachman also cried out upon. And presently they come up to some people that stood looking after it, and told our gallants that it was a mayde of Mr. Wright's carried away sick of the plague; which put the young gentleman into a fright had almost cost him his life, but is now well again. I, overtaking our young people, 'light, and into the coach to them, where mighty merry all the way; and anon come to the Blockhouse, over against Gravesend, where we staid a great while, in a little drinking-house. Sent back our coaches to Dagenhams. I, by and by, by boat to Gravesend, where no newes of Sir G. Carteret come yet; so back again, and fetched them all over, but the two saddle-horses that were to go with us, which could not be brought over in the horse-boat, the wind and tide being against us, without towing; so we had some difference with some watermen, who would not tow them over under 20s., whereupon I swore to send one of them to sea and will do it. Anon some others come to me and did it for 10s. By and by comes Sir G. Carteret, and so we set out for Chatham: in my way overtaking some company, wherein was a lady, very pretty, riding singly, her husband in company with her. We fell into talke, and I read a copy of verses which her husband showed me, and he discommended, but the lady commended: and I read them, so as to make the husband turn to commend them. By and by he and I fell into acquaintance, having known me formerly at the Exchequer. His name is Nokes, over against Bow Church. He was servant to Alderman Dashwood. We promised to meet, if ever we come both to London again; and, at parting, I had a fair salute on horseback, in Rochester streets, of the lady, and so parted. Come to Chatham mighty merry, and anon to supper, it being near 9 o'clock ere we come thither.

My Lady Carteret come thither in a coach, by herself, before us. Great mind they have to buy a little *hacquenée* that I rode on from Greenwich, for a woman's horse. Mighty merry, and after supper, all being withdrawn, Sir G. Carteret did take an opportunity to speak with much value and kindness to me, which is of great joy to me. So anon to bed. Mr. Brisband and I together to my content.

August 31st. Up; and, after putting several things in order to my removal, to Woolwich; the plague having a great encrease this week, beyond all expectation of almost 2,000, making the general Bill 7,000, odd 100; and the plague above 6,000. I down by appointment to Greenwich, to our office, where I did some business, and there dined with our company and Sir W. Boreman, and Sir The. Biddulph, at Mr. Boreman's, where a good venison pasty, and after a good merry dinner I to my office, and there late writing letters, and then to Woolwich by water, where pleasant with my wife and people, and after supper to bed. Thus this month ends with great sadness upon the publick, through the greatness of the plague every where through the kingdom almost. Every day sadder and sadder news of its encrease. In the City died this week 7,496, and of them 6,102 of the plague. But it is feared that the true number of the dead this week is near 10,000; partly from the poor that cannot be taken notice of, through the greatness of the number, and partly from the Quakers and others that will not have any bell ring for them. Our fleete gone out to find the Dutch, we having about 100 sail in our fleete, and in them the *Soveraigne* one; so that it is a better fleete than the former with the Duke was. All our fear is that the Dutch should be got in before them; which would be a very great sorrow to the publick, and to me particularly, for my Lord Sandwich's sake. A great deal of money being spent, and the kingdom not in a condition to spare, nor a parliament without much difficulty to meet to give more. And to that; to have it said, what hath been done by our late fleetes? As to myself I am very well, only in fear of the plague, and as much of an ague by being forced to go early and late to Woolwich, and my family to lie there continually. My late gettings have been very great to my great content, and am likely to have yet a few more profitable jobbs in a little while; for which Tangier and Sir W. Warren I am wholly obliged to.

September 10th (Lord's day). Walked home; being forced thereto by one of my watermen falling sick yesterday, and it was God's great mercy I did not go by water with them yesterday, for he fell sick on Saturday night, and it is to be feared of the plague. So I sent him away to London with his fellow; but another boat come to me this morning, whom I sent to Blackewall for Mr. Andrews. I walked to Woolwich, and there find Mr. Hill, and he and I all the morning at musique and a song he hath set of three parts, methinks, very good. Anon comes Mr. Andrews, though it be a very ill day, and so after dinner we to musique and sang till about 4 or 5 o'clock, it blowing very hard, and now and then raining, and wind and tide being against us, Andrews and I took leave and walked to Greenwich. My wife before I come out telling me the ill news that she hears that her father is very ill, and then I told her I feared of the plague, for that the house is shut up. And so she much troubled she did desire me to send them something; and I said I would, and will do so. But before I come out there happened newes to come to me by an expresse from Mr. Coventry, telling me the most happy news of my Lord Sandwich's meeting with part of the Dutch; his taking two of their East India ships, and six or seven others, and very good prizes: and that he is in search of the rest of the fleet, which he hopes to find upon the Wellbancke, with the loss only of the *Hector*, poor Captain Cuttle. This news do so overjoy me that I know not what to say enough to express it, but the better to do it I did walk to Greenwich, and there sending away Mr. Andrews, I to Captain Cocke's, where I find my Lord Bruncker and his mistress, and Sir J. Minnes. Where we supped (there was also Sir W. Doyly and Mr. Evelyn); but the receipt of this news did put us all into such an extacy of joy, that it inspired into Sir J. Minnes and Mr. Evelyn such a spirit of mirth, that in all my life I never met with so merry a two hours as our company this night was. Among other humours, Mr. Evelyn's repeating of some verses made up of nothing but the various acceptations of *may* and *can*, and doing it so aptly upon occasion of something of that nature, and so fast, did make us all die almost with laughing, and did so stop the mouth of Sir J. Minnes in the middle of all his mirth (and in a thing agreeing with his own manner of genius), that I never saw any man so out-done in all my life; and Sir J. Minnes's mirth too to see himself out-done, was the crown of all our mirth. In this humour we sat till about ten at night, and so my Lord and his mistress home, and we to bed, it being one of the times of my life wherein I was the fullest of true sense of joy.

November 5th (Lord's day). Up, and after being trimmed, by boat to the Cockpitt, where I heard the Duke of Albemarle's chaplin make a simple sermon: among other things, reproaching the imperfection of humane learning, he cried: "All our physicians cannot tell what an ague is, and all our arithmetique is not able to number the days of a man;" which, God knows, is not the fault of arithmetique, but that our understandings reach not the thing. To dinner, where a great deale of silly discourse, but the worst is I hear that the plague increases much at Lambeth, St. Martin's and Westminster, and fear it will all over the city. Thence I to the Swan, thinking to have seen Sarah but she was at church, and so I by water to Deptford, and there made a visit to Mr. Evelyn, who, among other things, showed me most excellent painting in little; in distemper, Indian incke, water colours: graveing; and, above all, the whole secret of mezzo-tinto, and the manner of it, which is very pretty, and good things done with it. He read to me very much also of his discourse, he hath been many years and now is about, about Guardenage; which will be a most noble and pleasant piece. He read me part of a play or two of his making, very good, but not as he conceits them, I think, to be. He showed me his

Hortus Hyemalis; leaves laid up in a book of several plants kept dry, which preserve colour, however, and look very finely, better than any Herball. In fine, a most excellent person he is, and must be allowed a little for a little conceitedness; but he may well be so, being a man so much above others. He read me, though with too much gusto, some little poems of his own, that were not transcendant, yet one or two very pretty epigrams; among others, of a lady looking in at a grate, and being pecked at by an eagle that was there. Here comes in, in the middle of our discourse Captain Cocke, as drunk as a dogg, but could stand, and talk and laugh. With him in his coach to Mr. Glanville's, where he sat with Mrs. Penington and myself a good while talking and then went away. After an houre's talke we to bed, the lady mightily troubled about a pretty little bitch she hath, which is very sicke, and will eat nothing, and the worst was, I could hear her in her chamber bemoaning the bitch, and by and by taking her into bed with her. This night I had a letter that Sir G. Carteret would be in towne to-morrow, which did much surprize me.

[1666] January 29th. Up, and to Court by coach, where to Council before the Duke of Yorke, the Duke of Albemarle with us, and after Sir W. Coventry had gone over his notes that he had provided with the Duke of Albemarle, I went over all mine with good successe, only I fear I did once offend the Duke of Albemarle, but I was much joyed to find the Duke of Yorke so much contending for my discourse about the pursers against Sir W. Pen, who opposes it like a foole; my Lord Sandwich come in in the middle of the business, and, poor man, very melancholy, methought, and said little at all, or to the business, and sat at the lower end, just as he come, no roome being made for him, only I did give him my stoole, and another was reached me. After council done, I walked to and again up and down the house, discoursing with this and that man. Anon others tooke occasion to thanke the Duke of Yorke for his good opinion in general of my service, and particularly his favour in conferring on me the Victualling business. He told me that he knew nobody so fit as I for it, and next, he was very glad to find that to give me for my encouragement, speaking very kindly of me. So to Sir W. Coventry's to dinner with him, whom I took occasion to thanke for his favour and good thoughts of what little service I did, desiring he would do the last act of friendship in telling me of my faults also. He told me he would be sure he would do that also, if there were any occasion for it. So that as much as it is possible under so great a fall of my Lord Sandwich's, and difference between them, I may conclude that I am thoroughly right with Sir W. Coventry. I dined with him with a great deale of company, and much merry discourse. I was called away before dinner ended to go to my company who dined at our lodgings. Thither I went with Mr. Evelyn (whom I met) in his coach going that way, but finding my company gone, but my Lord Bruncker left his coach for me; so Mr. Evelyn and I into my Lord's coach, and rode together with excellent discourse till we come to Clapham, talking of the vanity and vices of the Court, which makes it a most contemptible thing; and indeed in all his discourse I find him a most worthy person. Particularly he entertained me with discourse of an Infirmary, which he hath projected for the sick and wounded seamen against the next year, which I mightily approve of; and will endeavour to promote it, being a worthy thing, and of use, and will save money. He set me down at Mr. Gawden's, where nobody yet come home, I having left him and his sons and Creed at Court, so I took a book and into the gardens, and there walked and read till darke with great pleasure, and then in and in comes Osborne, and he and I to talk of Mr. Jaggard, who comes from London, and great hopes there is of a decrease this week also of the plague. Anon comes in Creed, and after that Mr. Gawden and his sons, and then they bringing in three ladies, who were in the house, but I do not know them, his daughter and two nieces, daughters of Dr. Whistler's, with whom and Creed mighty sport at supper, the ladies very pretty and mirthfull. I perceive they know

Creed's gut and stomach as well as I, and made as much mirthe as I with it at supper. After supper I made the ladies sing, and they have been taught, but, Lord! though I was forced to commend them, yet it was the saddest stuff I ever heard. However, we sat up late, and then I, in the best chamber like a prince, to bed, and Creed with me, and being sleepy talked but little.

March 10th. Up, and to the office, and there busy sitting till noon. I find at home Mrs. Pierce and Knipp come to dine with me. We were mighty merry; and, after dinner, I carried them and my wife out by coach to the New Exchange, and there I did give my valentine, Mrs. Pierce, a dozen payre of gloves, and a payre of silke stockings, and Knipp for company's sake, though my wife had, by my consent, laid out 20s. upon her the other day, six payre of gloves. Thence to Hales's to have seen our pictures, but could not get in, he being abroad, and so to the Cakehouse hard by, and there sat in the coach with great pleasure, and eat some fine cakes and so carried them to Pierce's and away home. It is a mighty fine witty boy, Mrs. Pierce's little boy. Thence home and to the office, where late writing letters and leaving a great deale to do on Monday, I home to supper and to bed. The truth is I do indulge myself a little the more in pleasure, knowing that this is the proper age of my life to do it; and out of my observation that most men that do thrive in the world, do forget to take pleasure during the time that they are getting their estate, but reserve that till they have got one, and then it is too late for them to enjoy it with any pleasure.

March 19th. Up betimes and upon a meeting extraordinary at the office most of the morning with Lord Bruncker, Sir W. Coventry, and Sir W. Pen, upon the business of the accounts. Where now we have got almost as much as we would have we begin to lay all on the Controller, and I fear he will be run down with it, for he is every day less and less capable of doing business. Thence with my Lord Bruncker, Sir W. Coventry to the ticket office, to see in what little order things are there, and there it is a shame to see how the King is served. Thence to the Chamberlain of London, and satisfy ourselves more particularly how much credit we have there, which proves very little. Thence to Sir Robert Long's, absent. About much the same business, but have not the satisfaction we would have there neither. So Sir W. Coventry parted, and my Lord and I to Mrs. Williams's, and there I saw her closett, where indeed a great many fine things there are, but the woman I hate. Here we dined, and Sir J. Minnes come to us, and after dinner we walked to the King's playhouse, all in dirt, they being altering of the stage to make it wider. But God knows when they will begin to act again; but my business here was to see the inside of the stage and all the tiring-rooms and machines; and, indeed, it was a sight worthy seeing. But to see their clothes, and the various sorts, and what a mixture of things there was; here a wooden-leg, there a ruff, here a hobby-horse, there a crown, would make a man split himself to see with laughing; and particularly Lacy's wardrobe, and Shotrell's. But then again, to think how fine they show on the stage by candle-light, and how poor things they are to look now too near hand, is not pleasant at all. The machines are fine, and the paintings very pretty. Thence mightily satisfied in my curiosity I away with my Lord to see him at her house again, and so take leave and by coach home and to the office, and thence sent for to Sir G. Carteret by and by to the Broad Streete, where he and I walked two or three hours till it was quite darke in his gallery talking of his affairs, wherein I assure him all will do well, and did give him (with great liberty, which he accepted kindly) my advice to deny the Board nothing they would aske about his accounts, but rather call upon them to know whether there was anything more they desired, or was wanting. But our great discourse and serious reflections was upon the bad state of the kingdom in general, through want of money and good conduct, which we fear will undo all. Thence mightily satisfied with this good fortune of this discourse with him I home, and there walked in the darke till 10 o'clock at night in the garden with Sir W. Warren, talking of many things belonging to us particularly, and I hope to get something considerably by him before the year be over. He gives me good advice of circumspection in my place, which I am now in great mind to improve; for I think our office stands on very ticklish terms, the Parliament likely to sit shortly and likely to be asked more money, and we able to give a very bad account of the expense of what we have done with what they did give before. Besides, the turning out the prize officers may be an example for the King giving us up to the Parliament's pleasure as easily, for we deserve it as much. Besides, Sir G. Carteret did tell me to-night how my Lord Bruncker himself, whose good-will I could have depended as much on as any, did himself to him take notice of the many places I have; and though I was a painful man, yet the Navy was enough for any man to go through with in his owne single place there, which much troubles me, and shall yet provoke me to more and more care and diligence than ever. Thence home to supper, where I find my wife and Mrs. Barbary with great colds, as I also at this time have. This day by letter from my father he propounds a match in the country for Pall, which pleased me well, of one that hath seven score and odd pounds land per annum in possession, and expects £1,000 in money by the death of an old aunt. He hath neither father, mother, sister, nor brother, but demands £600 down, and £100 on the birth of first child, which I had some inclination to stretch to. He is kinsman to, and lives with, Mr. Phillips, but my wife tells me he is a drunken, ill-favoured, ill-bred country fellow, which sets me off of it again, and I will go on with Harman. So after supper to bed.

March 26th. Up, and a meeting extraordinary there was of Sir W. Coventry, Lord Bruncker, and myself, about the business of settling the ticket office, where infinite room is left for abusing the King in the wages of seamen. Our meeting being done, my Lord Bruncker and I to the Tower, to see the famous engraver, to get him to grave a seale for the office. And did see some of the finest pieces of work in embossed work, that ever I did see in my life, for fineness and smallness of the images thereon, and I will carry my wife thither to shew them her. Here I also did see bars of gold melting, which was a fine sight. So with my Lord to the Pope's Head Taverne in Lumbard Streete to dine by appointment with Captain Taylor, whither Sir W. Coventry come to us, and were mighty merry, and I find reason to honour him every day more and more. Thence alone to Broade Street to Sir G. Carteret by his desire to confer with him, who is I find in great pain about the business of the office, and not a little, I believe, in fear of falling there, Sir W. Coventry having so great a pique against him, and herein I first learn an eminent instance how great a man this day, that nobody would think could be shaken, is the next overthrown, dashed out of countenance, and every small thing of irregularity in his business taken notice of, where nobody the other day durst cast an eye upon them, and next I see that he that the other day nobody durst come near is now as supple as a spaniel, and sends and speaks to me with great submission, and readily hears to advice. Thence home to the office, where busy late, and so home a little to my accounts publique and private, but could not get myself rightly to know how to dispose of them in order to passing.

April 29th (Lord's day). Up, and to church, where Mr. Mills, a lazy, simple sermon upon the Devil's having no right to any thing in this world. So home to dinner, and after dinner I and my boy down by water to Redriffe and thence walked to Mr. Evelyn's, where I walked in his garden till he come from Church, with great pleasure reading Ridly's discourse, all my way going and coming, upon the Civill and Ecclesiastical Law. He being come home, he and I walked together in the garden with mighty pleasure, he being a very ingenious man; and the more I know him, the more I love him. His chief business with me was to propose having my cozen Thomas Pepys in Commission of the Peace, which I do not know what to say to till I speake with him, but should be glad of it and will put him upon it. Thence walked back again reading and so took water and home, where I find my uncle and aunt Wight, and supped with them upon my leads with mighty pleasure and mirthe, and they being gone I mighty weary to bed, after having my haire of my head cut shorter, even close to my skull, for coolnesse, it being mighty hot weather.

July 10th. Up, and to the office, where busy all the morning, sitting, and there presented Sir W. Coventry with my little book made up of Lovett's varnished paper, which he and the whole board liked very well. At noon home to dinner and then to the office; the yarde being very full of women (I believe above three hundred) coming to get money for their husbands and friends that are prisoners in Holland; and they lay clamouring and swearing and cursing us, that my wife and I were afeard to send a venison-pasty that we have for supper to-night to the cook's to be baked, for fear of their offering violence to it: but it went, and no hurt done. Then I took an opportunity, when they were all gone into the fore-yarde, and slipt into the office and there busy all the afternoon, but by and by the women got into the garden, and come all to my closett window, and there tormented me, and I confess their cries were so sad for money, and laying down the condition of their families and their husbands, and what they have done and suffered for the King, and how ill they are used by us, and how well the Dutch are used here by the allowance of their masters, and what their husbands are offered to serve the Dutch abroad, that I do most heartily pity them, and was ready to cry to hear them, but cannot help them. However, when the rest were gone, I did call one to me that I heard complaine only and pity her husband and did give her some money, and she blessed me and went away. Anon my business at the office being done I to the Tower to speak with Sir John Robinson about business, principally the bad condition of the pressed men for want of clothes, so it is represented from the fleete, and so to provide them shirts and stockings and drawers. Having done with him about that, I home and there find my wife and the two Mrs. Bateliers walking in the garden. I with them till almost 9 at night, and then they and we and Mrs. Mercer, the mother, and her daughter Anne, and our Mercer, to supper to a good venison-pasty and other good things, and had a good supper, and very merry, Mistresses Bateliers being both very good-humoured. We sang and talked, and then led them home, and there they made us drink; and, among other things, did show us, in cages, some birds brought from about Bourdeaux, that are all fat, and, examining one of them, they are so, almost all fat. Their name is Ortolans, which are brought over to the King for him to eat, and indeed are excellent things. We parted from them and so home to bed, it being very late, and to bed.

August 14th (Thanksgiving day). Up, and comes Mr. Foley and his man, with a box of a great variety of carpenter's and joyner's tooles, which I had bespoke, to me, which please me mightily; but I will have more. Then I abroad down to the Old Swan, and to White Hall, where I find them at Chappell, and met with Povy, and he and I together, who tells me how mad my letter makes my Lord Peterborough, and what a furious letter he hath writ to me in answer, though it is not come yet. This did trouble me; for though there be no reason, yet to have a nobleman's mouth open against a man may do a man hurt; so I endeavoured to have found him out and spoke with him, but could not. So to the chappell, and heard a piece of the Dean of Westminster's sermon, and a special good anthemne before the King, after a sermon, and then home by coach with Captain Cocke, who is in pain about his hempe, of which he says he hath bought great quantities, and would gladly be upon good terms with us for it, wherein I promise to assist him. So we 'light at the 'Change, where, after a small turn or two, taking no pleasure now-a-days to be there, because of answering questions that would be asked there which I cannot answer; so home and dined, and after dinner, with my wife and Mercer to the Beare-garden, where I have not been, I think, of many years, and saw some good sport of the bull's tossing of the dogs: one into the very boxes. But it is a very rude and nasty pleasure. We had a great many hectors in the same box with us (and one very fine went into the pit, and played his dog for a wager, which was a strange sport for a gentleman), where they drank wine, and drank Mercer's health first, which I pledged with my hat off; and who should be in the house but Mr. Pierce the surgeon, who saw us and spoke to us. Thence home, well enough satisfied, however, with the variety of this afternoon's exercise; and so I to my chamber, till in the evening our company come to supper. We had invited to a venison pasty Mr. Batelier and his sister Mary, Mrs. Mercer, her daughter Anne, Mr. Le Brun, and W. Hewer; and so we supped, and very merry. And then about nine o'clock to Mrs. Mercer's gate, where the fire and boys expected us, and her son had provided abundance of serpents and rockets; and there mighty merry (my Lady Pen and Pegg going thither with us, and Nan Wright), till about twelve at night, flinging our fireworks, and burning one another and the people over the way. And at last our businesses being most spent, we into Mrs. Mercer's, and there mighty merry, smutting one another with candle grease and soot, till most of us were like devils. And that being done, then we broke up, and to my house; and there I made them drink, and upstairs we went, and then fell into dancing (W. Batelier dancing well), and dressing, him and I and one Mr. Banister (who with his wife come over also with us) like women; and Mercer put on a suit of Tom's, like a boy, and mighty mirth we had, and Mercer danced a jigg; and Nan Wright and my wife and Pegg Pen put on perriwigs. Thus we spent till three or four in the morning, mighty merry; and then parted, and to bed.

August 19th (Lord's day). Up and to my chamber, and there began to draw out fair and methodically my accounts of Tangier, in order to shew them to the Lords. But by and by comes by agreement Mr. Reeves, and after him Mr. Spong, and all day with them, both before and after dinner, till ten o'clock at night, upon opticke enquiries, he bringing me a frame he closes on, to see how the rays of light do cut one another, and in a dark room with smoake, which is very pretty. He did also bring a lanthorne with pictures in glasse, to make strange things appear on a wall, very pretty. We did also at night see Jupiter and his girdle and satellites, very fine, with my twelve-foote glasse, but could not Saturne, he being very dark. Spong and I had also several fine discourses upon the globes this afternoon, particularly why the fixed stars do not rise and set at the same houre all the yeare long, which he could not demonstrate, nor I neither, the reason of. So, it being late, after supper they away home. But it vexed me to understand no more from Reeves and his glasses touching the nature and reason of the several refractions of the several figured glasses, he understanding the acting part, but not one bit the theory, nor can make any body understand it, which is a strange dullness, methinks. I did not hear anything yesterday or at all to confirm either Sir Thos. Allen's news of the 10 or 12 ships taken, nor of the disorder at Amsterdam upon the news of the burning of the ships, that he De Witt should be fled to the Prince of Orange, it being generally believed that he was gone to France before.

September 2nd (Lord's day). Some of our mayds sitting up late last night to get things ready against our feast to-day, Jane called us up about three in the morning, to tell us of a great fire they saw in the City. So I rose and slipped on my night-gowne, and went to her window, and thought it to be on the back-side of Marke-lane at the farthest; but, being unused to such fires as followed, I thought it far enough off; and so went to bed again and to sleep. About seven rose again to dress myself, and there looked out at the window, and saw the fire not so much as it was and further off. So to my closett to set things to rights after yesterday's cleaning. By and by Jane comes and tells me that she hears that above 300 houses have been burned down to-night by the fire we saw, and that it is now burning down all Fish-street, by London Bridge. So I made myself ready presently, and walked to the Tower, and there got up upon one of the high places, Sir J. Robinson's little son going up with me; and there I did see the houses at that end of the bridge all on fire, and an infinite great fire on this and the other side the end of the bridge; which, among other people, did trouble me for poor little Michell and our Sarah on the bridge. So down, with my heart full of trouble, to the Lieutenant of the Tower, who tells me that it begun this morning in the King's baker's house in Pudding-lane, and that it hath burned St. Magnus's Church and most part of Fish-street already. So I down to the water-side, and there got a boat and through bridge, and there saw a lamentable fire. Poor Michell's house, as far as the Old Swan, already burned that way, and the fire running further, that in a very little time it got as far as the Steele-yard, while I was there. Everybody endeavouring to remove their goods, and flinging into the river or bringing them into lighters that lay off; poor people staying in their houses as long as till the very fire touched them, and then running into boats, or clambering from one pair of stairs by the water-side to another. And among other things, the poor pigeons, I perceive, were loth to leave their houses, but hovered about the windows and balconys till they were, some of them burned, their wings, and fell down. Having staid, and in an hour's time seen the fire rage every way, and nobody, to my sight, endeavouring to quench it, but to remove their goods, and leave all to the fire, and having seen it get as far as the Steele-yard, and the wind mighty high and driving it into the City; and every thing, after so long a drought, proving combustible, even the very stones of churches, and among other things the poor steeple by which pretty Mrs. —— lives, and whereof my old schoolfellow Elborough is parson, taken fire in the very top, and there burned till it fell down: I to White Hall (with a gentleman with me who desired to go off from the Tower, to see the fire, in my boat); to White Hall, and there up to the King's closett in the Chappell, where people come about me, and I did give them an account dismayed them all, and word was carried in to the King. So I was called for, and did tell the King and Duke of Yorke what I saw, and that unless his Majesty did command houses to be pulled down nothing could stop the fire. They seemed much troubled, and the King commanded me to go to my Lord Mayor from him, and command him to spare no houses, but to pull down before the fire every way. The Duke of York bid me tell him that if he would have any more soldiers he shall; and so did my Lord Arlington afterwards, as a great secret. Here meeting with Captain Cocke, I in his coach, which he lent me, and Creed with me to Paul's, and there walked along Watling-street, as well as I could, every creature coming away loaden with goods to save, and here and there sicke people carried away in beds. Extraordinary good goods carried in carts and on backs. At last met my Lord Mayor in Canning-street, like a man spent, with a handkercher about his neck. To the King's message he cried, like a fainting woman, "Lord! what can I do? I am spent: people will not obey me. I have been pulling down houses; but the fire overtakes us faster than we can do it." That he needed no more soldiers; and that, for himself, he must go and refresh himself, having been up all night. So he left me, and I him, and walked home, seeing people all almost distracted, and no manner of means used to quench the fire. The houses, too, so very thick thereabouts, and full of matter for burning, as pitch and tarr, in Thames-street; and warehouses of oyle, and wines, and brandy, and other things. Here I saw Mr. Isaake Houblon, the handsome man, prettily dressed and dirty, at his door at Dowgate, receiving some of his brother's things, whose houses were on fire; and, as he says, have been removed twice already; and he doubts (as it soon proved) that they must be in a little time removed from his house also, which was a sad consideration. And to see the churches all filling with goods by people who themselves should have been quietly there at this time. By this time it was about twelve o'clock; and so home, and there find my guests, which was Mr. Wood and his wife

Barbary Sheldon, and also Mr. Moone: she mighty fine, and her husband, for aught I see, a likely man. But Mr. Moone's design and mine, which was to look over my closett and please him with the sight thereof, which he hath long desired, was wholly disappointed; for we were in great trouble and disturbance at this fire, not knowing what to think of it. However, we had an extraordinary good dinner, and as merry as at this time we could be. While at dinner Mrs. Batelier come to enquire after Mr. Woolfe and Stanes (who, it seems, are related to them), whose houses in Fish-street are all burned, and they in a sad condition. She would not stay in the fright. Soon as dined, I and Moone away, and walked through the City, the streets full of nothing but people and horses and carts loaden with goods, ready to run over one another, and removing goods from one burned house to another. They now removing out of Canning-streete (which received goods in the morning) into Lumbard-streete, and further; and among others I now saw my little goldsmith, Stokes, receiving some friend's goods, whose house itself was burned the day after. We parted at Paul's; he home, and I to Paul's Wharf, where I had appointed a boat to attend me, and took in Mr. Carcasse and his brother, whom I met in the streete, and carried them below and above bridge to and again to see the fire, which was now got further, both below and above, and no likelihood of stopping it. Met with the King and Duke of York in their barge, and with them to Queenhithe, and there called Sir Richard Browne to them. Their order was only to pull down houses apace, and so below bridge at the water-side; but little was or could be done, the fire coming upon them so fast. Good hopes there was of stopping it at the Three Cranes above, and at Buttolph's Wharf below bridge, if care be used; but the wind carries it into the City, so as we know not by the water-side what it do there. River full of lighters and boats taking in goods, and good goods swimming in the water, and only I observed that hardly one lighter or boat in three that had the goods of a house in, but there was a pair of Virginalls in it. Having seen as much as I could now, I away to White Hall by appointment, and there walked to St. James's Parke, and there met my wife and Creed and Wood and his wife, and walked to my boat; and there upon the water again, and to the fire up and down, it still encreasing, and the wind great. So near the fire as we could for smoke; and all over the Thames, with one's face in the wind, you were almost burned with a shower of fire-drops. This is very true; so as houses were burned by these drops and flakes of fire, three or four, nay, five or six houses, one from another. When we could endure no more upon the water, we to a little ale-house on the Bankside, over against the Three Cranes, and there staid till it was dark almost, and saw the fire grow; and, as it grew darker, appeared more and more, and in corners and upon steeples, and between churches and houses, as far as we could see up the hill of the City, in a most horrid malicious bloody flame, not like the fine flame of an ordinary fire. Barbary and her husband away before us. We staid till, it being darkish, we saw the fire as only one entire arch of fire from this to the other side the bridge, and in a bow up the hill for an arch of above a mile long: it made me weep to see it. The churches, houses, and all on fire and flaming at once; and a horrid noise the flames made, and the cracking of houses at their ruine. So home with a sad heart, and there find every body discoursing and lamenting the fire; and poor Tom Hater come with some few of his goods saved out of his house, which is burned upon Fish-streete Hill. I invited him to lie at my house, and did receive his goods, but was deceived in his lying there, the newes coming every moment of the growth of the fire; so as we were forced to begin to pack up our owne goods, and prepare for their removal; and did by moonshine (it being brave dry, and moonshine, and warm weather) carry much of my goods into the garden, and Mr. Hater and I did remove my money and iron chests into my cellar, as thinking that the safest place. And got my bags of gold into my office, ready to carry away, and my chief papers of accounts also there, and my tallys into a box by themselves. So great was our fear, as Sir W. Batten hath carts come out of the country to fetch away his goods this night. We did put Mr. Hater, poor man, to bed a little; but he got but very little rest, so much noise being in my house, taking down of goods.

September 3rd. About four o'clock in the morning, my Lady Batten sent me a cart to carry away all my money, and plate, and best things, to Sir W. Rider's at Bednall-greene. Which I did, riding myself in my night-gowne in the cart; and, Lord! to see how the streets and the highways are crowded with people running and riding, and getting of carts at any rate to fetch away things. I find Sir W. Rider tired with being called up all night, and receiving things from several friends. His house full of goods, and much of Sir W. Batten's and Sir W. Pen's. I am eased at my heart to have my treasure so well secured. Then home, with much ado to find a way, nor any sleep all this night to me nor my poor wife. But then and all this day she and I, and all my people labouring to get away the rest of our things, and did get Mr. Tooker to get me a lighter to take them in, and we did carry them (myself some) over Tower Hill, which was by this time full of people's goods, bringing their goods thither; and down to the lighter, which lay at the next quay, above the Tower Docke. And here was my neighbour's wife, Mrs. ——, with her pretty child, and some few of her things, which I did willingly give way to be saved with mine; but there was no passing with any thing through the postern, the crowd was so great. The Duke of Yorke come this day by the office, and spoke to us, and did ride with his guard up and down the City to keep all quiet (he being now Generall, and having the care of all). This day, Mercer being not at home, but against her mistress's order gone to her mother's, and my wife going thither to speak with W. Hewer, met her there, and was angry; and her mother saying that she was not a 'prentice girl, to ask leave every time she goes abroad, my wife with good reason was angry, and, when she came home, bid her be gone again. And so she went away, which troubled me, but yet less than it would, because of the condition we are in, fear of coming into in a little time of being less able to keepe one in her quality. At night lay down a little upon a quilt of W. Hewer's in the office, all my owne things being packed up or gone; and after me my poor wife did the like, we having fed upon the remains of yesterday's dinner, having no fire nor dishes, nor any opportunity of dressing any thing.

September 4th. Up by break of day to get away the remainder of my things; which I did by a lighter at the Iron gate: and my hands so few, that it was the afternoon before we could get them all away. Sir W. Pen and I to Tower-street, and there met the fire burning three or four doors beyond Mr. Howell's, whose goods, poor man, his trayes, and dishes, shovells, &c., were flung all along Tower-street in the kennels, and people working therewith from one end to the other; the fire coming on in that narrow streete, on both sides, with infinite fury. Sir W. Batten not knowing how to remove his wine, did dig a pit in the garden, and laid it in there; and I took the opportunity of laying all the papers of my office that I could not otherwise dispose of. And in the evening Sir W. Pen and I did dig another, and put our wine in it; and I my Parmazan cheese, as well as my wine and some other things. The Duke of Yorke was at the office this day, at Sir W. Pen's; but I happened not to be within. This afternoon sitting melancholy with Sir W. Pen in our garden, and thinking of the certain burning of this office, without extraordinary means, I did propose for the sending up of all our workmen from Woolwich and Deptford yards (none whereof yet appeared), and to write to Sir W. Coventry to have the Duke of Yorke's permission to pull down houses, rather than lose this office, which would much hinder the King's business. So Sir W. Pen he went down this night, in order to the sending them up to-morrow morning; and I wrote to Sir W. Coventry about the business, but received no answer. This night Mrs. Turner (who, poor woman, was removing her goods all this day, good goods into the garden, and knows not how to dispose of them), and her husband supped with my wife and I at night, in the office, upon a shoulder of mutton from the cook's, without any napkin or any thing, in a sad manner, but were merry. Only now and then walking into the garden, and saw how horridly the sky looks, all on a fire in the night, was enough to put us out of our wits; and, indeed, it was extremely dreadful, for it looks just as if it was at us, and the whole heaven on fire. I after supper walked in the darke down to Tower-streete, and there saw it all on fire, at the Trinity House on that side, and the Dolphin Taverne on this side, which was very near us; and the fire with extraordinary vehemence. Now begins the practice of blowing up of houses in Tower-streete, those next the Tower, which at first did frighten people more than any thing; but it stopped the fire where it was done, it bringing down the houses to the ground in the same places they stood, and then it was easy to quench what little fire was in it, though it kindled nothing almost. W. Hewer this day went to see how his mother did, and comes late home, telling us how he hath been forced to remove her to Islington, her house in Pye-corner being burned; so that the fire is got so far that way, and all the Old Bayly, and was running down to Fleete-streete; and Paul's is burned, and all Cheapside. I wrote to my father this night, but the post-house being burned, the letter could not go.

September 5th. I lay down in the office again upon W. Hewer's quilt, being mighty weary, and sore in my feet with going till I was hardly able to stand. About two in the morning my wife calls me up and tells me of new cryes of fire, it being come to Barking Church, which is the bottom of our lane. I up, and finding it so, resolved presently to take her away, and did, and took my gold, which was about £2,350, W. Hewer, and Jane, down by Proundy's boat to Woolwich; but, Lord! what a sad sight it was by moone-light to see the whole City almost on fire, that you might see it plain at Woolwich, as if you were by it. There, when I come, I find the gates shut, but no guard kept at all, which troubled me, because of discourse now begun, that there is plot in it, and that the French had done it. I got the gates open, and to Mr. Shelden's, where I locked up my gold, and charged my wife and W. Hewer never to leave the room without one of them in it, night or day. So back again, by the way seeing my goods well in the lighters at Deptford, and watched well by people. Home, and whereas I expected to have seen our house on fire, it being now about seven o'clock, it was not. But to the fire, and there find greater hopes than I expected; for my confidence of finding our Office on fire was such, that I durst not ask any body how it was with us, till I come and saw it not burned. But going to the fire, I find by the blowing up of houses, and the great helpe given by the workmen out of the King's yards, sent up by Sir W. Pen, there is a good stop given to it, as well as at Marke-lane end as ours; it having only burned the dyall of Barking Church, and part of the porch, and was there quenched. I up to the top of Barking steeple, and there saw the saddest sight of desolation that I ever saw; every where great fires, oyle-cellars, and brimstone, and other things burning. I became afeard to stay there long, and therefore down again as fast as I could, the fire being spread as far as I could see it; and to Sir W. Pen's, and there eat a piece of cold meat, having eaten nothing since Sunday, but the remains of Sunday's dinner. Here I met with Mr. Young and Whistler; and having removed all my things, and received good hopes that the fire at our end is stopped, they and I walked into the town, and find Fanchurch-streete, Gracious-streete, and Lumbard-streete all in dust. The Exchange a sad sight, nothing standing there, of all the statues or pillars, but Sir Thomas Gresham's picture in the corner. Walked into Moorefields (our feet ready to burn, walking through the towne among the hot coles), and find that full of people, and poor wretches carrying their goods there, and every body keeping his goods together by themselves (and a great blessing it is to them that it is fair weather for them to keep abroad night and day); drank there, and paid twopence for a plain penny loaf. Thence homeward, having passed through Cheapside and Newgate Market, all burned, and seen Anthony Joyce's house in fire. And took up (which I keep by me) a piece of glasse of Mercer's Chappell in the streete, where much more was, so melted and buckled with the heat of the fire like parchment. I also did see a poor cat taken out of a hole in the chimney, joyning to the wall of the Exchange, with the hair all burned off the body, and yet alive. So home at night, and find there good hopes of saving our office; but great endeavours of watching all night, and having men ready; and so we lodged them in the office, and had drink and bread and cheese for them. And I lay down and slept a good night about midnight, though when I rose I heard that there had been a great alarme of French and Dutch being risen, which proved nothing. But it is a strange thing to see how long this time did look since Sunday, having been always full of variety of actions, and little sleep, that it looked like a week or more, and I had forgot almost the day of the week.

September 6th. Up about five o'clock, and there met Mr. Gawden at the gate of the office (I intending to go out, as I used, every now and then to-day, to see how the fire is) to call our men to Bishop's-gate, where no fire had yet been near, and there is now one broke out: which did give great grounds to people, and to me too, to think that there is some kind of plot in this (on which many by this time have been taken, and it hath been dangerous for any stranger to walk in the streets), but I went with the men, and we did put it out in a little time; so that that was well again. It was pretty to see how hard the women did work in the cannells, sweeping of water; but then they would scold for drink, and be as drunk as devils. I saw good butts of sugar broke open in the street, and people go and take handsfull out, and put into beer, and drink it. And now all being pretty well, I took boat, and over to Southwarke, and took boat on the other side the bridge, and so to Westminster, thinking to shift myself, being all in dirt from top to bottom; but could not there find any place to buy a shirt or pair of gloves, Westminster Hall being full of people's goods, those in Westminster having removed all their goods, and the Exchequer money put into vessels to carry to Nonsuch; but to the Swan, and there was trimmed; and then to White Hall, but saw nobody; and so home. A sad sight to see how the River looks: no houses nor church near it, to the Temple, where it stopped. At home, did go with Sir W. Batten, and our neighbour, Knightly (who, with one more, was the only man of any fashion left in all the neighbourhood thereabouts, they all removing their goods and leaving their houses to the mercy of the fire), to Sir R. Ford's, and there dined in an earthen platter—a fried breast of mutton; a great many of us, but very merry, and indeed as good a meal, though as ugly a one, as ever I had in my life. Thence down to Deptford, and there with great satisfaction landed all my goods at Sir G. Carteret's safe, and nothing missed I could see, or hurt. This being done to my great content, I home, and to Sir W. Batten's, and there with Sir R. Ford, Mr. Knightly, and one Withers, a professed lying rogue, supped well, and mighty merry, and our fears over. From them to the office, and there slept with the office full of labourers, who talked, and slept, and walked all night long there. But strange it was to see Cloath-workers' Hall on fire these three days and nights in one body of flame, it being the cellar full of oyle.

December 31st. Rising this day with a full design to mind nothing else but to make up my accounts for the year past, I did take money, and walk forth to several places in the towne as far as the New Exchange, to pay all my debts, it being still a very great frost and good walking. I staid at the Fleece Tavern in Covent Garden while my boy Tom went to W. Joyce's to pay what I owed for candles there. Thence to the New Exchange to clear my wife's score, and so going back again I met Doll Lane (Mrs. Martin's sister), with another young woman of the Hall, one Scott, and took them to the Half Moon Taverne and there drank some burnt wine with them, without more pleasure, and so away home by coach, and there to dinner, and then to my accounts wherein, at last, I find them clear and right; but to my great discontent, do find that my gettings this year have been £573 less than my last: it being this year in all but £2,986; whereas, the last, I got £3,560. And then again my spendings this year have exceeded my spendings the last by £644: my whole spendings last year being but £509; whereas this year, it appears, I have spent £1,154, which is a sum not fit to be said that ever I should spend in one year, before I am master of a better estate than I am. Yet, blessed be God! and I pray God make me thankful for it, I do find myself worth in money, all good, above £6,200; which is above £1,800 more than I was the last year. This, I trust in God, will make me thankfull for what I have, and carefull to make up by care next year what by my negligence and prodigality I have lost and spent this year. The doing of this, and entering of it fair, with the sorting of all my expenses, to see how and in what points I have exceeded, did make it late work, till my eyes become very sore and ill, and then did give over, and supper, and to bed. Thus ends this year of publick wonder and mischief to this nation, and, therefore, generally wished by all people to have an end. Myself and family well, having four mayds and one clerk, Tom, in my house, and my brother, now with me, to spend time in order to his preferment. Our healths all well, only my eyes with overworking them are sore as candlelight comes to them, and not else; publick matters in a most sad condition; seamen discouraged for want of pay, and are become not to be governed: nor, as matters are now, can any fleete go out next year. Our enemies, French and Dutch, great, and grow more by our poverty. The Parliament backward in raising, because jealous of the spending of the money; the City less and less likely to be built again, every body settling elsewhere, and nobody encouraged to trade. A sad, vicious, negligent Court, and all sober men there fearful of the ruin of the whole kingdom this next year; from which, good God deliver us! One thing I reckon remarkable in my owne condition is, that I am come to abound in good plate, so as at all entertainments to be served wholly with silver plates, having two dozen and a half.

[1667] February 25th. Lay long in bed, talking with pleasure with my poor wife, how she used to make coal fires, and wash my foul clothes with her own hand for me, poor wretch! in our little room at my Lord Sandwich's; for which I ought for ever to love and admire her, and do; and persuade myself she would do the same thing again, if God should reduce us to it. So up and by coach abroad to the Duke of Albemarle's about sending soldiers down to some ships, and so home, calling at a beltmaker's to mend my belt, and so home and to dinner, where pleasant with my wife, and then to the office, where mighty busy all the day, saving going forth to the 'Change to pay for some things, and on other occasions, and at my goldsmith's did observe the King's new medall, where, in little, there is Mrs. Steward's face as well done as ever I saw anything in my whole life, I think: and a pretty thing it is, that he should choose her face to represent Britannia by. So at the office late very busy and much business with great joy dispatched, and so home to supper and to bed.

April 22nd. Up pretty betimes, my throat better, and so drest me, and to White Hall to see Sir W. Coventry, returned from Portsmouth, whom I am almost ashamed to see for fear he should have been told how often I have been at plays, but it is better to see him at first than afterward. So walked to the Old Swan and drank at Michell's, and then to White Hall and over the Park to St. James's to Sir W. Coventry, where well received, and good discourse. He seems to be sure of a peace; that the King of France do not intend to set out a fleete, for that he do design Flanders. Our Embassadors set out this week. Thence I over the Park to Sir G. Carteret, and after him by coach to the Lord Chancellor's house, the first time I have been therein; and it is very noble, and brave pictures of the ancient and present nobility, never saw better. Thence with him to London, mighty merry in the way. Thence home, and find the boy out of the house and office, and by and by comes in and hath been to Mercer's. I did pay his coat for him. Then to my chamber, my wife comes home with linen she hath been buying of. I then to dinner, and then down the river to Greenwich, and the watermen would go no further. So I turned them off, giving them nothing, and walked to Woolwich; there did some business, and met with Captain Cocke and back with him. He tells me our peace is agreed on; we are not to assist the Spanyard against the French for this year, and no restitution, and we are likely to lose Poleroone. I know not whether this be true or no, but I am for peace on any terms. He tells me how the King was vexed the other day for having no paper laid him at the Council-table, as was usual; and Sir Richard Browne did tell his Majesty he would call the person whose work it was to provide it: who being come, did tell his Majesty that he was but a poor man, and was out £400 or £500 for it, which was as much as he is worth; and that he cannot provide it any longer without money, having not received a penny since the King's coming in. So the King spoke to my Lord Chamberlain; and many such mementos the King do now-a-days meet withall, enough to make an ingenuous man mad. I to Deptford, and there scolded with a master for his ship's not being gone, and so home to the office and did business till my eyes are sore again, and so home to sing, and then to bed, my eyes failing me mightily.

May 11th. Up, and being called on by Mr. Commander, he and I out to the ground behind Sir W. Pen's, where I am resolved to take a lease of some of it for a stable and coach house, and so to keep a coach, unless some change come before I can do it, for I do see it is a greater charge to me now in hackneys, and I am a little dishonoured by going in them. We spoke with him that hath the letting it, and I do believe when I can tell how much it will be fit for me to have we shall go near to agree. So home, and there found my door open, which makes me very angry with Nell, and do think to put her away for it, though it do so go against me to part with a servant that it troubles me more than anything in the world. So to the office, where all the morning. At noon home to dinner, where Mr. Goodgroome and Creed, and I have great hopes that my wife will come to sing to my mind. After dinner my wife and Creed and I being entered a hackney coach to go to the other end of the town, we espied The. Turner coming in her coach to see us, which we were surprised at, and so 'light and took her and another young lady home, and there sat and talked with The., she being lately come out of the North after two or three years absence. She is come to put out her sister and brothers to school at Putney. After a little talk, I over Tower Hill with them to a lady's they go to visit, and so away with my wife, whose being dressed this day in fair hair did make me so mad, that I spoke not one word to her in our going, though I was ready to burst with anger. So to White Hall to the Committee of Tangier, where they were discoursing about laws for the civil government of the place, but so dull and so little to the purpose that I fell to slumber, when the fear of being seen by Sir W. Coventry did trouble me much afterwards, but I hope he did not. After that broke up. Creed and I into the Park, and walked, a most pleasant evening, and so took coach, and took up my wife, and in my way home discovered my trouble to my wife for her white locks, swearing by God, several times, which I pray God forgive me for, and bending my fist, that I would not endure it. She, poor wretch, was surprised with it, and made me no answer all the way home; but there we parted, and I to the office late, and then home, and without supper to bed, vexed.

May 28th. Up, and by coach to St. James's, where I find Sir W. Coventry, and he desirous to have spoke with me. It was to read over a draught of a letter which he hath made for his brother Commissioners and him to sign to us, demanding an account of the whole business of the Navy accounts; and I perceive, by the way he goes about it, that they will do admirable things. He tells me they have chosen Sir G. Downing their Secretary, who will be as fit a man as any in the world; and said, by the by, speaking of the bankers being fearful of Sir G. Downing's being Secretary, he being their enemy, that they did not intend to be ruled by their Secretary, but do the business themselves. My heart is glad to see so great hopes of good to the nation as will be by these men; and it do me good to see Sir W. Coventry so cheerfull as he now is on the same score. Thence home, and there fell to seeing my office and closet there made soundly clean, and the windows cleaned. At which all the morning, and so at noon to dinner. After dinner my wife away down with Jane and W. Hewer to Woolwich, in order to a little ayre and to lie there to-night, and so to gather May-dew to-morrow morning, which Mrs. Turner hath taught her as the only thing in the world to wash her face with; and I am contented with it. Presently comes Creed, and he and I by water to Fox-hall, and there walked in Spring Garden. A great deal of company, and the weather and garden pleasant: that it is very pleasant and cheap going thither, for a man may go to spend what he will, or nothing, all is one. But to hear the nightingale and other birds, and here fiddles, and there a harp, and here a Jew's trump, and here laughing, and there fine people walking, is mighty divertising. Among others, there were two pretty women alone, that walked a great while, which being discovered by some idle gentlemen, they would needs take them up; but to see the poor ladies how they were put to it to run from them, and they after them, and sometimes the ladies put themselves along with other company, then the other drew back; at last, the last did get off out of the house, and took boat and away. I was troubled to see them abused so; and could have found in my heart, as little desire of fighting as I have, to have protected the ladies. So by water, set Creed down at White Hall, and I to the Old Swan, and so home. My father gone to bed, and wife abroad at Woolwich, I to Sir W. Pen, where he and his Lady and Pegg and pretty Mrs. Lowther her sister-in-law at supper, where I sat and talked, and Sir W. Pen, half drunk, did talk like a fool and vex his wife, that I was half pleased and half vexed to see so much folly and rudeness from him, and so late home to bed.

June 10th. Up; and news brought us that the Dutch are come up as high as the Nore; and more pressing orders for fire-ships. W. Batten, W. Pen, and I to St. James's; where the Duke of York gone this morning betimes, to send away some men down to Chatham. So we three to White Hall, and met Sir W. Coventry, who presses all that is possible for fire-ships. So we three to the office presently; and thither comes Sir Fretcheville Hollis, who is to command them all in some exploits he is to do with them on the enemy in the River. So we all down to Deptford, and pitched upon ships and set men at work: but, Lord! to see how backwardly things move at this pinch, notwithstanding that, by the enemy's being now come up as high as almost the Hope, Sir J. Minnes, who has gone down to pay some ships there, hath sent up the money; and so we are possessed of money to do what we will with. Yet partly ourselves, being used to be idle and in despair, and partly people that have been used to be deceived by us as to money, won't believe us; and we know not, though we have it, how almost to promise it; and our wants such, and men out of the way, that it is an admirable thing to consider how much the King suffers, and how necessary it is in a State to keep the King's service always in a good posture and credit. Here I eat a bit, and then in the afternoon took boat and down to Greenwich, where I find the stairs full of people, there being a great riding there to-day for a man, the constable of the town, whose wife beat him. Here I was with much ado fain to press two watermen to make me a galley, and so to Woolwich to give order for the dispatch of a ship I have taken under my care to see dispatched, and orders being so given, I, under pretence to fetch up the ship, which lay at Grays (the *Golden Hand*), did do that in my way, and went down to Gravesend, where I find the Duke of Albemarle just come, with a great many idle lords and gentlemen, with their pistols and fooleries; and the bulwarke not able to have stood half an hour had they come up; but the Dutch are fallen down from the Hope and Shell-haven as low as Sheernesse, and we do plainly at this time hear the guns play. Yet I do not find the Duke of Albemarle intends to go thither, but stays here to-night, and hath, though the Dutch are gone, ordered our frigates to be brought to a line between the two blockhouses; which I took then to be a ridiculous thing. So I away into the town and took a captain or two of our ships (who did give me an account of the proceedings of the Dutch fleete in the river) to the taverne, and there eat and drank, and I find the townsmen had removed most of their goods out of the town, for fear of the Dutch coming up to them; and from Sir John Griffen, that last night there was not twelve men to be got in the town to defend it: which the master of the house tells me is not true, but that the men of the town did intend to stay, though they did indeed, and so had he, at the Ship, removed their goods. Thence went off to an Ostend man-of-war, just now come up, who met the Dutch fleete, who took three ships that he come convoying hither from him: says they are as low as the Nore, or thereabouts. So I homeward, as long as it was light reading Mr. Boyle's book of Hydrostatics, which is a most excellent book as ever I read, and I will take much pains to understand him through if I can, the doctrine being very useful. When it grew too dark to read I lay down and took a nap, it being a most excellent fine evening, and about one o'clock got home, and after having wrote to Sir W. Coventry an account of what I had done and seen (which is entered in my letter-book), I to bed.

June 11th. Up, and more letters still from Sir W. Coventry about more fire-ships, and so Sir W. Batten and I to the office, where Bruncker come to us, who is just now going to Chatham upon a desire of Commissioner Pett's, who is in a very fearful stink for fear of the Dutch, and desires help for God and the King and kingdom's sake. So Bruncker goes down, and Sir J. Minnes also, from Gravesend. This morning Pett writes us word that Sheernesse is lost last night, after two or three hours' dispute. The enemy hath possessed himself of that place; which is very sad, and puts us into great fears of Chatham. Sir W.

Batten and I down by water to Deptford, and there Sir W. Pen and we did consider of several matters relating to the dispatch of the fire-ships, and so Sir W. Batten and I home again, and there to dinner, my wife and father having dined, and after dinner, by W. Hewer's lucky advice, went to Mr. Fenn, and did get him to pay me above £400 of my wages, and W. Hewer received it for me, and brought it home this night. Thence I meeting Mr. Moore went toward the other end of the town by coach, and spying Mercer in the street, I took leave of Moore and 'light and followed her, and at Paul's overtook her and walked with her through the dusty street almost to home, and there in Lombard Street met The. Turner in coach, who had been at my house to see us, being to go out of town to-morrow to the Northward, and so I promised to see her to-morrow, and then home, and there to our business, hiring some fire-ships, and receiving every hour almost letters from Sir W. Coventry, calling for more fire-ships; and an order from Council to enable us to take any man's ships; and Sir W. Coventry, in his letter to us, says he do not doubt but at this time, under an invasion, as he owns it to be, the King may, by law, take any man's goods. At this business late, and then home; where a great deal of serious talk with my wife about the sad state we are in, and especially from the beating up of drums this night for the trainbands upon pain of death to appear in arms to-morrow morning with bullet and powder, and money to supply themselves with victuals for a fortnight; which, considering the soldiers drawn out of Chatham and elsewhere, looks as if they had a design to ruin the City and give it up to be undone; which, I hear, makes the sober citizens to think very sadly of things. So to bed after supper, ill in my mind. This afternoon Mrs. Williams sent to me to speak with her, which I did, only about news. I had not spoken with her many a day before by reason of Carcasse's business.

June 12th. Up very betimes to our business at the office, there hiring of more fire-ships; and at it close all the morning.

At noon home, and Sir W. Pen dined with us. By and by, after dinner, my wife out by coach to see her mother; and I in another, being afraid, at this busy time, to be seen with a woman in a coach, as if I were idle, towards The. Turner's; but met Sir W. Coventry's boy; and there in his letter find that the Dutch had made no motion since their taking Sheernesse; and the Duke of Albemarle writes that all is safe as to the great ships against any assault, the boom and chaine being so fortified; which put my heart into great joy. When I come to Sir W. Coventry's chamber, I find him abroad; but his clerk, Powell, do tell me that ill news is come to Court of the Dutch breaking the Chaine at Chatham; which struck me to the heart. And to White Hall to hear the truth of it; and there, going up the back-stairs, I did hear some lacquies speaking of sad news come to Court, saying, that hardly anybody in the Court but do look as if he cried, and would not go into the house for fear of being seen, but slunk out and got into a coach, and to The. Turner's to Sir W. Turner's, where I met Roger Pepys, newly come out of the country. He and I talked aside a little, he offering a match for Pall, one Barnes, of whom we shall talk more the next time. His father married a Pepys; in discourse he told me further that his grandfather, my great grandfather, had £800 per annum, in Queen Elizabeth's time, in the very town of Cottenham; and that we did certainly come out of Scotland with the Abbot of Crowland. More talk I had, and shall have more with him, but my mind is so sad and head full of this ill news that I cannot now set it down. A short visit here, my wife coming to me, and took leave of The., and so home, where all our hearts do now ake; for the news is true, that the Dutch have broken the chaine and burned our ships, and particularly *The Royal Charles*: other particulars I know not, but most sad to be sure. And, the truth is, I do fear so much that the whole kingdom is undone, that I do this night resolve to study with my father and wife what to do with the little that I have in money by me, for I give up all the rest that I have in the King's hands, for Tangier, for lost. So God help us! and God knows what disorders we may fall into, and whether any violence on this office, or perhaps some severity on our persons, as being reckoned by the silly people, or perhaps may, by policy of State, be thought fit to be condemned by the King and Duke of York, and so put to trouble; though, God knows! I have, in my own person, done my full duty, I am sure. So having with much ado finished my business at the office, I home to consider with my father and wife of things, and then to supper and to bed with a heavy heart. The manner of my advising this night with my father was, I took him and my wife up to her chamber, and shut the door; and there told them the sad state of the times how we are like to be all undone; that I do fear some violence will be offered to this office, where all I have in the world is; and resolved upon sending it away—sometimes into the country—sometimes my father to lie in town, and have the gold with him at Sarah Giles's, and with that resolution went to bed full of fear and fright, hardly slept all night.

June 13th. No sooner up but hear the sad news confirmed of *The Royal Charles* being taken by them, and now in fitting by them—which Pett should have carried up higher by our several orders, and deserves, therefore, to be hanged for not doing it—and turning several others; and that another fleete is come up into the Hope. Upon which news the King and Duke of York have been below since four o'clock in the morning, to command the sinking of ships at Barking-Creeke, and other places, to stop their coming up higher: which put me into such a fear, that I presently resolved of my father's and wife's going into the country; and, at two hours' warning, they did go by the coach this day, with about £1,300 in gold in their night-bag. Pray God give them good passage, and good care to hide it when they come home! but my heart is full of fear. They gone, I continued in fright and fear what to do with the rest. W. Hewer hath been at the banker's, and hath got £500 out of Backewell's hands of his own money; but they are so called upon that they will be all broke, hundreds coming to them for money: and their answer is, "It is payable at twenty days—when the days are out we will pay you;" and those that are not so, they make tell over their money, and make their bags false, on purpose to give cause to retell it, and so spend time. I cannot have my 200 pieces of gold again for silver, all being bought up last night that were to be had, and sold for 24 and 25s. a-piece. So I must keep the silver by me, which sometimes I think to fling into the house of office, and then again know not how I shall come by it, if we be made to leave the office. Every minute some one or other calls for this or that order; and so I forced to be at the office, most of the day, about the fire-ships which are to be suddenly fitted out: and it's a most strange thing that we hear nothing from any of my brethren at Chatham; so that we are wholly in the dark, various being the reports of what is done there; in so much that I sent Mr. Clapham express thither to see how matters go. I did, about noon, resolve to send Mr. Gibson away after my wife with another 1,000 pieces, under colour of an express to Sir Jeremy Smith; who is, as I hear, with some ships at Newcastle; which I did really send to him, and may, possibly, prove of good use to the King; for it is possible, in the hurry of business, they may not think of it at Court, and the charge of an express is not considerable to the King. So though I intend Gibson no further than to Huntingdon, I direct him to send the packet forward. My business the most of the afternoon is listening to every body that comes to the office, what news? which is variously related, some better, some worse, but nothing certain. The King and Duke of York up and down all the day here and there: some time on Tower Hill, where the City militia was; where the King did make a speech to them, that they should venture themselves no further than he would himself. I also sent, my mind being in pain, Saunders after my wife and father, to overtake them at their night's lodgings, to see how matters go with them. In the evening, I sent for my cousin Sarah Gyles and her husband, who come; and I did deliver them my chest of writings about Brampton, and my brother Tom's papers, and my journalls, which I value much;

and did send my two silver flaggons to Kate Joyce's: that so, being scattered what I have, something might be saved. I have also made a girdle, by which, with some trouble, I do carry about me £300 in gold about my body, that I may not be without something in case I should be surprised: for I think, in any nation but our's, people that appear (for we are not indeed so) so faulty as we, would have their throats cut. In the evening comes Mr. Pelling, and several others, to the office, and tell me that never were people so dejected as they are in the City all over at this day; and do talk most loudly, even treason; as, that we are bought and sold—that we are betrayed by the Papists, and others, about the King; cry out that the office of the Ordnance hath been so backward as no powder to have been at Chatham nor Upnor Castle till such a time, and the carriages all broken; that Legg is a Papist; that Upnor, the old good castle built by Queen Elizabeth, should be lately slighted; that the ships at Chatham should not be carried up higher. They look upon us as lost, and remove their families and rich goods in the City; and do think verily that the French, being come down with his army to Dunkirke, it is to invade us, and that we shall be invaded. Mr. Clerke, the solicitor, comes to me about business, and tells me that he hears that the King hath chosen Mr. Pierpont and Vaughan of the West, Privy-councillors; that my Lord Chancellor was affronted in the Hall this day, by people telling him of his Dunkirke house; and that there are regiments ordered to be got together, whereof to be commanders my Lord Fairfax, Ingoldsby, Bethell, Norton, and Birch, and other Presbyterians; and that Dr. Bates will have liberty to preach. Now, whether this be true or not, I know not; but do think that nothing but this will unite us together. Late at night comes Mr. Hudson, the cooper, my neighbour, and tells me that he come from Chatham this evening at five o'clock, and saw this afternoon *The Royal James*, *Oake*, and *London*, burnt by the enemy with their fire-ships: that two or three men-of-war come up with them, and made no more of Upnor Castle's shooting, than of a fly; that those ships lay below Upnor Castle, but therein, I conceive, he is in an error; that the Dutch are fitting out *The Royal Charles*; that we shot so far as from the yard thither, so that the shot did no good, for the bullets grazed on the water; that Upnor played hard with their guns at first, but slowly afterwards, either from the men being beat off, or their powder spent. But we hear that the fleete in the Hope is not come up any higher the last flood; and Sir W. Batten tells me that ships are provided to sink in the River, about Woolwich, that will prevent their coming up higher if they should attempt it. I made my will also this day, and did give all I had equally between my father and wife, and left copies of it in each of Mr. Hater and W. Hewer's hands, who both witnessed the will, and so to supper and then to bed, and slept pretty well, but yet often waking.

June 14th. Up, and to the office; where Mr. Fryer comes and tells me that there are several Frenchmen and Flemish ships in the River, with passes from the Duke of York for carrying of prisoners, that ought to be parted from the rest of the ships, and their powder taken, lest they do fire themselves when the enemy comes, and so spoil us; which is good advice, and I think I will give notice of it; and did so. But it is pretty odd to see how every body, even at this high time of danger, puts business off of their own hands! He says that he told this to the Lieutenant of the Tower, to whom I, for the same reason, was directing him to go; and the Lieutenant of the Tower bade him come to us, for he had nothing to do with it; and yesterday comes Captain Crew, of one of the fire-ships, and told me that the officers of the Ordnance would deliver his gunner's materials, but not compound them, but that we must do it; whereupon I was forced to write to them about it; and one that like a great many come to me this morning by and by comes—Mr. Wilson, and by direction of his, a man of Mr. Gawden's; who come from Chatham last night, and saw the three ships burnt, they lying all dry, and boats going from the men-of-war and fire them.

But that, that he tells me of worst consequence is, that he himself, I think he said, did hear many Englishmen on board the Dutch ships speaking to one another in English; and that they did cry and say, "We did heretofore fight for tickets; now we fight for dollars!" and did ask how such and such a one did, and would commend themselves to them: which is a sad consideration. And Mr. Lewes, who was present at this fellow's discourse to me, did tell me, that he is told that when they took *The Royal Charles*, they said that they had their tickets signed, and showed some, and that now they come to have them paid, and would have them paid before they parted. And several seamen come this morning to me, to tell me that, if I would get their tickets paid, they would go and do all they could against the Dutch; but otherwise they would not venture being killed, and lose all they have already fought for: so that I was forced to try what I could do to get them paid. This man tells me that the ships burnt last night did lie above Upnor Castle, over against the Docke; and the boats come from the ships of war and burnt them: all which is very sad. And masters of ships, that we are now taking up, do keep from their ships all their stores, or as much as they can, so that we can despatch them, having not time to appraise them nor secure their payment; only some little money we have, which we are fain to pay the men we have with, every night, or they will not work. And indeed the hearts as well as affections of the seamen are turned away; and in the open streets in Wapping, and up and down, the wives have cried publickly, "This comes of your not paying our husbands; and now your work, is undone, or done by hands that understand it not." And Sir W. Batten told me that he was himself affronted with a woman, in language of this kind, on Tower Hill publickly yesterday; and we are fain to bear it, and to keep one at the office door to let no idle people in, for fear of firing of the office and doing us mischief. The City is troubled at their being put upon duty: summoned one hour, and discharged two hours after; and then again summoned two hours after that; to their great charge as well as trouble. And Pelling, the Potticary, tells me the world says all over, that less charge than what the kingdom is put to, of one kind or other, by this business, would have set out all our great ships. It is said they did in open streets yesterday, at Westminster, cry, "A Parliament! a Parliament!" and I do believe it will cost blood to answer for these miscarriages. We do not hear that the Dutch are come to Gravesend; which is a wonder. But a wonderful thing it is that to this day we have not one word yet from Bruncker, or Peter Pett, or J. Minnes, of any thing at Chatham. The people that come hither to hear how things go, make me ashamed to be found unable to answer them: for I am left alone here at the office; and the truth is, I am glad my station is to be here, near my own home and out of danger, yet in a place of doing the King good service. I have this morning good news from Gibson; three letters from three several stages, that he was safe last night as far as Royston, at between nine and ten at night. The dismay that is upon us all, in the business of the kingdom and Navy at this day, is not to be expressed otherwise than by the condition the citizens were in when the City was on fire, nobody knowing which way to turn themselves, while every thing concurred to greaten the fire; as here the easterly gale and spring-tides for coming up both rivers, and enabling them to break the chaine. D. Gawden did tell me yesterday, that the day before at the Council they were ready to fall together by the ears at the Council-table, arraigning one another of being guilty of the counsel that brought us into this misery, by laying up all the great ships. Mr. Hater tells me at noon that some rude people have been, as he hears, at my Lord Chancellor's, where they have cut down the trees before his house and broke his windows; and a gibbet either set up before or painted upon his gate, and these three words writ: "Three sights to be seen; Dunkirke, Tangier, and a barren Queene." It gives great matter of talk that it is said there is at this hour, in the Exchequer, as much money as is ready to break down the floor. This arises, I believe, from Sir G. Downing's late talk of the greatness of the sum lying there of people's money, that they would not fetch away, which he shewed me and a great many others. Most people that I speak with are in doubt how we shall do to secure our seamen from running over to the Dutch; which is a sad but very true consideration at this day. At noon I am told that my Lord Duke of Albemarle is made Lord High Constable; the meaning whereof at this time I know not, nor whether it be true or no. Dined, and Mr. Hater and W. Hewer with me; where they do speak very sorrowfully of the posture of the times, and how people do cry out in the streets of their being bought and sold; and both they, and every body that come to me, do tell me that people make nothing of talking treason in the streets openly: as, that we are bought and sold, and governed by Papists, and that we are betrayed by people about the King, and shall be delivered up to the French, and I know not what. At dinner we discoursed of Tom of the Wood, a fellow that lives like a hermit near Woolwich, who, as they say, and Mr. Bodham, they tell me, affirms that he was by at the Justice's when some did accuse him there for it, did foretell the burning of the City, and now says that a greater desolation is at hand. Thence we read and laughed at Lilly's prophecies this month, in his Almanack this year. So to the office after dinner; and thither comes Mr. Pierce, who tells me his condition, how he cannot get his money, about £500, which, he says, is a very great part of what he hath for his family and children, out of Viner's hand: and indeed it is to be feared that this will wholly undo the bankers. He says he knows nothing of the late affronts to my Lord Chancellor's house, as is said, nor hears of the Duke of Albemarle's being made High Constable; but says that they are in great distraction at White Hall, and that every where people do speak high against Sir W. Coventry: but he agrees with me, that he is the best Minister of State the King hath, and so from my heart I believe. At night come home Sir W. Batten and W. Pen, who only can tell me that they have placed guns at Woolwich and Deptford, and sunk ships below Woolwich and Blackewall, and are in hopes that they will stop the enemy's coming up. But strange our confusion! that among them that are sunk they have gone and sunk without consideration *The Franakin*, one of the King's ships, with stores to a very considerable value, that hath been long loaden for supply of the ships; and the new ship at Bristoll, and much wanted there; and nobody will own that they directed it, but do lay it on Sir W. Rider. They speak also of another ship, loaden to the value of £80,000, sunk with the goods in her, or at least was mightily contended for by him, and a foreign ship, that had the faith of the nation for her security: this Sir R. Ford tells us. And it is too plain a truth, that both here and at Chatham the ships that we have sunk have many, and the first of them, been ships completely fitted for fire-ships at great charge. But most strange the backwardness and disorder of all people, especially the King's people in pay, to do any work, Sir W. Pen tells me, all crying out for money; and it was so at Chatham, that this night comes an order from Sir W. Coventry to stop the pay of the wages of that Yard; the Duke of Albemarle having related, that not above three of 1,100 in pay there did attend to do any work there. This evening having sent a messenger to Chatham on purpose, we have received a dull letter from my Lord Bruncker and Peter Pett, how matters have gone there this week; but not so much, or so particularly, as we knew it by common talk before, and as true. I doubt they will be found to have been but slow men in this business; and they say the Duke of Albemarle did tell my Lord Bruncker to his face that his discharging of the great ships there was the cause of all this; and I am told that it is become common talk against my Lord Bruncker. But in that he is to be justified, for he did it by verbal order from Sir W. Coventry, and with good intent; and it was to good purpose, whatever the success be, for the men would have but spent the King so much the more in wages, and yet not attended on board to have done the King any service; and as an evidence of that, just now, being the 15th day in the morning that I am writing yesterday's passages, one is with me, Jacob Bryan, Purser of *The Princesse*, who confesses to me that he hath about 180 men borne at this day in victuals and wages on that ship lying at

Chatham, being lately brought in thither; of which 180 there was not above five appeared to do the King any service at this late business. And this morning also, some of the *Cambridge's* men come up from Portsmouth, by order from Sir Fretcheville Hollis, who boasted to us the other day that he had sent for 50, and would be hanged if 100 did not come up that would do as much as twice the number of other men: I say some of them, instead of being at work at Deptford, where they were intended, do come to the office this morning to demand the payment of their tickets; for otherwise they would, they said, do no more work; and are, as I understand from every body that has to do with them, the most debauched, damning, swearing rogues that ever were in the Navy, just like their prophane commander. So to Sir W. Batten's to sit and talk a little, and then home to my flageolet, my heart being at pretty good ease by a letter from my wife, brought by Saunders, that my father and wife got well last night to their Inne and out again this morning, and Gibson's being got safe to Caxton at twelve last night. So to supper, and then to bed. No news today of any motion of the enemy either upwards towards Chatham or this way.

June 15th. All the morning at the office. No news more than last night; only Purser Tyler comes and tells me that he being at all the passages in this business at Chatham, he says there have been horrible miscarriages, such as we shall shortly hear of: that the want of boats hath undone us; and it is commonly said, and Sir J. Minnes under his hand tells us, that they were employed by the men of the Yard to carry away their goods; and I hear that Commissioner Pett will be found the first man that began to remove; he is much spoken against, and Bruncker is complained of and reproached for discharging the men of the great ships heretofore. At noon Mr. Hater dined with me; and tells me he believes that it will hardly be the want of money alone that will excuse to the Parliament the neglect of not setting out a fleete, it having never been done in our greatest straits, but however unlikely it appeared, yet when it was gone about, the State or King did compass it; and there is something in it. In like manner all the afternoon busy, vexed to see how slowly things go on for want of money. At night comes, unexpectedly so soon, Mr. Gibson, who left my wife well, and all got down well with them, but not with himself, which I was afeard of, and cannot blame him, but must myself be wiser against another time. He had one of his bags broke, through his breeches, and some pieces dropped out, not many, he thinks, but two, for he 'light, and took them up, and went back and could find no more. But I am not able to tell how many, which troubles me, but the joy of having the greatest part safe there makes me bear with it, so as not to afflict myself for it. This afternoon poor Betty Michell, whom I love, sent to tell my wife her child was dying, which I am troubled for, poor girle! At night home and to my flageolet. Played with pleasure, but with a heavy heart, only it pleased me to think how it may please God I may live to spend my time in the country with plainness and pleasure, though but with little glory. So to supper and to bed.

June 19th. Up, and to the office, where all the morning busy with Fist again, beginning early to overtake my business in my letters, which for a post or two have by the late and present troubles been interrupted. At noon comes Sir W. Batten and Sir W. Pen, and we to Sir W. Pen's house, and there discoursed of business an hour, and by and by comes an order from Sir R. Browne, commanding me this afternoon to attend the Council-board, with all my books and papers touching the Medway. I was ready to fear some mischief to myself, though it appears most reasonable that it is to inform them about Commissioner Pett. I eat a little bit in haste at Sir W. Batten's, without much comfort, being fearful, though I shew it not, and to my office and get up some papers, and found out the most material letters and orders in our books, and so took coach and to the Council-chamber lobby, where I met Mr. Evelyn, who do miserably decry our follies that bring all this misery upon us. While we were discoursing over our publique misfortunes, I am called in to a large Committee of the Council: present the Duke of Albemarle, Anglesey, Arlington, Ashly, Carteret, Duncomb, Coventry, Ingram, Clifford, Lauderdale, Morrice, Manchester, Craven, Bridgewater. And after Sir W. Coventry's telling them what orders His Royal Highness had made for the safety of the Medway, I told them to their full content what we had done, and shewed them our letters. Then was Peter Pett called in, with the Lieutenant of the Tower. He is in his old clothes, and looked most sillily. His charge was chiefly the not carrying up of the great ships, and the using of the boats in carrying away his goods; to which he answered very sillily, though his faults to me seem only great omissions. Lord Arlington and Coventry very severe against him; the former saying that, if he was not guilty, the world would think them all guilty. The latter urged, that there must be some faults, and that the Admiral must be found to have done his part. I did say an unhappy word, which I was sorry for, when he complained of want of oares for the boats: and there was, it seems, enough, and good enough, to carry away all the boats with from the King's occasions. He said he used never a boat till they were all gone but one; and that was to carry away things of great value, and these were his models of ships; which, when the Council, some of them, had said they wished that the Dutch had had them instead of the King's ships, he answered, he did believe the Dutch would have made more advantage of the models than of the ships, and that the King had had greater loss thereby; this they all laughed at. After having heard him for an hour or more, they bid him withdraw. I all this while showing him no respect, but rather against him, for which God forgive me! for I mean no hurt to him, but only find that these Lords are upon their own purgation, and it is necessary I should be so in behalf of the office. He being gone, they caused Sir Richard Browne to read over his minutes; and then my Lord Arlington moved that they might be put into my hands to put into form, I being more acquainted with such business; and they were so. So I away back with my books and papers; and when I got into the Court it was pretty to see how people gazed upon me, that I thought myself obliged to salute people and to smile, lest they should think I was a prisoner too; but afterwards I found that most did take me to be there to bear evidence against P. Pett; but my fear was such, at my going in, of the success of the day, that at my going in I did think fit to give T. Hater, whom I took with me, to wait the event, my closet-key and directions where to find £500 and more in silver and gold, and my tallys, to remove, in case of any misfortune to me. Thence to Sir G. Carteret's to take my leave of my Lady Jem, who is going into the country to-morrow; but she being now at prayers with my Lady and family, and hearing here by Yorke, the carrier, that my wife is coming to towne, I did make haste home to see her, that she might not find me abroad, it being the first minute I have been abroad since yesterday was se'ennight. It is pretty to see how strange it is to be abroad to see people, as it used to be after a month or two's absence, and I have brought myself so to it, that I have no great mind to be abroad, which I could not have believed of myself. I got home, and after being there a little, she come, and two of her fellow-travellers with her, with whom we drunk: a couple of merchant-like men, I think, but have friends in our country. They being gone, I and my wife to talk, who did give me so bad an account of her and my father's method in burying of our gold, that made me mad: and she herself is not pleased with it, she believing that my sister knows of it. My father and she did it on Sunday, when they were gone to church, in open daylight, in the midst of the garden; where, for aught they knew, many eyes might see them: which put me into such trouble, that I was almost mad about it, and presently cast about, how to have it back again to secure it here, the times being a little better now: at least at White Hall they seem as if they were, but one way or other I am resolved to free them from the place if I can get them. Such was my trouble at this, that I fell out with my wife, that though new come to towne, I did not sup with her, nor speak to her to-night, but to bed and sleep.

July 14th (Lord's day). Up, and my wife, a little before four, and to make us ready; and by and by Mrs. Turner come to us, by agreement, and she and I staid talking below, while my wife dressed herself, which vexed me that she was so long about it keeping us till past five o'clock before she was ready. She ready; and, taking some bottles of wine, and beer, and some cold fowle with us into the coach, we took coach and four horses, which I had provided last night, and so away. A very fine day, and so towards Epsum, talking all the way pleasantly, and particularly of the pride and ignorance of Mrs. Lowther, in having of her train carried up. The country very fine, only the way very dusty. We got to Epsum by eight o'clock, to the well; where much company, and there we 'light, and I drank the water: they did not, but do go about and walk a little among the women, but I did drink four pints. Here I met with divers of our town, among others with several of the tradesmen of our office, but did talk but little with them, it growing hot in the sun, and so we took coach again and to the towne, to the King's Head, where our coachman carried us, and there had an ill room for us to go into, but the best in the house that was not taken up. Here we called for drink, and bespoke dinner; and hear that my Lord Buckhurst and Nelly are lodged at the next house, and Sir Charles Sidly with them: and keep a merry house. Poor girl! I pity her; but more the loss of her at the King's house. Here I saw Gilsthrop, Sir W. Batten's clerk that hath been long sick, he looks like a dying man, with a consumption got, as is believed, by the pox, but God knows that the man is in a sad condition, though he finds himself much better since his coming thither, he says. W. Hewer rode with us, and I left him and the women, and myself walked to church, where few people, contrary to what I expected, and none I knew, but all the Houblons, brothers, and them after sermon I did salute, and walk with towards my inne, which was in their way to their lodgings. They come last night to see their elder brother, who stays here at the waters, and away to-morrow. James did tell me that I was the only happy man of the Navy, of whom, he says, during all this freedom the people have taken of speaking treason, he hath not heard one bad word of me, which is a great joy to me; for I hear the same of others, but do know that I have deserved as well as most. We parted to meet anon, and I to my women into a better room, which the people of the house borrowed for us, and there to dinner, a good dinner, and were merry, and Pendleton come to us, who happened to be in the house, and there talked and were merry. After dinner, he gone, we all lay down after dinner (the day being wonderful hot) to sleep, and each of us took a good nap, and then rose; and Tom Wilson come to see me, and sat and talked an hour; and I perceive he hath been much acquainted with Dr. Fuller (Tom) and Dr. Pierson, and several of the great cavalier parsons during the late troubles; and I was glad to hear him talk of them, which he did very ingeniously, and very much of Dr. Fuller's art of memory, which he did tell me several instances of. By and by he parted, and we took coach and to take the ayre, there being a fine breeze abroad; and I went and carried them to the well, and there filled some bottles of water to carry home with me; and there talked with the two women that farm the well, at £12 per annum, of the lord of the manor, Mr. Evelyn (who with his lady, and also my Lord George Barkeley's lady, and their fine daughter, that the King of France liked so well, and did dance so rich in jewells before the King at the Ball I was at, at our Court, last winter, and also their son, a Knight of the Bath, were at church this morning). Here W. Hewer's horse broke loose, and we had the sport to see him taken again. Then I carried them to see my cozen Pepys's house, and 'light, and walked round about it, and they like it, as indeed it deserves, very well, and is a pretty place; and then I walked them to the wood hard by, and there got them in the thickets till they had lost themselves, and I could not find the way into any of the walks in the wood, which indeed are very pleasant, if I could have found them. At last got out of the wood again; and I, by leaping down the little bank, coming out of the wood, did sprain my right foot, which brought me great present pain, but presently, with walking, it went away for the present, and so the women and W. Hewer and I walked upon the Downes, where a flock of sheep was; and the most pleasant and innocent sight that ever I saw in my life—we find a shepherd and his little boy reading, far from any houses or sight of people, the Bible to him; so I made the boy read to me, which he did, with the forced tone that children do usually read, that was mighty pretty, and then I did give him something, and went to the father, and talked with him; and I find he had been a servant in my cozen Pepys's house, and told me what was become of their old servants. He did content himself mightily in my liking his boy's reading, and did bless God for him, the most like one of the old patriarchs that ever I saw in my life, and it brought those thoughts of the old age of the world in my mind for two or three days after. We took notice of his woolen knit stockings of two colours mixed, and of his shoes shod with iron shoes, both at the toe and heels, and with great nails in the soles of his feet, which was mighty pretty: and, taking notice of them, "Why," says the poor man, "the downes, you see, are full of stones, and we are faine to shoe ourselves thus; and these," says he, "will make the stones fly till they sing before me." I did give the poor man something, for which he was mighty thankful, and I tried to cast stones with his horne crooke. He values his dog mightily, that would turn a sheep any way which he would have him, when he goes to fold them: told me there was about eighteen scoare sheep in his flock, and that he hath four shillings a week the year round for keeping of them: so we posted thence with mighty pleasure in the discourse we had with this poor man, and Mrs. Turner, in the common fields here, did gather one of the prettiest nosegays that ever I saw in my life. So to our coach, and through Mr. Minnes's wood, and looked upon Mr. Evelyn's house; and so over the common, and through Epsum towne to our inne, in the way stopping a poor woman with her milk-pail, and in one of my gilt tumblers did drink our bellyfulls of milk, better than any creame; and so to our inne, and there had a dish of creame, but it was sour, and so had no pleasure in it; and so paid our reckoning, and took coach, it being about seven at night, and passed and saw the people walking with their wives and children to take the ayre, and we set out for home, the sun by and by going down, and we in the cool of the evening all the way with much pleasure home, talking and pleasing ourselves with the pleasure of this day's work, Mrs. Turner mightily pleased with my resolution, which, I tell her, is never to keep a country-house, but to keep a coach, and with my wife on the Saturday to go sometimes for a day to this place, and then quit to another place; and there is more variety and as little charge, and no trouble, as there is in a country-house. Anon it grew dark, and as it grew dark we had the pleasure to see several glow-worms, which was mighty pretty, but my foot begins more and more to pain me, which Mrs. Turner, by keeping her warm hand upon it, did much ease; but so that when we come home, which was just at eleven at night, I was not able to walk from the lane's end to my house without being helped, which did trouble me, and therefore to bed presently, but, thanks be to God, found that I had not been missed, nor any business happened in my absence. So to bed, and there had a cere-cloth laid to my foot and leg alone, but in great pain all night long.

October 5th. Up, and to the office; and there all the morning; none but my Lord Anglesey and myself; but much surprized with the news of the death of Sir W. Batten, who died this morning, having been but two days sick. Sir W. Pen and I did dispatch a letter this morning to Sir W. Coventry, to recommend Colonel Middleton, who we think a most honest and understanding man, and fit for that place. Sir G. Carteret did also come this morning, and walked with me in the garden; and concluded not to concern himself or have any advice made to Sir W. Coventry, in behalf of my Lord Sandwich's business; so I do rest satisfied, though I do think they are all mad, that they will judge Sir W. Coventry an enemy, when he is indeed no such man to any body, but is severe and just, as he ought to be, where he sees things ill done. At noon home, and by coach to Temple Bar to a India shop, and there bought a gown and sash, which cost me 26s., and so she (Mrs. Pepys) and Willet away to the 'Change, and I to my Lord Crew, and there met my Lord Hinchingbroke and Lady Jemimah, and there dined with them and my Lord, where pretty merry, and after dinner my Lord Crew and Hinchingbroke and myself went aside to discourse about my Lord Sandwich's business, which is in a very ill state for want of money, and so parted, and I to my tailor's, and there took up my wife and Willet, who staid there for me, and to the Duke of York's playhouse, but the house so full, it being a new play, *The Coffee House*, that we could not get in, and so to the King's house: and there, going in, met with Knepp, and she took us up into the tireing-rooms: and to the women's shift, where Nell was dressing herself, and was all unready, and is very pretty, prettier than I thought. And so walked all up and down the house above, and then below into the scene-room, and there sat down, and she gave us fruit: and here I read the questions to Knepp, while she answered me, through all her part of *Flora's Figary's* which was acted to-day. But, Lord! to see how they were both painted would make a man mad, and did make me loath them; and what base company of men comes among them, and how lewdly they talk! and how poor the men are in clothes, and yet what a shew they make on the stage by candle-light, is very observable. But to see how Nell cursed, for having so few people in the pit, was pretty; the other house carrying away all the people at the new play, and is said, now-a-days, to have generally most company, as being better players. By and by into the pit, and there saw the play, which is pretty good, but my belly was full of what I had seen in the house, and so, after the play done, away home, and there to the writing my letters, and so home to supper and to bed.

November 29th. Waked about seven o'clock this morning with a noise I supposed I heard, near our chamber, of knocking, which, by and by, increased: and I, more awake, could distinguish it better. I then waked my wife, and both of us wondered at it, and lay so a great while, while that increased, and at last heard it plainer, knocking, as if it were breaking down a window for people to get out; and then removing of stools and chairs; and plainly, by and by, going up and down our stairs. We lay, both of us, afeard; yet I would have rose, but my wife would not let me. Besides, I could not do it without making noise; and we did both conclude that thieves were in the house, but wondered what our people did, whom we thought either killed, or afeard, as we were. Thus we lay till the clock struck eight, and high day. At last, I removed my gown and slippers safely to the other side of the bed over my wife: and there safely rose, and put on my gown and breeches, and then, with a fire-brand in my hand, safely opened the door, and saw nor heard any thing. Then (with fear, I confess), went to the maid's chamber-door, and all quiet and safe. Called Jane up, and went down safely, and opened my chamber door, where all well. Then more freely about, and to the kitchen, where the cook-maid up, and all safe. So up again, and when Jane come, and we demanded whether she heard no noise, she said, "yes, and was afeard," but rose with the other maid, and found nothing; but heard a noise in the great stack of chimnies that goes from Sir J. Minnes through our house; and so we sent, and their chimnies have been swept this morning, and the noise was that, and nothing else. It is one of the most extraordinary accidents in my life, and gives ground to think of Don Quixote's adventures how people may be surprised, and the more from an accident last night, that our young gibb-cat did leap down our stairs from top to bottom, at two leaps, and frighted us, that we could not tell well whether it was the cat or a spirit, and do sometimes think this morning that the house might be haunted. Glad to have this so well over, and indeed really glad in my mind, for I was much afeard. I dressed myself and to the office both forenoon and afternoon, mighty hard putting papers and things in order to my extraordinary satisfaction, and consulting my clerks in many things, who are infinite helps to my memory and reasons of things, and so being weary, and my eyes akeing, having over-wrought them to-day reading so much shorthand, I home and there to supper, it being late, and to bed. This morning Sir W. Pen and I did walk together a good while, and he tells me that the Houses are not likely to agree after their free conference yesterday, and he fears what may follow.

[1668] January 1st. Up, and all the morning in my chamber making up some accounts against this beginning of the new year, and so about noon abroad with my wife, who was to dine with W. Hewer and Willet at Mrs. Pierce's, but I had no mind to be with them, for I do clearly find that my wife is troubled at my friendship with her and Knepp, and so dined with my Lord Crew, with whom was Mr. Browne, Clerk of the House of Lords, and Mr. John Crew. Here was mighty good discourse, as there is always: and among other things my Lord Crew did turn to a place in the *Life of Sir Philip Sidney*, wrote by Sir Fulke Greville, which do foretell the present condition of this nation, in relation to the Dutch, to the very degree of a prophecy; and is so remarkable that I am resolved to buy one of them, it being quite throughout, a good discourse. Here they talk much of the present cheapness of corne, even to a miracle; so as their farmers can pay no rent, but do fling up their lands; and would pay in corne: but, which I did observe to my Lord, and he liked well of it, our gentry are grown so ignorant in every thing of good husbandry, that they know not how to bestow this corne: which, did they understand but a little trade, they would be able to joyne together, and know what markets there are abroad, and send it thither, and thereby ease their tenants and be able to pay themselves. They did talk much of the disgrace the Archbishop is fallen under with the King, and the rest of the Bishops also. Thence I after dinner to the Duke of York's playhouse, and there saw *Sir Martin Mar-all*; which I have seen so often, and yet am mightily pleased with it, and think it mighty witty, and the fullest of proper matter for mirth that ever was writ; and I do clearly see that they do improve in their acting of it. Here a mighty company of citizens, 'prentices, and others; and it makes me observe, that when I begun first to be able to bestow a play on myself, I do not remember that I saw so many by half of the ordinary 'prentices and mean people in the pit at 2s. 6d. a-piece as now; I going for several years no higher than the 12d. and then the 18d. places, though I strained hard to go in then when I did; so much the vanity and prodigality of the age is to be observed in this particular. Thence I to White Hall, and there walked up and down the house a while, and do hear nothing of anything done further in this business of the change of Privy-counsellors: only I hear that Sir G. Saville, one of the Parliament Committee of nine, for examining the Accounts, is by the King made a Lord, the Lord Halifax; which, I believe, will displease the Parliament. By and by I met with Mr. Brisband; and having it in my mind this Christmas to (do what I never can remember that I did) go to see the manner of the gaming at the Groome-Porter's, I having in my coming from the playhouse stepped into the two Temple-halls, and there saw the dirty 'prentices and idle people playing; wherein I was mistaken, in thinking to have seen gentlemen of quality playing there, as I think it was when I was a little child, that one of my father's servants, John Bassum, I think, carried me in his arms thither. I did tell Brisband of it, and he did lead me thither, where, after staying an hour, they begun to play at about eight at night, where to see how differently one man took his losing from another, one cursing and swearing, and another only muttering and grumbling to himself, a third without any apparent discontent at all: to see how the dice will run good luck in one hand, for half an hour together, and another have no good luck at all: to see how easily here, where they play nothing but guinnys, a £100 is won or lost: to see two or three gentlemen come in there drunk, and putting their stock of gold together, one 22 pieces, the second 4, and the third 5 pieces; and these to play one with another, and forget how much each of them brought, but he that brought the 22 thinks that he brought no more than the rest: to see the different humours of gamesters to change their luck, when it is bad, how ceremonious they are as to call for new dice, to shift their places, to alter their manner of throwing, and that with great industry, as if there was anything in it: to see how some old gamesters, that have no money now to spend as formerly, do come and sit and look on, as among others, Sir Lewis Dives, who was here, and hath been a great gamester in his time: to hear their cursing and damning to no purpose, as one man being to throw a seven if he could, and, failing to do it after a great many throws, cried he would be damned if ever he flung seven more while he lived, his despair of throwing it being so great, while others did it as their luck served almost every throw: to see how persons of the best quality do here sit down, and play with people of any, though meaner; and to see how people in ordinary clothes shall come hither, and play away 100, or 2 or 300 guinnys, without any kind of difficulty: and lastly, to see the formality of the groome-porter, who is their judge of all disputes in play and all quarrels that may arise therein, and how his under-officers are there to observe true play at each table, and to give new dice, is a consideration I never could have thought had been in the world, had I not now seen it. And mighty glad I am that I did see it, and it may be will find another evening, before Christmas be over, to see it again, when I may stay later, for their heat of play begins not till about eleven or twelve o'clock; which did give me another pretty observation of a man, that did win mighty fast when I was there. I think he won £100 at single pieces in a little time. While all the rest envied him his good fortune, he cursed it, saying, "A pox on it, that it should come so early upon me, for this fortune two hours hence would be worth something to me, but then, God damn me, I shall have no such luck." This kind of prophane, mad entertainment they give themselves. And so I, having enough for once, refusing to venture, though Brisband pressed me hard, and tempted me with saying that no man was ever known to lose the first time, the devil being too cunning to discourage a gamester; and he offered me also to lend me ten pieces to venture; but I did refuse, and so went away, and took coach and home about 9 or 10 at night, where not finding my wife come home, I took the same coach again, and leaving my watch behind me for fear of robbing, I did go back and to Mrs. Pierce's, thinking they might not have broken up yet, but there I find my wife newly gone, and not going out of my coach spoke only to Mr. Pierce in his nightgown in the street, and so back again home, and there to supper with my wife and to talk about their dancing and doings at Mrs. Pierce's to-day, and so to bed.

January 21st. Up, and while at the office comes news from Kate Joyce that if I would see her husband alive, I must come presently. So, after the office was up, I to him, and W. Hewer with me, and find him in his sick bed (I never was at their house, this Inne, before) very sensible in discourse and thankful for my kindness to him, and his breath rattled in his throate, and they did lay pigeons to his feet while I was in the house, and all despair of him, and with good reason. But the story is that it seems on Thursday last he went sober and quiet out of doors in the morning to Islington, and behind one of the inns, the White Lion, did fling himself into a pond, was spied by a poor woman and got out by some people binding up hay in a barn there, and set on his head and got to life, and known by a woman coming that way; and so his wife and friends sent for. He confessed his doing the thing, being led by the devil; and do declare his reason to be, his trouble that he found in having forgot to serve God as he ought, since he come to this new employment: and I believe that, and the sense of his great loss by the fire, did bring him to it, and so everybody concludes. He stayed there all that night, and come home by coach next morning, and there grew sick, and worse and worse to this day. I stayed awhile among the friends that were there, and they being now in fear that the goods and estate would be seized on, though he lived all this while, because of his endeavouring to drown himself, my cozen did endeavour to remove what she could of plate out of the house, and desired me to take my flagons; which I was glad of, and did take them away with me in great fear all the way of being seized; though there was no reason for it, he not being dead, but yet so fearful I was. So home, and there eat my dinner, and busy all the afternoon, and troubled at this business. In the evening with Sir D. Gawden, to Guild Hall, to advise with the Town-Clerke about the practice of the City and nation in this case: and he thinks that it cannot be found self-murder; but if it be, it will fall, all the estate, to the King. So we parted, and I to my cozen's again; where I no sooner come but news was brought down from his chamber that he was departed. So, at their entreaty, I presently took coach to White Hall, and there find Sir W. Coventry; and he carried me to the King, the Duke of York being with him, and there told my story which I had told him: and the King, without more ado, granted that, if it was found, the estate should be to the widow and children. I presently to each Secretary's office, and there left caveats, and so away back again to my cozen's, leaving a chimney on fire at White Hall, in the King's closet, but no danger. And so, when I come thither, I find her all in sorrow, but she and the rest mightily pleased with my doing this for them; and, indeed, it was a very great courtesy, for people are looking out for the estate, and the coroner will be sent to, and a jury called to examine his death. This being well done to my and their great joy, I home, and there to my office, and so to supper and to bed.

February 9th (Lord's day). Up, and at my chamber all the morning and the office doing business, and also reading a little of *L'escholle des filles*, which is a mighty lewd book, but yet not amiss for a sober man once to read over to inform himself in the villainy of the world. At noon home to dinner, where by appointment Mr. Pelling come and with him three friends, Wallington, that sings the good base, and one Rogers, and a gentleman, a young man, his name Tempest, who sings very well indeed, and understands anything in the world at first sight. After dinner we into our dining-room, and there to singing all the afternoon. (By the way, I must remember that

Pegg Pen was brought to bed yesterday of a girl; and, among other things, if I have not already set it down, that hardly ever was remembered such a season for the smallpox as these last two months have been, people being seen all up and down the streets, newly come out after the smallpox.) But though they sang fine things, yet I must confess that I did take no pleasure in it, or very little, because I understood not the words, and with the rests that the words are set, there is no sense nor understanding in them though they be English, which makes me weary of singing in that manner, it being but a worse sort of instrumental musick. We sang until almost night, and drank mighty good store of wine, and then they parted, and I to my chamber, where I did read through *L'escholle des filles*, a lewd book, but what do no wrong once to read for information sake. And after I had done it I burned it, that it might not be among my books to my shame, and so at night to supper and to bed.

February 27th. All the morning at the office, and at noon home to dinner, and thence with my wife and Deb. to the King's House, to see *The Virgin Martyr*, the first time it hath been acted a great while: and it is mighty pleasant; not that the play is worth much, but it is finely acted by Becke Marshal. But that which did please me beyond any thing in the whole world was the wind-musique when the angel comes down, which is so sweet that it ravished me, and indeed, in a word, did wrap up my soul so that it made me really sick, just as I have formerly been when in love with my wife; that neither then, nor all the evening going home, and at home, I was able to think of any thing, but remained all night transported, so as I could not believe that ever any musick hath that real command over the soul of a man as this did upon me: and makes me resolve to practise wind-musique, and to make my wife do the like.

March 5th. With these thoughts I lay troubling myself till six o'clock, restless, and at last getting my wife to talk to me to comfort me, which she at last did, and made me resolve to quit my hands of this Office, and endure the trouble of it no longer than till I can clear myself of it. So with great trouble, but yet with some ease, from this discourse with my wife, I up, and to my Office, whither come my clerks, and so I did huddle the best I could some more notes for my discourse to-day, and by nine o'clock was ready, and did go down to the Old Swan, and there by boat, with T. Hater and W. Hewer with me, to Westminster, where I found myself come time enough, and my brethren all ready. But I full of thoughts and trouble touching the issue of this day; and to comfort myself did go to the Dog and drink half-a-pint of mulled sack, and in the Hall (Westminster) did drink a dram of brandy at Mrs. Hewlett's; and with the warmth of this did find myself in better order as to courage, truly. So we all up to the lobby; and between eleven and twelve o'clock, were called in, with the mace before us, into the House, where a mighty full House; and we stood at the bar, namely, Brouncker, Sir J. Minnes, Sir T. Harvey, and myself, W. Pen being in the House, as a Member. I perceive the whole House was full, and full of expectation of our defence what it would be, and with great prejudice. After the Speaker had told us the dissatisfaction of the House, and read the Report of the Committee, I began our defence most acceptably and smoothly, and continued at it without any hesitation or losse, but with full scope, and all my reason free about me, as if it had been at my own table, from that time till past three in the afternoon; and so ended, without any interruption from the Speaker; but we withdrew. And there all my Fellow-Officers, and all the world that was within hearing, did congratulate me, and cry up my speech as the best thing they ever heard; and my Fellow-Officers overjoyed in it; we were called in again by and by to answer only one question, touching our paying tickets to ticket-mongers; and so out; and we were in hopes to have had a vote this day in our favour, and so the generality of the House was; but my speech, being so long, many had gone out to dinner, and come in again half drunk; and then there are two or three that are professed enemies to us and every body else; among others,

Sir T. Littleton, Sir Thomas Lee, Mr. Wiles, the coxcomb whom I saw heretofore at the cock-fighting and a few others; I say, these did rise up and speak against the coming to a vote now, the House not being full, by reason of several being at dinner, but most because that the House was to attend the King this afternoon, about the business of religion, wherein they pray him to put in force all the laws against Nonconformists and Papists; and this prevented it, so that they put it off to to-morrow come se'nnight. However, it is plain we have got great ground; and everybody says I have got the most honour that any could have had opportunity of getting; and so with our hearts mightily overjoyed at this success, we all to dinner to Lord Brouncker's —that is to say, myself, T. Harvey, and W. Pen, and there dined; and thence with Sir Anthony Morgan, who is an acquaintance of Brouncker's, a very wise man, we after dinner to the King's house, and there saw part of *The Discontented Colonel*, but could take no great pleasure in it, because of our coming in in the middle of it. After the play, home with W. Pen, and there to my wife, whom W. Hewer had told of my success, and she overjoyed, and I also as to my particular; and, after talking awhile, I betimes to bed, having had no quiet rest a good while.

April 10th (Friday). All the morning at Office. At noon with W. Pen to Duke of York, and attended Council. So to piper and Duck Lane, and there kissed bookseller's wife, and bought Legend. So home, coach. Sailor. Mrs. Hannan dead. News of Peace. Conning my gamut.

May 22nd. Up, and all the morning at the office busy. At noon home with my people to dinner, where good discourse and merry. After dinner comes Mr. Martin, the purser, and brings me his wife's starling, which was formerly the King's bird, that do speak and whistle finely, which I am mighty proud of and shall take pleasure in it. Thence to the Duke of York's house to a play, and saw *Sir Martin Marr-all*, where the house is full; and though I have seen it, I think, ten times, yet the pleasure I have is yet as great as ever, and is undoubtedly the best comedy ever was wrote. Thence to my tailor's and a mercer's for patterns to carry my wife of cloth and silk for a bed, which I think will please her and me, and so home, and fitted myself for my journey to-morrow, which I fear will not be pleasant, because of the wet weather, it raining very hard all this day; but the less it troubles me because the King and Duke of York and Court are at this day at Newmarket, at a great horse-race, and proposed great pleasure for two or three days, but are in the same wet. So from the office home to supper, and betimes to bed.

June 11th (Thursday). Up, and W. Hewer and I up and down the town (Salisbury), and find it a very brave place. The river goes through every street; and a most capacious market-place. The city great, I think greater than Hereford. But the Minster most admirable; as big, I think, and handsomer than Westminster: and a most large Close about it, and houses for the Officers thereof, and a fine palace for the Bishop. So to my lodging back, and took out my wife and people to shew them the town and Church; but they being at prayers, we could not be shewn the Quire. A very good organ; and I looked in, and saw the Bishop, my friend Dr. Ward. Thence to the inne; and there not being able to hire coach-horses, and not willing to use our own, we got saddle-horses, very dear. Boy that went to look for them, 6d. So the three women behind W. Hewer, Murford, and our guide, and I single to Stonage, over the Plain and some great hills, even to fright us. Come thither, and find them as prodigious as any tales I ever heard of them, and worth going this journey to see. God knows what their use was! they are hard to tell, but yet may be told. Give the shepherd-woman, for leading our horses, 4d. So back by Wilton, my Lord Pembroke's house, which we could not see, he being just coming to town; but the situation I do not like, nor the house promise much, it being in a low but rich valley. So back home; and there being 'light, we to the Church, and there find them at prayers again, so could not see the Quire; but I sent the women home, and I did go in, and saw very many fine tombs, and among the rest some very ancient, of the Montagus. So home to dinner; and, that being done, paid the reckoning, which was so exorbitant, and particular in rate of my horses, and 7s. 6d. for bread and beer, that I was mad, and resolved to trouble the master about it, and get something for the poor; and come away in that humour: £2 5s. 6d. Servants, 1s. 6d; poor, 1s.; guide to the Stones, 2s.; poor woman in the street, 1s.; ribbands, 9d.; washwoman, 1s.; sempstress for W. Hewer, 3s.; lent W. Hewer, 2s. Thence about six o'clock, and with a guide went over the smooth Plain indeed till night; and then by a happy mistake, and that looked like an adventure, we were carried out of our way to a town where we would lye, since we could not go so far as we would. And there with great difficulty come about ten at night to a little inn, where we were fain to go into a room where a pedlar was in bed, and made him rise; and there wife and I lay, and in a truckle-bed Betty Turner and Willett. But good beds, and the master of the house a sober understanding man, and I had good discourse with him about this country's matters, as wool, and corne, and other things. And he also merry, and made us mighty merry at supper, about manning the new ship, at Bristol, with none but men whose wives do master them; and it seems it is become in reproach to some men of estate that are such hereabouts, that this is become common talk. By and by to bed, glad of this mistake, because, it seems, had we gone on as we intended, we could not have passed with our coach, and must have lain on the Plain all night. This day from Salisbury I wrote by the post my excuse for not coming home, which I hope will do, for I am resolved to see the Bath, and, it may be, Bristol.

June 12th (Friday). Up, finding our beds good, but lousy; which made us merry. We set out, the reckoning and servants coming to 9s. 6d.; my guide thither, 2s.; coachman, advanced, 10s. So rode a very good way, led to my great content by our landlord to Philips-Norton, with great pleasure, being now come into Somersetshire; where my wife and Deb. mightily joyed thereat, I commending the country, as indeed it deserves. And the first town we came to was Brekington, where, we stopping for something for the horses, we called two or three little boys to us, and pleased ourselves with their manner of speech, and did make one of them kiss Deb., and another say the Lord's Prayer (hallowed be thy kingdom come). At Philips-Norton I walked to the Church, and there saw a very ancient tomb of some Knight Templar, I think; and here saw the tombstone whereon there were only two heads cut, which, the story goes, and credibly, were two sisters, called the Fair Maids of Foscott, that had two bodies upward and one belly, and there lie buried. Here is also a very fine ring of six bells, and they mighty tuneable. Having dined very well, 10s., we come before night to the Bath; where I presently stepped out with my landlord, and saw the baths, with people in them. They are not so large as I expected, but yet pleasant; and the town most of stone, and clean, though the streets generally narrow. I home, and being weary, went to bed without supper; the rest supping.

June 13th (Saturday). Up at four o'clock, being by appointment called up to the Cross Bath, where we were carried one after one another, myself, and wife, and Betty Turner, Willet, and W. Hewer. And by and by, though we designed to have done before company come, much company come; very fine ladies; and the manner pretty enough, only methinks it cannot be clean to go so many bodies together in the same water. Good conversation among them that are acquainted here, and stay together. Strange to see how hot the water is; and in some places, though this is the most temperate bath, the springs so hot as the feet not able to endure. But strange to see, when women and men herein, that live all the season in these waters, that cannot but be parboiled, and look like the creatures of the bath! Carried away, wrapped in a sheet, and in a chair home; and there one after another thus carried, I staying above two hours in the water, home to bed, sweating for an hour; and by and by, comes musick to play to me, extraordinary good as ever I heard at London almost, or anywhere: 5s. Up, to go to Bristol, about eleven o'clock, and paying my landlord that was our guide from Chiltern, 10s., and the serjeant of the bath, 10s., and the man that carried us in chairs, 3s. 6d. Set out towards Bristoll, and come thither (in a coach hired to spare our own horses); the way bad, but country good, about two o'clock, where set down at the Horseshoe, and there, being trimmed by a very handsome fellow, 2s., walked with my wife and people through the city, which is in every respect another London, that one can hardly know it, to stand in the country, no more than that. No carts, it standing generally on vaults, only dog-carts. So to the Three Crowns Tavern I was directed; but, when I come in, the master told me that he had newly given over the selling of wine; it seems, grown rich; and so went to the Sun; and there Deb. going with W. Hewer and Betty Turner to see her uncle Butts, and leaving my wife with the mistress of the house, I do see the quay, which is a most large and noble place; and to see the new ship building by Bally, neither he nor Furzer being in town. It will be a fine ship. Spoke with the foreman, and did give the boys that kept the cabin 2s. Walked back to the Sun, where I find Deb. come back, and with her, her uncle, a sober merchant, very good company, and so like one of our sober, wealthy, London merchants, as pleased me mightily. Here we dined, and much good talk with him, 7s. 6d.: a messenger to Sir John Knight, who was not at home, 6d. Then walked with him (Butts) and my wife and company round the quay, and to the ship; and he shewed me the Custom-house, and made me understand many things of the place, and led us through Marsh Street, where our girl was born. But, Lord! the joy that was among the old poor people of the place, to see Mrs. Willet's daughter, it seems her mother being a brave woman and mightily beloved! And so brought us a back way by surprize to his house, where a substantial good house, and well furnished; and did give us good entertainment of strawberries, a whole venison-pasty, cold, and plenty of brave wine, and above all Bristoll milk: where comes in another poor woman, who, hearing that Deb. was here, did come running hither, and with her eyes so full of tears, and heart so full of joy, that she could not speak when she come in, that it made me weep too: I protest that I was not able to speak to her, which I would have done, to have diverted her tears. His wife a good woman, and so sober and substantiall as I was never more pleased anywhere. Servant-maid, 2s. So thence took leave, and he with us, through the city, where in walking I find the city pay him great respect, and he the like to the meanest, which pleased me mightily. He shewed us the place where the merchants meet here, and a fine Cross yet standing, like Cheapside. And so to the Horseshoe, where paid the reckoning, 2s. 6d. We back, and by moonshine to the Bath again, about ten o'clock: bad way; and giving the coachman 1s., went all of us to bed.

July 14th. Up, and to my office, where sat all the morning. At noon home to dinner, and thence all the afternoon hard at the office, we meeting about the Victualler's new contract; and so into the garden, my Lady Pen, Mrs. Turner and her daughter, my wife and I, and there supped in the dark and were merry, and so to bed. This day Bossc finished his copy of my picture, which I confess I do not admire, though my wife prefers him to Browne; nor do I think it like. He do it for W. Hewer, who hath my wife's also, which I like less. This afternoon my Lady Pickering come to see us: I busy, saw her not. But how natural it is for us to slight people out of power, and for people out of power to stoop to see those that while in power they contemned!

[1669] January 23rd. Up, and again to look after the setting things right against dinner, which I did to very good content.

So to the office, where all the morning till noon, when word brought me to the Board that my Lord Sandwich was come; so I presently rose, leaving the Board ready to rise, and there I found my Lord Sandwich, Peterborough, and Sir Charles Harbord; and presently after them comes my Lord Hinchingbroke, Mr. Sidney, and Sir William Godolphin. And after greeting them, and some time spent in talk, dinner was brought up, one dish after another, but a dish at a time, but all so good; but, above all things, the variety of wines, and excellent of their kind, I had for them, and all in so good order, that they were mightily pleased, and myself full of content at it: and indeed it was, of a dinner of about six or eight dishes, as noble as any man need to have, I think; at least, all was done in the noblest manner that ever I had any, and I have rarely seen in my life better anywhere else, even at the Court. After dinner, my Lords to cards, and the rest of us sitting about them and talking, and looking on my books and pictures, and my wife's drawings, which they commend mightily; and mighty merry all day long, with exceeding great content, and so till seven at night; and so took their leaves, it being dark and foul weather. Thus was this entertainment over, the best of its kind, and the fullest of honour and content to me, that ever I had in my life: and shall not easily have so good again. The truth is, I have some fear that I am more behind-hand in the world for these last two years, since I have not, or for some time could not, look after my accounts, which do a little allay my pleasure. But I do trust in God I am pretty well yet, and resolve, in a very little time, to look into my accounts, and see how they stand. So to my wife's chamber, and there supped, and got her cut my hair and look my shirt, for I have itched mightily these 6 or 7 days, and when all comes to all she finds that I am lousy, having found in my head and body about twenty lice, little and great, which I wonder at, being more than I have had I believe these 20 years. I did think I might have got them from the little boy, but they did presently look him, and found none. So how they come I know not, but presently did shift myself, and so shall be rid of them, and cut my hair close to my head, and so with much content to bed.

February 3rd. So up, and to the Office till noon, and then home to a little dinner, and thither again till night, mighty busy, to my great content, doing a great deal of business, and so home to supper, and to bed; I finding this day that I may be able to do a great deal of business by dictating, if I do not read myself, or write, without spoiling my eyes, I being very well in my eyes after a great day's work.

February 8th. Up, and dressed myself; and by coach, with W. Hewer and my wife, to White Hall, where she set us two down; and in the way, our little boy, at Martin, my bookseller's shop, going to 'light, did fall down; and, had he not been a most nimble boy (I saw how he did it, and was mightily pleased with him for it), he had been run over by the coach. I to visit my Lord Sandwich; and there, while my Lord was dressing himself, did see a young Spaniard, that he hath brought over with him, dance, which he is admired for, as the best dancer in Spain, and indeed he do with mighty mastery; but I do not like his dancing as the English, though my Lord commends it mightily: but I will have him to my house, and show it my wife. Here I met with Mr. Moore, who tells me the state of my Lord's accounts of his embassy, which I find not so good as I thought: for, though it be passed the King and his Cabal (the Committee for Foreign Affairs as they are called), yet they have cut off from £19,000 full £8,000, and have now sent it to the Lords of the Treasury, who, though the Committee have allowed the rest, yet they are not obliged to abide by it. So that I do fear this account may yet be long ere it be passed—much more, ere that sum be paid: I am sorry for the family, and not a little for what it owes me. So to my wife, took her up at Unthank's, and in our way home did shew her the tall woman, in Holborne, which I have seen before; and I measured her, and she is, without shoes, just six feet five inches high, and they say not above twenty-one years old. Thence home, and there to dinner, and my wife in a wonderful ill humour; and so I to the Office, with a very light heart, and there close at my business all the afternoon. This day I was told by Mr. Wren, that Captain Cox, Master-Attendant at Deptford, is to be one of us very soon, he and Tippets being to take their turns for Chatham and Portsmouth, which choice I like well enough; and Captain Annesley is to come in his room at Deptford. This morning also, going to visit Roger Pepys, at the potticary's in King's Street, he tells me that Roger is gone to his wife's, so that they have been married, as he tells me, ever since the middle of last week: it was his design, upon good reasons, to make no noise of it; but I am well enough contented that it is over. Dispatched a great deal of business at the office, and there pretty late, till finding myself very full of wind, by my eating no dinner to-day, being vexed, I was forced to go home, and there supped W. Batelier with us, and so with great content to bed.

March 25th. Up, and by and by, about eight o'clock, come Rear-Admiral Kempthorne and seven Captains more, by the Duke of York's order, as we expected, to hold the Court-martiall about the loss of *The Defyance*; and so presently we by boat to *The Charles*, which lies over against Upnor Castle, and there we fell to the business; and there I did manage the business, the Duke of York having, by special order, directed them to take the assistance of Commissioner Middleton and me, forasmuch as there might be need of advice in what relates to the government of the ships in harbour. And so I did lay the law open to them, and rattle the Master-Attendants out of their wits almost; and made the trial last till seven at night, not eating a bit all the day; only when we had done examination, and I given my thoughts that the neglect of the Gunner of the ship was as great as I thought any neglect could be, which might by the law deserve death, but Commissioner Middleton did declare that he was against giving the sentence of death, we withdrew, as not being of the Court, and so left them to do what they pleased; and, while they were debating it, the Boatswain of the ship did bring us out of the kettle a piece of hot salt beef, and some brown bread and brandy; and there we did make a little meal, but so good as I never would desire to eat better meat while I live, only I would have cleaner dishes. By and by they had done, and called us down from the quarter-deck; and there we find they do sentence that the Gunner of *The Defyance* should stand upon *The Charles* three hours with his fault writ upon his breast, and with a halter about his neck, and so be made incapable of any office. The truth is, the man do seem, and is, I believe, a good man; but his neglect, in trusting a girl to carry fire into his cabin, is not to be pardoned. This being done, we took boat and home; and there a good supper was ready for us, which should have been our dinner. The Captains, desirous to be at London, went away presently for Gravesend, to get thither by this night's tide; and so we to supper, it having been a great snowy and mighty cold, foul day; and so after supper to bed.

April 25th (Lord's day). Up, and to my Office awhile, and thither comes Lead with my vizard, with a tube fastened within both eyes; which, with the help which he prompts me to, of a glass in the tube, do content me mightily. So to church, where a stranger made a dull sermon, but I mightily pleased to look upon Mr. Buckworth's little pretty daughters, and so home to dinner, where W. Howe come and dined with us; and then I to my Office, he being gone, to write down my Journal for the last twelve days: and did it with the help of my vizard and tube fixed to it, and do find it mighty manageable, but how helpfull to my eyes this trial will shew me. So abroad with my wife, in the afternoon, to the Park, where very much company, and the weather very pleasant. I carried my wife to the Lodge, the first time this year, and there in our coach eat a cheese-cake and drank a tankard of milk. I showed her this day also first the Prince of Tuscany, who was in the Park, and many very fine ladies, and so home, and after supper to bed.

April 30th. Up, and by coach to the coachmaker's: and there I do find a great many ladies sitting in the body of a coach that must be ended by to-morrow: they were my Lady Marquess of Winchester, Bellassis, and other great ladies, eating of bread and butter, and drinking ale. I to my coach, which is silvered over, but no varnish yet laid on, so I put it in a way of doing; and myself about other business, and particularly to see Sir W. Coventry, with whom I talked a good while to my great content; and so to other places—among others, to my tailor's: and then to the belt-maker's, where my belt cost me 55s., of the colour of my new suit; and here, understanding that the mistress of the house, an oldish woman in a hat, hath some water good for the eyes, she did dress me, making my eyes smart most horribly, and did give me a little glass of it, which I will use, and hope it will do me good. So to the cutler's, and there did give Tom, who was with me all day, a sword cost me 12s. and a belt of my owne; and set my own silver-hilt sword a-gilding against to-morrow. This morning I did visit Mr. Oldenburgh, and did see the instrument for perspective made by Dr. Wren, of which I have one making by Browne; and the sight of this do please me mightily. At noon my wife come to me at my tailor's, and I sent her home, and myself and Tom dined at Hercules' Pillars; and so about our business again, and particularly to Lilly's, the varnisher, about my prints, whereof some of them are pasted upon the boards, and to my full content. Thence to the frame-maker's, one Norris, in Long Acre, who shewed me several forms of frames to choose by, which was pretty, in little bits of mouldings, to choose by. This done, I to my coachmaker's, and there vexed to see nothing yet done to my coach, at three in the afternoon; but I set it in doing, and stood by it till eight at night, and saw the painter varnish it, which is pretty to see how every doing it over do make it more and more yellow; and it dries as fast in the sun as it can be laid on almost; and most coaches are, now-a-days, done so, and it is very pretty when laid on well, and not too pale, as some are, even to shew the silver. Here I did make the workmen drink, and saw my coach cleaned and oyled; and, staying among poor people there in the alley, did hear them call their fat child Punch, which pleased me mightily, that word being become a word of common use for all that is thick and short. At night home, and there find my wife hath been making herself clean against to-morrow; and late as it was, I did send my coachman and horses to fetch home the coach to-night, and so we to supper, myself most weary with walking and standing so much, to see all things fine against to-morrow, and so to bed. God give a blessing to it! Meeting with Mr. Sheres, he went with me up and down to several places, and, among others, to buy a perriwig, but I bought none; and also to Dancre's, where he was about my picture of Windsor, which is mighty pretty, and so will the prospect of Rome be.

May 1st. Up betimes. Called up by my tailor, and there first put on a summer suit this year; but it was not my fine one of flowered tabby vest, and coloured camelott tunique, because it was too fine with the gold lace at the hands, that I was afeard to be seen in it; but put on the stuff suit I made the last year, which is now repaired; and so did go to the Office in it, and sat all the morning, the day looking as if it would be fowle. At noon home to dinner, and there find my wife extraordinary fine, with her flowered tabby gown that she made two years ago, now laced exceeding pretty; and, indeed, was fine all over; and mighty earnest to go, though the day was very lowering; and she would have me put on my fine suit, which I did. And so anon we went alone through the town with our new liveries of serge, and the horses' manes and tails tied with red ribbons, and the standards there gilt with varnish, and all clean, and green reines, that people did mightily look upon us; and, the truth is, I did not see any coach more pretty, though more gay, than ours, all the day. But we set out, out of humour—I because Betty, whom I expected, was not come to go with us; and my wife that I would sit on the same seat with her, which she likes not, being so fine: and she then expected to meet Sheres, which we did in the Pell Mell, and, against my will, I was forced to take him into the coach, but was sullen all day almost, and little complaisant: the day also being unpleasing, though the Park full of coaches, but dusty and windy, and cold, and now and then a little dribbling rain; and, what made it worst, there were so many hackney-coaches as spoiled the sight of the gentlemen's; and so we had little pleasure. But here was W. Batelier and his sister in a borrowed coach by themselves, and I took them and we to the lodge; and at the door did give them a syllabub, and other things, cost me 12s., and pretty merry. And so back to the coaches, and there till the evening, and then home, leaving Mr. Sheres at St. James's Gate, where he took leave of us for altogether, he being this night to set out for Portsmouth post, in his way to Tangier, which troubled my wife mightily, who is mighty, though not, I think, too fond of him. But she was out of humour all the evening, and I vexed at her for it. So home, and after a little supper, to bed.

May 24th. To White Hall, and there all the morning, and thence home, and giving order for some business and setting my brother to making a catalogue of my books, I back again to W. Hewer to White Hall, where I attended the Duke of York, and was by him led to the King, who expressed great sense of my misfortune in my eyes, and concernment for their recovery; and accordingly signified, not only his assent to my desire therein, but commanded me to give them rest this summer, according to my late petition to the Duke of York. W. Hewer and I dined alone at the Swan; and thence, having thus waited on the King, spent till four o'clock in St. James's Park, where I met my wife at Unthanke's, and so home.

May 25th. Dined at home; and the rest of the day, morning and afternoon, at the Office.

May 31st. Up very betimes, and so continued all the morning with W. Hewer, upon examining and stating my accounts, in order to the fitting myself to go abroad beyond sea, which the ill condition of my eyes, and my neglect for a year or two, hath kept me behindhand in, and so as to render it very difficult now, and troublesome to my mind to do it; but I this day made a satisfactory entrance therein. Dined at home, and in the afternoon by water to White Hall, calling by the way at Michell's. And thence had another meeting with the Duke of York, at White Hall, on yesterday's work, and made a good advance: and so, being called by my wife, we to the Park, Mary Batelier, and a Dutch gentleman, a friend of hers, being with us. Thence to "The World's End", a drinking-house by the Park; and there merry, and so home late.

And thus ends all that I doubt I shall ever be able to do with my own eyes in the keeping of my Journal, I being not able to do it any longer, having done now so long as to undo my eyes almost every time that I take a pen in my hand; and, therefore, whatever comes of it, I must forbear: and, therefore, resolve, from this time forward, to have it kept by my people in long-hand, and must therefore be contented to set down no more than is fit for them and all the world to know; or, if there be any thing, which cannot be much, now my amours to Deb. are past, and my eyes hindering me in almost all other pleasures, I must endeavour to keep a margin in my book open, to add, here and there, a note in short-hand with my own hand.

And so I betake myself to that course, which is almost as much as to see myself go into my grave: for which, and all the discomforts that will accompany my being blind, the good God prepare me!

S. P.

NOTES

[The references are to page numbers of this edition.]

27 *the White-Crosse*: an inn.
Mr. Secretary: the Secretary of State—Sir Edward Nicholas.

28 Between April and October 1644 Evelyn visited Tours, Bourges, Lyons and Avignon.
Free-stone: sand or lime-stone.

30 *spiring:* breathing gently.
Prattique-house: the house of the quarantine officer.
Syndics: officers of the government.
Between the two entries on this page Evelyn visited Pisa, Florence, Siena, and Rome, where he stayed for about six months. He arrived in Venice in June 1645.

31 *Strigil*: a brush.

32 *Bucentoro*: the Bucentaur or state barge.
Channell to Chanell: an interesting example of the freedom in spelling prevailing at the time.

34 Most of the description of St. Mark's Church has been taken by Evelyn from guide-books of the time. Hence I have omitted much of it. Most of my other selections from his travels are his original work.
faciata: The façade. Evelyn is using the Italian word.

35 *Choppines*: unlikely to have been over two feet high.
strakes: sections of different coloured hair.

36 *oriency*: lustre.

37 *sumptuarie Laws*: laws to prevent wasteful expenditure.
pouderd beefe: salted beef.
Gunns: flagons of ale.

38 *pasquils*: lampoons.

39 *those rare Tables*: These can still be seen in the museum of the Royal College of Surgeons.

40 *Treacle*: Venetian treacle was thought to have valuable medicinal qualities. It was a proprietary medicine of the time.

pompous: it is interesting to note the difference in meaning of this word from that current today.

On his way to Milan Evelyn visited Vicenza, Verona and Brescia, and he arrived in Milan some time in May 1646.

the Course: the fashionable place for driving or riding.

41 *Cavalerizzo*: a riding-school.

42 *Marguzzo*: a village on Lake Maggiore.

the rubbish of the Earth: the use of the word "rubbish" is worthy of note.

43 *Duomo*: the town of Domodossola.

44 *strumous*: affected by goitres.

Evelyn spent some time in Geneva, and crossed into France early in July 1646.

45 *tedious*: here used by Evelyn in the sense of long and tiring. He does not mean tiresome.

46 *aberrations*: wanderings.

I return'd home: i.e. from London to Sayes Court, Deptford. This was his home until 1696.

Liberty & Servitude: Evelyn displayed his Royalist sympathies in the Preface.

Evelyn returned to France in July 1649 and remained there, mainly in Paris, until his return to England in February 1652.

Sennock: Sevenoaks in Kent.

Canters: a nickname for the sectarian preachers.

50 *the rock of St. Vincent*: a cliff on the banks of the Avon, near the Clifton suspension bridge.

confragose: rough with breaks. (O.E.D.)

51 *Darneford magna*: Great Durnford, near Salisbury.

52 *Tan-hill*: St. Anne's Hill, near Devizes.

52 *Grebner*: Paulus Grebner who in 1574 wrote what he claimed to be a prophetic work.

53 *contignation*: the joining together of the beams.

Sturbridge faire: from 1211 until the eighteenth century this was one of the most important fairs in England. A big trade was done there, and in woollen manufactures alone as much as £100,000 often changed hands within a week. There were also the usual theatrical performances and amusements.

Dr. Collins: Samuel Collins, D.D., Provost of King's College.

Emanuel Coll: at that time the most puritan of the Cambridge Colleges.

54 *Hobsons*: Thomas Hobson (1544?-1631), the carrier, from whom we get our phrase "Hobson's choice".

Oxford: Evelyn was, of course, an Oxford man.

Lubicer: Thomas Baltzar (1630?-1663). Evelyn calls him Lubicer as he was born in Lubeck.

55 *King of Denmark*: King Erik Eiegod (1095-1103), who was so moved by the playing of a musician that he is said to have killed four men.

Bedlame: Bethlehem Hospital for lunatics. It was open to the public who could watch the inmates as a form of "entertainment".

Charter-house: it was also a school for forty boys.

Christ-Church & Hospital: then near Newgate Street in the City.

59 *Mund*: the orb of gold.

60 *μετ'* . . . "With great pomp". Evelyn quotes from the Acts of the Apostles, xxv, 23.

Gen: Monke: George Monk (1608-1670). He was Commander-in-Chief of all the forces, and for his part in helping to restore Charles II to the throne he was created Duke of Albemarle in 1660. He was in charge of the Admiralty in 1665 and in command of the Fleet in 1666. There are many references to him in Pepys's diary.

62 *the Philosophic Society*: this eventually became the Royal Society which was established by royal charter in 1662. It began as a society meeting weekly for the discussion of scientific subjects.

the Phanatics: these were some Fifth-monarchy men, religious fanatics led by Thomas Venner who believed that they would establish the millennium.

the Torricellian experiment: Evangelista Torricelli (1608-1647) devised an experiment to prove that the atmosphere has weight.

the first Solemn Fast: this entry should be compared with that of Pepys for the 30th January 1663.

63 *the Coronation*: I have omitted most of Evelyn's account of the procession as it is of little interest and is copied from a newspaper of the time.

64 *Panegyric*: it was the custom of the time to write "Panegyrics", fulsome eulogies, on great men of the period. Evelyn's on Charles II was fourteen pages long.

65 *Fumifugium*: see Introduction, page 11.

my Traduction of Naudeus: his translation of Gabriel Naudé's "Avis pour dresser une Bibliothèque".

66 *at the Groome-porters*: the groom-porter was appointed by the King to supervise the gaming which was a part of the Christmas festivities at Court. The King himself usually took part on Twelfth Night. Compare Pepys's entry for the 1st January 1668.

to sit with him coverd: it was still customary for men to wear hats at meals, but not if there was a person of superior rank present.

67 *Tallè doucès of the Paralelles*: the engravings of his book on architecture.

68 *None-such house*: near Ewell in Surrey. It was pulled down later in the century.

poincons: short upright pieces of wood used as supports.

Compartiments: Evelyn probably means heraldic shields.

69 *entretices*: horizontal pieces of wood connecting two vertical pieces. (O.E.D.)

70 *the French Queene-mother*: Queen Anne of Austria who died on the 20th January.

72 *the Royal Charles*: this ship had been called the *Naseby* during the Commonwealth.

73 *Salt-peter*: an important ingredient in the making of gunpowder.

74 *Sir Geo: Downing* (1623?-1684): one of the Tellers of the Receipt of the Exchequer in the Commonwealth, and Secretary to the Treasury and Commissioner of the Customs under Charles II. He gave his name to Downing St. For a time Pepys was one of his clerks.

a greate . . .: Evelyn leaves a blank.

pomerid: Evelyn's abbreviation of *Postmeridiano*, i.e. in the afternoon.

75 *Bow-dyed Scarlet*: a special dye made probably at Bow in Middlesex.

Mr. Povy: the holder of several important offices under Cromwell and Charles II. He was the first Treasurer of Tangier, but he knew little about accounts and resigned the position to Pepys in 1665.

Brainford: Brentford.

76 *Mercator*: the Latinized form of the name of Nicholas Kauffman (1620-1687), a famous mathematician and Fellow of the Royal Society.

77 *This fatal night*: a great deal can be learnt from a close comparison of Evelyn's description of the Fire with that of Pepys.

78 *ten thousand houses all in one flame*: during the whole fire about 13,000 houses are thought to have been burnt.

granados: grenades.

79 *interdict*: in the sense of prevented from taking action.

the invective: *Fumifugium*.

80 *Lot*: Genesis xix.

the French Prisoners: Evelyn emphasises the need for vigilance as it was generally thought that the Fire had been begun by French or Dutch incendiaries.

the Graft: the moat.

82 *surbated*: bruised or sore with much walking. (O.E.D.)

84 *Scorbut*: scurvy.

90 *Mr. Pepys*: this is Evelyn's first reference in his diary to Pepys, who had stopped writing his own diary the previous May. Pepys's first mention of Evelyn occurs on the 9th September 1665: "Here was Sir W. Doyly, lately come from Ipswich about the sicke and wounded, and Mr. Evelyn and Captain Cocke . . . full of discussion of the neglect of our masters, the great officers of State, about all business, and especially that of money." In this entry Evelyn refers to his younger brother, Richard. His elder brother, George, who had inherited the Wotton Estate in 1640, did not die until 1699.

Finding my brother . . .: in spite of the visit of Pepys with his stone "as big as a tenis-ball", Richard was not able to face what was then a very dangerous and painful operation.

91 *Gibson*: Grinling Gibbons (1648-1720). He was one of the world's greatest wood-carvers. Fine examples of his work can still be seen at Hampton Court, and he was employed by Sir C. Wren to carve the stalls in St. Paul's Cathedral.

curiosity: proficiency attained by careful application. (O.E.D.)

92 *Sir R: Brownes*: Clerk of the Privy Council. He had been Charles I's ambassador in France, and Evelyn had married his daughter in Paris in 1646.

Ewrie: the Ewery which was responsible for the ewers, table-linen and towels used at Court.

94 17 (*Oct*): the King was at Newmarket and Evelyn was staying in the neighbourhood.

95 *stoopes*: stupes. Pieces of tow, flannel, or other soft substances, wrung out of hot liquor and medicated, for fomenting wounds or ailing parts. (O.E.D.)

the engagement of the 28: the battle of Solebay.

96 *with Mr. Pepys at the Tower*: see Introduction, page 19.

98 *Artists*: here in the sense of proficient in their various skilled occupations.

Exercise: spiritual studies or private worship.

Ensiforme: in the shape of a sword.

99 *Annimadversions*: punishments.

a Royal Hospital: at Chelsea. It is still the home of the Chelsea Pensioners.

100 *Sir Anth: Deane* (1638?-1721): a well-known ship-builder of the time. He was a Commissioner of the Navy and friend of Pepys.

Sybillas: the famous Sibylline Books. These were supposed to have been written by the Sibyllae, a name given to a number of prophetic women of antiquity. The books were consulted as oracles.

101 *Carduus posset*: a drink made of hot milk curdled with ale or wine. To this is added a preparation made from the thistle plant.

103 *Horace's Mouse*: *Satires*, II, vi.

Bish: Andrews's method: Lancelot Andrewes (1555-1626). An eminent preacher and writer who became Bishop of Winchester. As a preacher he excelled in the old style of sermon with its quotations from the classics, play upon words and close analysis of the text. By the middle of the seventeenth century this style had become unpopular.

the late Plot & Conspiracy: the Rye-House plot. An attempted rising by certain Whig leaders against Charles II. It was planned to murder him at the Rye House on the way from Newmarket races.

104 *L. Chancelor Hydes*: Edward Hyde, Earl of Clarendon (1609-1674), was a great statesman and historian. He was chief adviser to Charles II during his exile and was appointed Lord Chancellor in 1658. In 1660 at the Restoration he became virtual head of the Government. He lost popularity because of the sale of Dunkirk, and the Dutch War, and was dismissed from Office in 1667. He died in exile.

106 *Dr. Tenison*: Thomas Tenison (1636-1715). He championed Protestantism in the reign of James II, and became Archbishop of Canterbury in 1694.

108 *Jesuits powder*: the name at this time for quinine.

111 *Basset*: a game of cards.

Was sentenc'd Oates: at the Revolution in 1688 Oates was stated to have been wrongly convicted and he was granted a pension by William. The wheel of fortune revolved quickly during this period.

Monmoth: the illegitimate son of Charles II. His ill-fated attempt to overthrow James II and establish his own right to the throne had ended at Sedgemoor in June.

112 *the fellow*: the executioner was the well-known Jack Ketch.

113 *The Trinity Company*: this body, now known as Trinity House, has been responsible since the time of Henry VIII for "erecting and maintaining lighthouses and other marks and signs of the sea". To be chosen Master is a considerable honour.

immunities: privileges granted by the King.

116 *Portals*: a mistake for portas, a portable breviary or prayer-book containing the Divine Office.

some the Mathematics: Charles II had founded a Mathematical School in 1673 in order to train forty boys from the Hospital in navigation.

117 *the Declaration for Liberty of Conscience*: this was James II's Declaration of Indulgence. The clergy were ordered to read it from their parish pulpits. It suspended the laws against Roman Catholics and Dissenters and admitted them to civil and military posts.

A young Prince borne: James Stuart, the Old Pretender. The words "which will cost dispute" were a later addition of Evelyn's.

119 *riant*: smiling.

120 *Mr. Kneller*: Sir Godfrey Kneller (1646-1723). Born in Germany, he studied art in Holland, settled in England in 1674 and soon built up a large and profitable practice. He was the leading portrait painter in England at this time.

121 *Sir Den: Gauden*: often mentioned in Pepys's diary as Mr. Gawden. He was an important business man and Victualler to the Navy.

Mr. Ewers: William Hewer. He was Pepys's clerk and there are many references to him in the diary. He came from a humble family but rose to be Deputy Judge Advocate of the Fleet, and Commissioner of the Navy. On his retirement Pepys went to live in Hewer's house at Clapham.

122 *Mr. Jackson*: the son of Pepys's sister, Paulina.

127 *my old pain*: Pepys had suffered from a stone in the kidneys and had been successfully operated on for this on 26th March 1658. He used to give a dinner each year on the anniversary of the operation. See also Evelyn's entry for 10 June 1669.

Axe Yard: in King's Street, Westminster.

Mr. Downing: see note on page 74.

128 *Mrs. The. Turner*: Theophila Turner, second-cousin to Pepys, who was very friendly with her and her mother, Jane.

Mr. Crew's: John, later Lord, Crew (1598-1679). Well known to Pepys because he was father-in-law of Edward Montague, the Earl of Sandwich. See *my Lord* below.

129 *March 25th*: at this time Pepys was acting as secretary to Edward Montague aboard the *Swiftsure*, lying in the Thames.

my Lord: Admiral Sir Edward Montague (1625-1672). He was created Earl of Sandwich at the Restoration for his part in bringing Charles II back to England. Pepys was related to him, and it was through his influence that Pepys was made Clerk of the Acts to the Navy Board in June 1660. It can generally be taken that the words "my Lord" in the diary refer to him. See Introduction, page 17.

Captain Cuttance: Captain of the *Naseby*.

Oct. 13th: see also Evelyn's entry for 17th October 1660. Major-General Harrison had signed the warrant for the execution of Charles I.

130 *the Comptroller's*: the Navy Board at this time consisted of the Duke of York; a Comptroller, Sir Robert Slingsby; a Surveyor, Sir William Batten; a Treasurer, Sir George Carteret; three Commissioners; and a Clerk of the Acts, Samuel Pepys.

Fifth Monarchy men: see note on page 236.

Sir G. Carteret (1599-1679): served Charles I in the Civil War, and at the Restoration was appointed Vice-Chamberlain to the King. He was also made a Privy Councillor, and Treasurer of the Navy, a position which brought Pepys very much into contact with him.

My Lady: just as "my Lord" in the diary normally refers to the Earl of Sandwich, "my Lady" refers to the Countess of Sandwich.

my Will: see note on Mr. Ewers on page 241.

by link: a boy with a torch who lighted travellers along the streets at night. There was very little street lighting at this time.

131 *Standing's*: a tavern in Fleet Street.

Dr. Fairbrother: a fellow of King's College Cambridge. Pepys's brother, John (1641-1677), was at this time a scholar of Christ's College, Cambridge.

Sir W. Batten: Vice-Admiral and Surveyor of the Navy Board.

132 *Sir W. Pen*: Sir William Pen or Penn. Vice-Admiral and Commissioner of the Navy. His son, William, was the founder of Pennsylvania. Pepys, Sir W. Batten and Sir W. Penn were neighbours at the Navy Office in Seething Lane, near the Tower of London, and there are many references to "Sir Williams both" in the diary.

133 *mum*: a kind of beer.

135 *William Howe*: an attendant of the Earl of Sandwich, and at one time close friend of Pepys. He was Deputy Treasurer of the Navy in 1665.

136 *Serjt. Glynne*: the people were pleased at his mishap because he had been Chief Justice in Cromwell's time.

Maynard: an eminent lawyer who had served under Cromwell.

137 *Brampton*: near Huntingdon. The Pepys family came from the fen villages north of Cambridge. On the death of Uncle Robert, Pepys's father went to live in Brampton.

Sir J. Minnes (1598-1671): a well-known seaman and traveller. He was appointed Vice-Admiral in May 1661, and became Comptroller of the Navy on the death of Sir R. Slingsby in October 1661.

138 *Mrs. Pierce's*: she and her husband, James Pierce, Surgeon-General of the Fleet, were close friends of Pepys.

139 *Captain Cocke*: he held various official positions under Charles II, including that of Treasurer of the Sick and Wounded Seamen, a position which led to frequent meetings with Evelyn and Pepys.

my brother Tom: Pepys made several attempts to find a suitable wife for Tom (1634-1664), but was unsuccessful.

the Paynter's: Pepys and his wife had their portraits painted by several painters of the time. The one referred to here was Savill who lived in Cheapside.

140 *to sail for Portugall*: in order to bring Catharine of Braganza to England to marry Charles II.

141 *an Oxford man*: Pepys was, of course, a Cambridge man.

from my Lord: Sandwich was then on a visit to Tangier which was to be part of Catharine of Braganza's dowry when she married Charles II, and from Tangier he was to proceed to Lisbon in order to bring home the new Queen.

the Duke of York's chamber: the Duke was Lord High Admiral.

Mr. Moore: a lawyer and friend of Pepys. He was in the service of John Crew.

Mr. Hater: one of Pepys's clerks.

144 *Mr. Coventry's coach*: William Coventry (1628-1686). He was private secretary to the Duke of York from 1660, appointed Secretary to the Lord High Admiral in 1664, and an extra Commissioner of the Navy in 1662. He was knighted in 1665. We hear a good deal about him in Pepys's diary and it is clear that Pepys had a great respect for him.

Bullen: Boulogne.

145 *vialls*: Musical instruments having five, six or seven strings, and played by means of a bow. (O.E.D.)

Sarah: Lord Sandwich's housekeeper.

Mr. Creed: John Creed was Sandwich's secretary. A clever and very efficient man, he was made Secretary to the Commissioners for Tangier in 1662.

147 *Sarah*: the maid referred to on page 139. She had been a member of Pepys's household until December 1662 when he gave her notice. Mrs. Pepys was constantly quarrelling with her maids, and the diary records the coming, and going, of many of them. This Sarah should not be confused with Lord Sandwich's housekeeper.

scallop: a lace covering for the neck with the edges decorated with a scallop pattern.

Jane: Jane Wayneman. Another maid, who after giving Mrs. Pepys some "saucy words" left the Pepys's employment in February 1663.

150 *Lacy's*: a famous actor of the time who was greatly admired by Pepys.

the other house: the number of theatre companies at this time was limited by Royal Patent to two: the King's (or Killigrew's), and the Duke's (or Davenant's).

152 *Argier*: Algiers.
Hambrough: Hamburg.

153 *December 4th*: the punctuation of this passage is interesting.
Luellin, Mount, and W. Symons: friends of Pepys from the days when he was a clerk to Sir George Downing.

154 *to my brother's*: Pepys's brother, Tom, had died on the 15th March.

155 *Besse*: Elizabeth, Pepys's new maid.

156 *scotoscope*: an instrument which enables the user to see in the dark. (O.E.D.)

157 *Sir William Petty* (1623-1687): a talented mathematician and political economist who was one of the authors of the first book on vital statistics. He was very interested in science and was one of the founders of the Royal Society.
Mr. Barlow: Thomas Barlow had been Pepys's predecessor as Clerk of the Acts and Pepys had agreed in 1660 to pay him part of the salary of the position.

158 *the making . . . of bread in France*: this paper was written by Evelyn.

159 *Sir Ph. Warwicke*: Secretary to the Treasury until 1667.
the abuse of Tickets: the Navy Board was always short of money and devised the scheme of paying off seamen by means of tickets and allowing them 8 per cent. interest until the tickets were cashed. We hear about these tickets frequently in the diary as they were a great worry to Pepys.

160 *in this late business*: Pepys had successfully negotiated a marriage between Sandwich's daughter, Lady Jemimah, and Sir George Carteret's eldest son.

163 *Lord Bruncker* (1620-1684): a distinguished mathematician who became the first President of the Royal Society. He was made an extra Commissioner of the Navy in 1664.

164 *Mr. Evelyn's repeating of some verses*: Evelyn's reference to this occasion in his diary reads: "I dined with the Commissioners of the Navy, retreated hither, and with whom I had business."

the Cockpitt: the Duke of Albemarle's residence in Whitehall Palace, probably on the site of the present Treasury. About this time Albemarle was Acting Lord Admiral.

165 *Lord Sandwich . . . very melancholy*: there had been an outcry against him because of his conduct in allowing some prize ships to be plundered before being handed over to the Prize Commissioners.

166 *Mr. Gawden's*: see note on Sir Den: Gauden on page 241.

167 *Knipp:* Mrs. Knipp or Knepp. A prominent actress at the King's House.

Hales's: John Hales, a well-known portrait painter. It is an interesting comment on the taste of the time that Pepys made him paint out the landscape background to his portrait.

169 *Pall*: Pepys's sister, Paulina, was seven years younger than he. Pepys made several attempts to find a husband for her before finding John Jackson whom she married in March 1668.

172 *our Mercer*. Mrs. Pepys eventually prevailed upon her husband to let her have a companion, and this difficult position was filled for some time by Mary Mercer.

175 *Steele-yard*: a place where many merchants did business. It was on the present site of Cannon Street Station.

176 *Lord Arlington* (1618-1685): Secretary of State under Charles II from 1662 to 1674.

Mr. Isaake Houblon: the brothers, Isaac and James Houblon, were members of an important London family of merchants. Pepys knew them well.

178 *tallys*: "Formerly accounts were kept, and large sums of money paid and received, by the King's Exchequer,

with little other form than the exchange or delivery of tallies, pieces of wood notched or scored, corresponding blocks being kept by the parties to the account." (Lord Braybrooke.)

185 *my brother*: John.

186 *pay his coat*: beat him.

187 *Poleroone*: a small but valuable island in the East Indies.

ingenuous: here in the sense of noble or high-minded.

189 *Jane*: Jane Birch. Another in the long procession of Pepys's maids.

Fox-hall: Vauxhall.

190 *the Hope*: a reach of the Thames, near to its mouth.

riding: a ludicrous procession, formerly common in villages and country districts, usually intended to bring ridicule or odium upon a woman or her husband in cases where the one ill-treated the other. (O.E.D.) There is a description of one in Hardy's *The Mayor of Casterbridge*.

the bulwarke: the block-house at Gravesend.

191 *Mr. Boyle's book*: This is a well-known book of the famous physicist, the Hon. Robert Boyle (1627-1691) He was one of the first members of the Royal Society, and gave his name to the law that the volume of a gas varies inversely as the pressure.

193 *but slunk out*: note how well Pepys chooses his words.

194 *Backewell's*: Backewell was a goldsmith and merchant-banker.

195 *Mr. Gibson*: one of Pepys's clerks.

Saunders: a porter.

196 *Mr. Pelling*: an apothecary and friend of Pepys.

Dr. Bates: an eminent Puritan preacher.

197 *but not compound them*: they would hand over the ingredients separately but not mix them as gunpowder.

199 *Peter Pett*: Peter Pett, who was Commissioner of the Navy at Chatham, was made the scapegoat for the Dutch attack, and was removed from office.

207 *Mr. Evelyn*: John Evelyn's brother, Richard, who had an estate near Epsom.

208 *shod with iron shoes*: by shoes Pepys here means iron or steel plates.

209 *a cere-cloth*: a cloth forming a plaster.

Lord Anglesey: he had succeeded Sir George Carteret as Treasurer of the Navy in June 1667.

210 *Willet*: Deborah Willet became maid to Mrs. Pepys in September 1667 and was discharged in November 1668.

Lord Hinchingbroke: Sandwich's son.

211 *gibb-cat*: a male cat.

213 *the Groome-Porter's*: see the note on page 236.

215 *Kate Joyce*: Pepys's cousin.

to this new employment: he had become a publican at the Three Stags Tavern at Holborn.

the goods and estate would be seized on: it was customary at this time for the property of suicides to be forfeited to the Crown.

217 *With these thoughts*: the Principal Officers of the Navy had been summoned to the Bar of the House of Commons to answer charges of corruption and inefficiency, and Pepys had gone to bed the night before full of worries.

219 *April 10th*: at this place in the MS. of the diary eight pages have been left blank as if for the entries from the 10th to the 19th April, which do not appear. Pepys has, however, inserted his rough notes for these days in the bound volume. He had probably intended to complete the diary from the rough notes, but left it until the details had faded in his mind.

Legend: possibly a book called the *Golden Legend* by Jac. de Voragine.

Conning my gamut: studying his musical scales.

220 *Salisbury*: compare Evelyn's account of his visit, page 50.

223 *No carts*: it seems that the Council, in order to prevent the shaking of the sherry for which Bristol was famous and which was stored in vaults, prohibited the use of carts and wagons. Heavy goods were drawn on sledges.

224 *Bristoll milk*: a type of sherry.

Bossc: Bossc and Alexander Browne were engravers.

226 *a young Spaniard*: Sandwich had just returned from Spain where he had been ambassador.

Unthank's: Mrs. Pepys's tailor.

227 *Roger Pepys*: a cousin of Pepys's father. He was a lawyer and M.P.

229 *Tom*: Tom Edwards, Pepys's boy.

231 *syllabub*: a drink made of milk or cream, curdled by the admixture of wine, cider, or other acid, and often sweetened or flavoured. (O.E.D.)

May 25th: almost the shortest entry in the diary. Pepys's eyes must have been causing him great trouble.

TIME-CHART

1620 Evelyn born. Francis Bacon: *Novum Organum.*
1623 Publication of First Folio of Shakespeare's Plays.
1625 Death of James I. Accession of Charles I.
1633 Pepys born.
1637 Descartes: *Le Discours de la Methode.*
1642 The beginning of the Civil War.
1643 Accession of Louis XIV.
1649 Execution of Charles I.
1651 Hobbes: *Leviathan.*
1658 Death of Cromwell.
1660 Restoration of Monarchy.
1662 Discovery of Boyle's Law. Royal Society founded.
1663 Opening of Drury Lane Theatre.
1665 War with Dutch. The Plague.
1666 The Great Fire of London. Moliere: *Le Misanthrope.*
1667 The Dutch in the Medway. Treaty of Breda. Dryden: *Annus Mirabilis.* Milton: *Paradise Lost.* Racine: *Andromaque.*
1668 La Fontaine: *Fables Choisies.*
1672 War with Dutch.
1674 Peace with Dutch.
1676 Greenwich Observatory (built by Sir C. Wren) opened.
1677 Marriage of Princess Mary and William of Orange.
1678 The Popish Plot. Bunyan: *The Pilgrim's Progress.*
1682 Newton's discovery of the Laws of Gravitation.
1683 The Rye House Plot.
1685 Death of Charles II. Accession of James II. Monmouth's Rising. The Bloody Assizes.
1687 Declaration of Indulgence. Newton: *Philosophiae Naturalis Principia Mathematica.*

1688 Revolution. Arrival of William and Mary.
1690 Locke: *An Essay concerning Human Understanding.*
1694 Death of Mary.
1700 Congreve: *The Way of the World.*
1702 Death of William. Accession of Anne.
1703 Death of Pepys.
1704 Battle of Blenheim.
1706 Death of Evelyn.

LIST OF BOOKS

E. S. de Beer (editor): THE DIARY OF JOHN EVELYN (*Clarendon*, 1955)

This is the authoritative edition of the diary. It not only provides the complete text, but it is also a masterpiece of editing. A great deal of information about the seventeenth century can be obtained from Dr de Beer's notes.

Lord Ponsonby: JOHN EVELYN (*Heinemann*, 1933)

Although suffering from the fact that it was written long before the publication of Dr de Beer's edition of the diary, this book remains a useful guide to Evelyn's life, writings, and friends.

Virginia Woolf: "Rambling around Evelyn" in THE COMMON READER: First Series (*Hogarth*, 1925)

This is a fine piece of writing and a penetrating comment on Evelyn.

W. G. Hiscock: JOHN EVELYN AND HIS FAMILY CIRCLE (*Routledge*, 1955)

An interesting guide to Evelyn's life based on the latest information available.

Boris Ford (editor): FROM DONNE TO MARVELL (*Penguin*, 1956)

Volume 3 of the Pelican Guide to English Literature. This provides a useful survey of the social and literary background of the period.

H. B. Wheatley (editor): THE DIARY OF SAMUEL PEPYS (*Bell*, 1899)

The most complete and satisfactory edition of the diary at present available. It has useful notes. A new edition of the diary is in preparation, but the date of publication has not yet been announced.

EVELYN AND PEPYS

R. G. Howarth (editor): THE LETTERS AND THE SECOND DIARY OF SAMUEL PEPYS (*Dent*, 1932)

A very interesting book for anyone who wishes to delve a little deeper into Pepys's life.

Sir Arthur Bryant: SAMUEL PEPYS, THE MAN IN THE MAKING (*Collins*, 1947)

THE YEARS OF PERIL (*Collins*, 1948)

THE SAVIOUR OF THE NAVY (*Collins*, 1949)